The Institute of Early American History and Culture is sponsored jointly by the College of William and Mary and Colonial Williamsburg, Incorporated.

DOCUMENTARY PROBLEMS IN EARLY AMERICAN HISTORY

THE GREAT AWAKENING

The Great Awakening

DOCUMENTS ON THE REVIVAL OF RELIGION, 1740–1745

Edited by

Richard L. Bushman

Published for the

INSTITUTE OF EARLY AMERICAN HISTORY AND CULTURE
AT WILLIAMSBURG, VIRGINIA

ATHENEUM   NEW YORK   1970

ACKNOWLEDGMENTS

F OR permission to quote from manuscripts in their custody, I am grateful to the Trustees of Dartmouth College (the Eleazar Wheelock papers, No. 10); the Connecticut Historical Society (Spiritual Travels of Nathan Cole, No. 20); the Connecticut State Library (Connecticut Archives, Ecclesiastical Affairs, and Papers Relating to the First Church in Norwich, Nos. 26A, 26B, 26D, 26E, 37). I have used with permission excerpts from the edition of George Whitefield's *Journals* published by the Banner of Truth Trust, and from Jonathan Edwards, *The Nature of True Virtue,* edited by Clarence H. Faust and Thomas H. Johnson and published in *Jonathan Edwards: Representative Selections . . . ,* rev. ed. (New York: Hill and Wang, 1962).

Miss Silke-Maria Garrels of the Charles Warren Center was both efficient typist and helpful critic. Mr. Stephen G. Kurtz, editor of publications for the Institute of Early American History and Culture, and Joy Dickinson, assistant editor, ably assisted from start to finish.

Boston University   Richard L. Bushman
May, 1969

CONTENTS

INTRODUCTION

THE persistence of revivals in the United States, down to our own time, may easily distort our understanding of the Great Awakening of the 1740s. The obvious similarities in eighteenth- and twentieth-century revivals, while somewhat helpful in recovering the past, can be misleading. It is true that in both centuries preachers condemned their audiences for slighting God, warned them of terrible punishments, and urged them to rely on Christ for salvation. In both times hearers experienced intense personal anguish as they confronted their guilt and equally intense exaltation when grace brought relief. It may even be argued that in both centuries revivals have restored the psychically alienated and helped men recommit themselves to life. Yet for all the similarities, the Great Awakening and the revivals of Billy Sunday and Billy Graham occupy quite different places in history. Our knowledge of recent revivals is a faulty guide to the past.

The reason is not just that most twentieth-century Americans know only the caricatures of revivals and fail to appreciate the power of Christian conversion. Nor is it that important eighteenth-century words like sin and damnation have lost credibility in our time. The revivals themselves have a different meaning. They have moved from the center to the periphery of American culture. The common disdain in this secular age for impassioned religious emotion and language is merely symptomatic of the shift in values that has shunted revivals to the sidelines. What was once of critical importance to the majority of people is now of marginal interest. We inevitably will underestimate the effect of the Awakening on eighteenth-century society if we compare it to revivals today. The Awakening was more like the civil rights demonstrations, the campus disturbances, and the urban riots of the 1960s combined. All together these may approach, though certainly not surpass, the Awakening in their impact on national life.

The very magnitude of the revivals, which won for the Awakening the appellation "Great," is one indication of their importance. From

Whitefield's 1740 tour until 1743, the period when the revival was at
its peak, thousands were converted. People from all ranks of society, of
all ages, and from every section underwent the new birth. In New
England virtually every congregation was touched. It was not uncommon for ten or twenty percent of a town, having experienced grace, to
join the church in a single year. In the middle colonies, the Presbyterians were most affected, although Whitefield, himself an Anglican,
preached to people of all denominations. The Awakening did not
penetrate far into the South until after 1744, but then Presbyterian
evangelists made rapid inroads into Anglican strongholds in Virginia
as well as among their own congregations in the backcountry. It is safe
to say that most of the colonists in the 1740s, if not converted themselves, knew someone who was, or at least heard revival preaching.

The Awakening reached so many people because Protestant beliefs,
which controlled the colonists' view of the world, placed so much
importance on conversion. The Awakening was a critical event in the
intellectual as well as the ecclesiastical life of the colonies. Particularly
in Calvinist theology, to which far the larger part of the population
subscribed, the most crucial occurrence in human life was the bestowal
of divine grace. Sin separated men from God and from their best selves.
Nothing a reprobate did was truly good, none of his happiness was
satisfying, because he was always running from God. The grace which
came in conversion reconciled men to the divine and allowed them to
know the joy of sincere, unselfish love. Besides assuring admission to
God's presence in the hereafter, divine grace prepared a person for a
fullness of life on earth. Calvinist doctrine made a man's eternal fate
and his immediate well-being depend on conversion.

For decades preachers had lamented the absence of grace and the
apparent indifference of their congregations. In sermon after sermon
ministers unsuccessfully urged sleepy sinners to awake to their danger.
An individual now and again detected signs of the Spirit operating in
him, and in the 1720s and 1730s a number of congregations reported
seasons of spiritual refreshment. But not until the 1740s did men
in large numbers lay claim to the divine power which their theology
offered them. Then they suddenly awoke to God's glory and experienced a moral transformation as promised. In the Awakening the
clergy's pleas of half a century came to fulfillment.

The president of Harvard and the governor of Massachusetts welcomed Whitefield just as country pastors did. The learned and the
simple honored him for his power to turn men toward God. The
prevailing view of what really mattered in life compelled people of all
sorts to take the Awakening seriously. Conversion was equally impor-

tant to backcountry farmers and to Jonathan Edwards, the most subtle and intricate thinker of the age. The revivals' theological significance, not just their unusual size, made them front-page news.

Not that everyone agreed that God was working in the Awakening. Many believed Whitefield to be a demagogue, notable chiefly for his skill in stirring up animal spirits. The revival was an emotional orgy that needlessly disturbed the churches and frustrated the true work of God. But even opposers agreed on the importance of the issue. The intensity of the debate attested to the significance of the question: Was the Spirit of God descending on men in the revivals? Each convert confidently believed that he wrestled with a cosmic problem. People might think him deceived about the true nature of his guilt and the succeeding joy, but none dared say that religious conversion was a trivial matter.

The converts of the eighteenth century thus proceeded with much more boldness than those of the twentieth. Placement in the center of the regnant American theology gave people courage. In the belief that God was with them, obscure men demanded more passionate preaching or a voice in ecclesiastical politics or even the right to preach themselves. Some broke free of their churches; others stayed within and reformed the existing ecclesiastical structures. In one way or another, they wished to create a new society, beginning with the church, that accorded with a vision of life opened in the Awakening. Powerful allies enabled common people to withstand all opposition. The reborn were not alone, out on the margins of colonial life. Jonathan Edwards, John Dickinson, Gilbert Tennent, and a host of others whose personal and intellectual capacities commanded universal respect, shared the Awakening vision and provided moral support.

The masses of converts in turn emboldened ministers and redirected their thinking. The alliance of popular forces with clerical intellectuals was mutually advantageous. The palpable evidence of grace among thousands of awakened men helped turn back the rationalist schemes which began to gain ground in the 1730s. So long as dramatic conversions were infrequent, men might convincingly assert that reasoned obedience to the moral law was the most sensible path to salvation. But when people in every congregation were experiencing the ecstasy of God's grace, Calvinists could more easily claim validity for their doctrines of depravity and new birth.

The forces of the Enlightenment were not to be denied. Arminianism, the belief that men could attain salvation through rational conviction and their own efforts, won adherents among the Old Lights—the enemies of the Awakening—despite the revival and even in reaction against its excesses. But the Awakening was an incentive for New Lights—the friends of the Awakening—to strengthen traditional Calvinism and to tailor it to evangelistic purposes. Encouraged by success in the 1740s, the New Lights forged a theological tradition which was to sustain future awakenings for over a century to come.

Measured by the numbers involved or its intellectual and social significance, the Great Awakening was a major movement in the eighteenth century. It released forces that were to have lasting effect on American theology and church life and, indirectly, on politics as well. From 1740 to 1745 no other subject received more attention in books and pamphlets, and for years afterward the issues the revival raised were debated in the press and fought over in the churches. We would be the losers if the revivals were to slip from sight in our secular age when religious elements in our history may be inadvertently neglected. Fortunately for our understanding of the past and of ourselves, the intensity of theological concerns, the passions conversion aroused, and the implications for thought and society can be recovered in the writings of men who experienced the Awakening. Through them we can vicariously participate in both the ecstasy and the rage generated in our first national revival.

THE GREAT AWAKENING

CHAPTER ONE

PREPARATIONS

THE New Light ministry themselves created the picture of the pre-Awakening years which has prevailed down to our time. Thomas Prince, Jr., of Boston, the first historian to compile documents on the revivals, in his *Christian History* of 1744 and 1745 described the previous seventy years as a time of religious declension. Like Cotton Mather before him and Perry Miller afterwards, Prince believed that piety had deteriorated as the saintly men of the first generation passed from the scene. The people continued to go through the motions of religion without partaking of its power and joy. Admonitions from the clergy were to no avail. The hearts of the people were set on their lands and cattle rather than on righteousness and the word of God. By the end of the seventeenth century the actual disdain for religion showed itself in sabbath-breaking, tippling, and the neglect of family prayer. Not until the Awakening did the dispiriting decline come to a halt.

The discourse of Samuel Willard (1640–1707) on the *Perils of the Time* (No. 1) was one of the sermons Prince cited to prove the point. Willard cataloged the besetting sins of his generation, beginning with dead formality in religion, that listlessness which was the bane of the conscientious clergy. Although vice-president of Harvard and noted for his grasp of theology (a series of his lectures was published posthumously in a fat volume entitled *The Compleat Body of Divinity*), Willard's diagnosis of the spiritual sickness of his generation was not unusual. Indeed by 1700 when he preached the sermon, his catalog was quite conventional. Many ministers, aware that people were slipping away from God, were similarly warning their audiences and urging people to awake.

Prince noted a few bright spots amidst the general gloom. Solomon Stoddard (1643–1729), the dominant figure in the valley of the Connecticut River, enjoyed revival seasons from time to time when his congregation in Northampton seemed to arouse itself and show signs of grace. Stoddard had dropped the conversion requirement for admission to his church, a startling departure from the usual practice, and argued that only God knew the recipients of grace and that participation in communion might bring unregenerate men to Christ. But he did not mean to depreciate conversion. He strenuously prepared his listeners to accept God and admonished his brethren in the ministry to do the same. Part of the blame for spiritual sluggishness he attributed to poor preaching. Ministers preferred elegance to power and left people secure in their sins. In the *Defects of Preachers Reproved* (No. 2), Stoddard advocated more impassioned attacks on this false security, including the resort to sheer terror. Undoubtedly he employed these methods himself during the revivals in Northampton. The style of the itinerants in the Great Awakening, far from being an innovation in New England, was merely the continuation of the tradition Stoddard represented. Whitefield recommended Stoddard's works to Harvard students, and in 1747 the *Defects of Preachers Reproved* was reprinted for the instruction of the ministry.

Jonathan Edwards (1703–1758), Stoddard's grandson, took over the Northampton pulpit in 1729 and brought his grandfather's practices to a culmination. In 1734 and 1735 a more powerful and extensive revival than any Stoddard had known began in Northampton and spread down the valley into many congregations in Connecticut. Edwards's success proved that sleepy sinners could be awakened if spoken to in the right tone of voice.

A number of preachers in Pennsylvania and the Jerseys were of a mind with Stoddard and Edwards. In the 1720s, when Stoddard was urging New England preachers to bear down on their congregations, Theodore Frelinghuysen (*ca.* 1691–*ca.* 1747), a minister in the Dutch Reformed Church in the Raritan Valley in New Jersey, was calling his listeners to confront their sins more directly and to come to Christ. Among the Presbyterians, William Tennent (1673–1746), an immigrant from northern Ireland and an effective preacher himself, was training a handful of fervent young men, among them his four sons, for service in the ministry. These graduates of the Log College, as Tennent's school at Neshaminy, Pennsylvania, came to be called, were characterized by deep personal piety, a talent for argumentation, and a passion for lively preaching. Later they were the mainstays of the Awakening in the middle colonies and among the moving spirits in the founding of the College of New Jersey, which was initially organized to carry on the Log College tradition after William Tennent died.

Through the 1730s the most prominent of Tennent's sons, Gilbert
Tennent (1703–1764), contended with conservatives among middle-
colony Presbyterians just as Stoddard prodded his colleagues in New
England. At New Brunswick, New Jersey, where he had accepted a
call, Tennent was inspired by the example of Frelinghuysen, who had
made a number of converts in the area. Recognizing the kinship of
purpose and method, the two men sometimes spoke in succession to the
same congregation. Tennent's *Solemn Warning* (No. 3), published in
1735 when news of the Northampton revival was beginning to filter
down from New England, exemplifies the kind of appeal by which
these "burning and shining lights," as Whitefield described them,
hoped to humble sinners and open them to grace.

1. The Decline of Piety: Samuel Willard, *The Peril of the Times Displayed*, 1700

[Samuel Willard, *The Peril of the Times Displayed, Or The Danger of Mens taking up with a Form of Godliness, But Denying the Power of it* . . . (Boston, 1700), 88–97, 99–102, 104–108, 112–117]

That there is a *Form of Godliness* among us, is manifest. Let us take the notion of a *form* in either of the senses before observed in the explication of the Doctrine, and it will appear to be so. If we look upon it as intending an outward *species, shew* or *pretence,* whether the thing it self be sincere, or only in pretence; it is certain that the generality of this people do give it out, that they are the people of God, that they acknowledge him to be their Soveraign, that they are engaged in his Service, and that they do stand up for the Gospel Ordinances and Order. Or if we take it for the *Rule* that men declare themselves to be under the obligation of; we have a sound *confession of the Faith,* which we declare that we adhere unto; and are not a little zealous for the upholding of those Ordinances which Christ hath Instituted in his Gospel; these things are evident, and possibly there may be more of this among us, than in most other places.

But the great enquiry is, whether there be not too much of a general denying of the power of it? God forbid that any discouragement should be offered to those who are serious and watchful Christians, whose hearts are truly set for the Glory of God, and the promoting of his interest: and let it be the encouragement of all such, that if there be but a *few names* in a degenerate *Sardis,* God doth not overlook them, nor will he forget them. See how comfortably he speaks to such, Rev. 3. 4. *thou hast a few names even in Sardis, that have not defiled their garments, and they shall walk with me in white, for they are worthy.* But if the other frame be grown too general and prevailing, the *Symptoms* are bad; and let us remember, that there are many discoveries which may be made of such a spirit, which, though they are not all found in every one, yet if they are found distributively, and spread generally, it will amount to the thing that we are enquiring after. When God chargeth a people in this regard, he doth not always say you are all thus and so, but such *are found in thee,* see Ezek. 22. 7, etc. and is it not too much thus with us? Whence else is it, that there are such things as these that follow, to be observed.

That there is such a prevalency of so many *immoralities* among Professors? I confess that it must be granted, that in the best times, and in places where the power of Godliness is most flourishing, there have been, and will be those that have not the fear of God before their eyes: there were so in the times of the greatest *Reformation* that we read of in the Book of God. In this world we must expect that *Wicked men will be mixed with the Godly,* and such as will dare to shew their wickedness in their Lives, and not be afraid to *Transgress in a Land of Uprightness.* But when such are not countenanced, but due testimony is born against them; when they are contemned in the places where they live, and a note of infamy and scandal is put upon them; this will not be charged on such a people for *Apostasy:* But when such sins grow frequent, and those that have taken on themselves a name of being Religious, begin to indulge themselves herein; and men that allow themselves in such things are not *Reproached* for it, but are in as good Credit as the best, it then becomes a bad symptom, and faith that the times are declining and perilous. Much more when such as these will undertake to justify, and patronize such things: and are there not sad complaints made on this account? I shall here instance only in some that are more notorious. Are not Gods *Sabbaths* wofully neglected? How little care is there used in making of due preparation for them? How wofully can such as would be esteemed Godly, encroach upon holy time, and be engaged, either in secular business, or in vain Company, and possibly in publick houses, when they should be at home, in

their Closets, or with their Families, Sanctifying of Gods day, and shewing of the *Honourable esteem* they have for it? And I am well satisfyed, that *where the strict Observation of Gods Sabbath is lost, there the Power of Godliness is gone.* How much complaint is there made of woful *Dishonesty* in their dealings, practised by such as can talk high of their Religion? How many fallacious tricks they can use in their Commerce? How deceitful in their Labour? How false to their words and promises? as if dissembling and lying were no reproach to the name of Christians. How many *Intemperate Church Members* are there reported to be, who spend their precious time in frequenting Publick Houses, and keeping of loose and lewd Company? who can come to the *Lords Table* on the Sabbath, and wrong themselves by excessive Drinking on the week days? How much *Animosity, Contention,* and implacable bitterness of Spirit, breaking forth in indecent words and carriages, between such as are bound in the strongest Evangelical ties to *Love one another, and meekly to bear with each others infirmities?* How much raising, spreading, and receiving of *Slanders* and *Defamations* one of another; contrary to that Charity which ought to *Cover a Multitude of sins?* These, and a great many more of like nature, which might have been added, so far as they spread and prevail, and begin to grow common, are an ill Omen; for, they are indisputable denials of the power of Godliness, at least in the vigour of it, in those who are Guilty of them, for *that teacheth men to Live Soberly, Righteously and Godly.*

That there is so little *Success of the Gospel,* notwithstanding the clear dispensations of it that are enjoyed among us. The Gospel is the Great instrument which God hath seen meet to make use of, both for the sowing of the seeds of

Godliness in the hearts of men, in the great work of Conversion, and for the strengthening and establishing of it where it is already sown: and this efficacy it will have when it becomes *the power of God to Salvation* in men, as we are told it is, *in all that believe, Rom* 1.16. True Godliness discovereth itself in a Cordial compliance with the Gospel in its designs, which are these: and when these fail, and the work of Conversion and edification are at a stay, it is a sign that Piety is gone to decay: and the more plenty God affords to a People of these means; and the more of light and life they are dispensed withal, the more notorious is this symptom. What there hath been enjoyed among us upon this account, God knows, and this people also shall be made to *know that there have been Prophets among them.* How few through Conversions are to be observed? How scarce and seldom? Men go from Ordinance to Ordinance, and that from year to year, and it may be they are sometimes a little touched, awakened, affected, and make some stir for a while; but how few are there who are effectually and throughly turned from sin to God? It is to be hoped that there are more than we know of; this work of God is Secret, and in some it is wrought without a noise: however, this is a certain observation which may safely be made, that where there is no *outward Conversion,* Charity hath no ground to proceed upon, to believe that there is an *inward* one; for, were the heart savingly changed, that would influence and alter the life. Yea, were men but *pricked at their hearts* under the Ordinances that they frequent, they would cry out for help and direction, and we should hear of them: So that if men take a great deal of delight in the means of Grace, and yet can be content without setling a saving interest in Christ, who is presented and offered to them therein, it

saith that they are seded on a form without the power; it is a sad complaint which the Church maketh in, Isa. 64 7. *There is none that calleth on thy name, that stirreth himself up to take hold on thee.* And may not there be found just reason to revive it in this day? And how little is there to be discerned of a *growing Grace,* in them who pretend to have experienced a work of Conversion in them? Grace is of a thriving nature, when it is indeed *Planted in a good heart,* made so by the operation of the Spirit; and more especially when it is planted by *many Waters;* when it hath plenty of suitable means afforded to it, and the Spirit of God influencing them: and if men did savingly profit by the Gospel, would it not make some discernible discoveries of it self? would there be no fruits by which it might be judged to thrive? and yet what do many, who have had all manner of helps afforded them in *Gods Vineyard,* for a great many years; and that have used much diligence in their outward attendance upon them, more than they did at first? do they not seem rather to grow downward than upward, to have lost rather than gained? did they not seem to express more of life, vigour, watchfulness over themselves, endeavour to walk worthy of the Gospel, when they first sat out, then they do now? do not the things that formerly looked lively and flourishing, now languish, and appear as if they were ready to expire? whereas we are told, in Prov. 4. 18. *the path of the just is as the shining light, which shineth more and more unto the perfect day.*

. . . .

That there is so much of *Contempt* cast upon the *Gospel Ministry:* The Lord Jesus Christ hath appointed a Ministry for the outward Dispensation of his Gospel unto men, and for the promoting of Godliness among them; and hath made it an ordinary necessary medium to this great end, according to that, Rom.10.14. *How shall they believe in whom they have not heard? and how shall they hear without a Preacher? and how shall he Preach except he be sent?* and for this reason, there is a good esteem to be had for this *Ordinance* of his, by all that would approve themselves pious. It is true, there is a difference to be acknowledged between the *work* it self, and the *persons* that are employed in it. As to the *persons* in the Ministry; though it be scarcely probable that men should profit by their Ministration, whiles they despise their persons, or entertain a low and a base esteem for them, and therefore it is said of the better times, *Isa. 52. 7. how beautiful are the feet of him that bringeth good tidings, that publisheth peace?* etc. yet certainly when God hath put them in this Service, and hath made them both wise and faithful in the discharge of their work, they are to be well accounted of *for their works sake.* When therefore their zeal for the glory of God, and their fidelity in *not shunning to declare the whole counsel of God* to men, makes them to be scorned and reproached, it bodes ill: and such carriages to them, speaks in his language, I *King. 22. 8. I hate him, for he doth not Prophesie good concerning me, but evil.* But this must be confessed, that the work it self is an Ordinance of Christ; and when men grow weary of the thing, look upon it as a needless charge, had rather live without a Ministry, than to bear the burden of it; or count so meanly of the work it self, that they think any one fit enough to be employed in it, who is so bold as to thrust himself upon it, though he hath nothing else to commend himself to it, but noise and nonsense; and those that are both able and faithful are despised; as also, when men think it no great matter to neglect their attendance on the Dispensation of the Ordinances by them, every small occasion is enough to make an excuse of, from *Coming to the House of*

God: or if men do come, and afford their bodily presence there, yet they little regard the Doctrines taught, but at best, carry it like them, Ezek. 33. 31. *they hear thy words, but they will not do them,* etc. If they *reprove sin,* and come close to their darling lusts, they are either enraged at and revile them, or scorn them; if they *urge Duty* never so clearly and earnestly, yet if they like it not, they will not believe them, nor be at the pains of those *Bereans, who searched the Scriptures daily, to see whether those things were so,* Acts 17. 11. and how much of this nature are we acquainted withal?

. . . .

The grievous neglect of *Family Worship.* There is a Worship which is due to God from men; and it doth not only concern men personally, but relatively too, in the several combinations which God hath ordained to be among them. The most publick Religious Worship which was at first performed by men, seems to have been in *Families,* before it came to be attended in the more open and frequented Asemblies, which is thought to have begun in the days of *Enos,* Gen 4.26. nor doth the making of this latter a duty now give men a discharge from the former any more than that did from secret Worship. The principal parts of *Family Worship,* are the *Reading of the Scriptures* and *Prayer;* and the reason of it is, because every Governour of a Family hath a charge lying upon him, to see to the Religious management of it, that so it may be a Family consecrated to God. As to *Prayer,* it is of it self a piece of *Natural Worship:* and the light of nature in meer *Heathen,* taught them, not only to pray to him whom they accounted God, but to perform it in and with their Families; and that they had a Worship in their Houses, is fully testified in Pagan Antiquity; for this reason there is such an imprecation used against the *Heathen Families that call not on Gods*

Name, Jer. 10.21. and it shews them to have been guilty of sinning against the Law given to man at first, else this neglect would not have laid them open to such a curse; and this is certain, that Family which is without their daily joynt prayers unto God, is an irreligious Family, and exposed to the dreadful vengeance of Heaven; and for men whom God hath betrusted with the care and charge of Families, to bring up their Children and Servants without prayer, is to bring them up in *Atheism;* and yet there is lamentable complaint of this neglect even in this place, where there is so much of conviction offered unto men of their duty: and how many have there been, who, when God hath opened their eyes, and given them a true sight of things, have bitterly lamented themselves, that they have lived in *Prayerless Families?* and that which maketh it to be the more doleful, is that they have not been the Families of such as have made no profession, but been openly profane, but of such as have made an acknowledgment of their Engagement to God, and have before men espoused the *Gospel Covenant,* and made promises to God that they would observe his Commandments to do them. There are some who pray not at all with their Families from one end of the year to the other; others who it may be on a Sabbath day find a time to pray for all the week. If Godliness had any power in them, it would not be so: Their sense of the need of Gods blessing upon their Family Affairs; their belief that it is of him to preserve their Houses from Desolation, their Substance from Casualties, their Families from mischief; their apprehension of the need which their Children and Servants have of being brought up in the fear of God, and the danger of their losing the very face of Religion, by such neglects as these; yea, the aw of Gods indignation for such contempt offered him, would make them afraid of living in the frequent,

much more the constant omission of this duty. If this grow to be a common distemper in the midst of us, saith, *we are departed from God,* and we have just cause to look for some fearful departure of his from us.

. . . . : . .

The bad *Symptoms* that are upon the *Rising Generation.* It hath been a frequent observation, that if one Generation begins to decline, the next that followeth usually grows worse, and so on, till God poureth out his Spirit again upon them; and for the most part some desolating Judgments intervene. Thus it was with *Israel* soon after they came into *Canaan,* Judg. 2. 10. *there arose another Generation, which knew not the Lord;* and then, verse 14. *the anger of the Lord was hot against Israel,* &c. The decayes which we do already languish under, are sad, and what tokens are there on our Children that it is like to be better hereafter? we are going off, and they are coming apace on the Stage, and the management of the great concerns of Religion will in a little time be devolved upon them; and what aspect hath this upon it in the observation of serious Souls? God be thanked, that there are so many among them that promise well, and the Lord add to, and greatly encrease their number; But alas, how doth vanity, and a fondness after new things abound among them? how do young persons grow weary of the strict profession of their fathers, and become strong disputants for those things which their Progenitors forsook a pleasant Land for the avoidance of, and that not only for themselves, but that their posterity might be removed from the temptations of? Besides, it is almost a general complaint of Family Governours, that their Children and Servants are weary of the yoke, and are not willing to be under their Command, or observe the good order in the Family which they require them to attend: that they are in combination one with another, and do joyn hand in hand in refusing of that subjection which they owe to their Superiours, and debauching of themselves with their night revels, and meetings in bad houses, to drink and game: they force the reins into their necks, and will be no way curbed in from their exorbitances; and these also the Children of Godly Parents, and such as have been carefully and religiously Educated, and many a time solemnly charged with tears and earnest adjurations, to *Serve the God of their Fathers with a perfect heart, and a willing mind,* and warned of his fearful *departure* from them if they do not. How far this decay is to be imputed to the neglect of Family Governours, either in a prudent managing of their authority, or in a careful setting of a good and holy example before their Families, is a matter of awful consideration; for certainly they are sorely afflicted in this matter, and ought to judge themselves upon the account: however, this plainly discovereth that the life of Religion is panting and gasping among us.

The inefficaciousness of Gods severe Judgments. The Judgments which God brings upon a professing people, are witnesses of great decays in Godliness, for that is even the controversy which he manageth by them. But when these Judgments come upon a people, and are often repeated, and God followeth them with a long series thereof, and they are bruised, and broken, and brought exceeding low by them, and yet they do not work to the declared end of them, which is to reclaim them from their lifelessness, and to quicken them to express the vigour and power of Grace, but they are stupid and sottish children, and do not lay to heart these Dispensations of his, as he complains, Isa. 42. 25. *he poured on him the fury of his anger; and it hath set him on fire round about, yet he knew not, and it burned him, yet*

he laid it not to heart; yea, when God complains as one that is weary of correcting them, and upon it threatens to leave off, because it is fruitless, and there is no good cometh of it, as Isa. 1. 5. *Why should you be smitten any more? ye will revolt more and more.* Hos. 4. 17. *Ephraim is joyned to his Idols, let him alone.* This is a token that the power is not only decayed, but expired; and let us make diligent enquiry upon this account; we have been for a long time harassed with Judgments which have been brought upon us, and wasted us; there have been many of them, and they have been continued: God hath manifestly witnessed his Anger and our Apostasy by them; and he hath *waited long in the way of his Judgments,* for our Repentance; and after all he hath changed the course of his Providence to us-ward, and hath again restored us to peace and plenty, and afforded large measures of health among us: but it is still a solemn enquiry to be made by us, *viz* whether Gods holding back his correcting hand, and opening of his bountiful hand to us, be because he is reconciled to us, or because his patience is wearied with our insensibleness of, and stupidity under his judicial dispensations: if it be the former, all is well, and we may abundantly rejoyce in it; but if it be the latter, there is then a sad *prognostick* in it. Well, this may soon be determined. What of the power of Godliness is recovered among us by all this? nay, what outward Reformation is there wrought by it? or are we not more stupid and senseless under all? let us not account these remarks to be trifles, or things not worthy our enquiring after; but let us be serious in our observation; and if it be thus we may be sure that we live in *perilous times,* and may by thus doing obtain the character of *Prudent,* for we are told, Prov. 27.12. *the prudent foreseeth the evil.*

2. A Plea for Fervent Preaching: Solomon Stoddard, *Defects of Preachers Reproved*, 1723

[Solomon Stoddard, *The Defects of Preachers Reproved in a Sermon Preached at Northampton, May 19, 1723* (New London, 1724), 7–18, 24–27]

Learning and Morality will qualify men to make many good and profitable Sermons, much for the Edification of the Hearers. Learning qualifies men to clear up many Principles of Religion; and a Moral disposition may fit men zealously to Reprove vicious Practices: But men may be Learned men, yet drink in very Corrupt Doctrines. Learning is no security against Erroneous Principles: The Pharisees and Sadducees were men of Liberal Education, yet leavened with many false Principles: Mat. 16.6. *Beware of the leaven of the Pharisees and Sadducees.* And ver. 12. *Then understood they that he bid them not beware of the leaven of bread; but of the doctrine of the Pharisees and of the Sadducees.* Learning will not cure those distempers of the Heart that do expose men to false Opinions; Learning will not cure the Pride and Conceitedness of mens Hearts. Men of learning may lean too much to their own Understanding. Men of Learning may be led aside by Reading Erronious Books. Learned Education will not deliver men from Carnal Reason: Men of corrupt Affections are very inclinable to imbibe bad Principles: Men of Learning may be blind men. Christ says of the Pharisees, *They be blind, leaders of the blind,* Mat. 15.14. Most of the Errors in the world in matters of Religion, have been hatched by men of Learning. *Arius, Socinus,* and *Arminius,* and *Pelagius* were Learned men: Errors in Religion have been generally the Off-spring of great Scholars, have been propagated by them. And men may be Moral men that have no experience of the work of God upon their Hearts. Men may be Zealous men against Drunkenness and Whoredom, that have no Saving Knowledge of Christ. Many Moral men have no Communion with God; no Experience of a Saving Change in their own Souls. Men may be very Moral and have no experience of a work of Humiliation, or being bro't off from their own Righteousness, or a work of Faith; of the difference that is between the Common and Special work of the Spirit; of the difference between Saving and Common Illumination, of the working of the heart under Temptation, of the way wherein godly men are wont to find Relief. Every Learned and Moral man is not a Sincere Convert, and so not able to speak exactly and experimentally to such things as Souls want to be instructed in. It is as with a man that has seen a Map of a Country, or has read a great deal about it; he can't tell the way between Town and Town, and hundreds of particular Circumstances, as a man that has Travelled or Lived there is able to do. Experience fits men to Teach others. A man that has himself had only a common work of the Spirit and judges it saving, is very unfit to judge of the State of other men. Men would not put their Lives into the hands of an unskilful Physician, or trust their Ship with an unskilful Pilot, or an intricate Case depending in the Law with an unskilful Lawyer.

USE, I. *Of Examination,* Whether it be not thus in this Country? It is notoriously known by those that are acquainted with the state of the Christian World, that tho' there be many eminent Truths taught, yet there is a great want of good Preaching; whence it comes to pass, that among Professors a spirit of Piety runs exceeding low. But it is proper for us to take notice how it is among our selves; and tho' it be very evident that there is a great deal of good Preaching in the Land, and the way of Salvation is Preached with a great deal of plainness and power, and many men are very faithful to declare all the Counsel of God; yet there may be cause of Lamentation, that there is a great deal wanting in some places: Some may be very much to blame in not Preaching as they ought to do.

1. *If any be taught that frequently men are ignorant of the Time of their Conversion, that is not good Preaching.* Some are of that Opinion, and its like they may drink it in from their Ministers. This is a delusion, and it may do them a great deal of hurt; it hardens men in their Natural Condition. *Paul* knew the time of his Conversion; *At Midday, O King, I saw a Light from Heaven, above the brightness of the Sun,* Act. 26.13. Men are frequently at a loss whether their Conversion were true or not; but surely men that are Converted must take some notice of the Time when God made a Change in them: Conversion is a great change, from darkness to light, from death to life, from the borders of despair to a spirit of faith in Christ. As for the outward Conversation, there is sometimes little difference; men might carry very well before; But as to the frame of mens Hearts, there is a very great difference. Formerly they were under the reigning power of Objections against the Gospel, when Converted they receive it as a Divine Truth; before they were Converted they were under a sentence of Condemnation, now they have Peace with God through Jesus Christ. Men are

generally a long time seeking Conversion, labouring to get an interest in Christ; and it would be much if when God reveals Christ to them, they should not take notice of it when the change is made; Ten to one but Conscience will take notice of it. When a Seaman comes into the Harbour, when a Prisoner is pardoned, when a Victory is obtained, when a Disease is broke, it would be much if men should take no notice of them; Conversion is the greatest change that men undergo in this world, surely it falls under Observation. The Prodigal knew well enough the time of his return to his Fathers House: The Children of Israel knew the time of their passing over Jordan.

2. *If any be taught that Humiliation is not necessary before Faith, that is not good Preaching.* Such Doctrine has been taught privately and publickly, and is a means to make some men mistake their condition, and think themselves happy when they are miserable: For men must be brought off from their own Righteousness before they be brought to Christ. Men that think they have any thing to appease the Wrath of God and ingratiate themselves, will not accept the Calls of the Gospel in Sincerity. While People have a Foundation to build upon, they will not build upon Christ. A Self-righteous spirit is quite contrary to the Gospel: If men be Self-righteous men, they will not judge it fair for God to cast them off. Men that depend upon the Justice of God, will not depend upon the meer Mercy of God. Men that lay claim to Heaven from their own Works, will not depend on that Plea that Christ has given his life a Ransom for many, and has redeemed us from the Curse being made a Curse for us. Multitudes of Men are ruined by building upon a Sandy Foundation. Men must see their Malady, before they see their Remedy. Men must be led into the Understanding of the

badness of their Hearts and the strictness of the Law, before they will be convinced of the Preciousness of Christ. Men that can heal their own Consciences, will not come to Christ for healing. Men must be driven by necessity indeed before they come to Christ. Tho' men feel great terrors and live a tormented Life, yet they will not come to Christ, till driven out of themselves. Men must feel themselves dead in sin, in order to their Believing; Rom. 7.9. *Sin revived, and I died.* Men must see themselves poor and miserable, wretched and blind and naked, before they receive that Counsel of buying of Christ gold tried in the fire, and white raiment, *Rev* 3.17,18.

3. *When Men don't Preach much about the danger of Damnation, there is want of good Preaching.* Some Ministers Preach much about moral Duties and the blessed Estate of godly Men, but don't seek to awaken Sinners and make them sensible of their danger; they cry for Reformation: These things are very needful in their places to be spoken unto; but if Sinners don't hear often of Judgment and Damnation, few will be Converted. Many men are in a deep Sleep and flatter themselves as if there was no Hell, or at least that God will not deal so harshly with them as to *Damn* them. Psal. 36.2. *He flattereth himself in his own eyes, until his iniquity be found to be hateful.* They need to be told of the Terrors of the Lord, that they may flee from Wrath to come: A little matter will not scare men, their hearts be as hard as a stone, as hard as a piece of the nether milstone, and they will be ready to laugh at the shaking of the Spear. Ministers must give them no rest in such a condition: They must pull them as Brands out of the burnings. It is well if Thunder and Lightning will awaken them: They had need to fear that they may work out their Salvation with fear and trembling. Ministers are

faulty when they speak to them with gentleness, as *Eli* rebuked his Sons. Christ Jesus often warned them of the danger of Damnation: Mat. 5.29.30. *It is better that one of thy members should perish, and not that thy whole body should be cast into hell.* Mat 7.13. *Broad is the gate and wide is the way that leadeth to destruction, and many there be that go in thereat.* Mat. 13.42. *The Angels shall cast them into a furnace of fire, there shall be wailing and gnashing of teeth.* So also, *Mat.* 22.13. *Mat.* 25, 41,46. This for our imitation. Christ knew how to deal with Souls, and *Paul* followed His Example. Men need to be terrified and have the arrows of the Almighty in them that they may be Converted. Ministers should be Sons of Thunder: Men had need have Storms in their hearts, before they will betake themselves to Christ for Refuge: When they are pricked at the Heart, then they will say, What must we do to be Saved? Men must be fired out of their worldliness and sloth: Men must be driven as *Lot* was out of *Sodom.* Reason will govern men in other things; but it is Fear that must make them diligently to seek Salvation: If they be but thoroughly Convinced of their danger, that will make them go to God and take Pains.

4. *If they give a wrong account of the nature of Justifying Faith, that is not good Preaching.* Justifying Faith is set forth in the Scripture by many figurative Expressions; Coming to Christ, Opening to Him, sitting under his Shadow, flying to Him for Refuge, building on Him as on a Foundation, feeding on Him, etc. These Expressions do imply not only an act of the Understanding, but also an act of the Will, accepting of Him, depending on Him. This Doctrine is despised by some, and Faith in Christ is said to be only a Perswasion of the truth of the Christian Religion. This is the way to make multitudes of Carnal men secure, and to flat-

ter themselves as if they were in a good Condition: They say they are no Heathens, nor Turks, nor Papists, nor Jews, but they believe that Jesus Christ is the Eternal Son of God, they hope they are Believers; but multitudes of People have such a Faith that will fall short of Eternal Life: Joh. 2.23,24 *Many believed in his name, when they saw the miracles that he did; but Jesus did not commit himself unto them.* Joh. 12.42,43. *Among the chief rulers many believed on him, but because of the Pharisees they did not confess him.* The Faith of some men is only a Perswasion from their Education: As Heathens do receive the Religion of their Forefathers by Tradition, so these do receive the Christian Religion from Hear-say. But Justifying Faith is wrought in men by the mighty Power of God; 2 Thess. 1.11. *That he would work in you the work of faith with power.* Eph. 1, 19, 20. *And what is the exceeding greatness of his power to us-ward who believe, according to the working of his mighty power; which he wrought in Christ when he raised him from the dead?* By Justifying Faith, men answer the Calls of God, relinquishing their own Righteousness, place their Dependance only on the Mediation of Christ; Heb. 6.18. *They flee for refuge, to lay hold on the hope that is set before them.* Justifying Faith is a living Principle that Sanctifies men; Act. 15.9. *Purifying their hearts by faith.* Many men have a common Perswasion of the truth of the Gospel, that are utterly destitute of Holiness: But true Justifying Faith is always accompanied with an Holy Life. Where there is Faith, there is every other Grace: Act. 26.18. *Sanctified by faith that is in me.*

5. *If any do give false Signs of Godliness, that is not good Preaching.* Signs of Grace are of two Sorts: Some are Probable, and they must be spoken of only as Probable; a Score of them may make the thing more Probable, but don't make it Certain: Probabilities make no Demonstration; Probable Signs are not Conclusive. There are two Errors in laying down Signs; one is when those things that may flow from Common Principles, as natural Temper, natural Conscience, fear of Hell, false Imaginations, are given as sure Signs of Grace: But those things that may flow from Common Principles, don't truly distinguish between Saints and Hypocrites; As a good Conversation, savoury Discourse, zeal against Sin, strong religious Affections, sorrow for Sin, quietness under Afflictions, delight in Ordinances, suffering for Religion, etc. From such loose Signs People are in danger to take up a false Perswasion of their godliness. Such Signs are full of Delusion; and many men do bless themselves who are in a miserable Condition. Such probable Signs may be, where there be certain Signs of the contrary. Men are apt to flatter themselves, and when they hear such Signs, they are strengthned in their carnal Confidence. There is no infallible Sign of Grace, but Grace. Grace is known only by intuition: All the External Effects of Grace may flow from other Causes. Another Error is when men are too strict in their Signs; As when they give that as a Sign, that there is a constant care to glorify GOD, and a continual living upon JESUS CHRIST, and a constant watchfulness against the workings of Corruption. There is no godly man but has at times ill Frames of spirit: *David* and *Jonah* and *Peter* had so. When *David* committed Adultery, he had not a due care to glorify God; nor *Jonah* when he was in a Fret, nor the *Psalmist* when he was as a Beast before God, nor *Paul* when he was led into Captivity by the law of sin that was in his Members. There is no godly man that can comfort himself with such Signs as these: It is well if godly men do see now and then the workings of a spirit of Grace: Grace is

many times under Hatches and invisible.

. . . .

The reading of Sermons is a dull way of Preaching. Sermons when Read are not delivered with Authority and in an affecting way. It is Prophesied of Christ, Mic. 5.4. *He shall stand and feed in the Strength of the Lord, in the Majesty of the Name of the Lord his God.* When Sermons are delivered without Notes, the looks and gesture of the Minister, is a great means to command Attention and stir up Affection. Men are apt to be Drowsy in hearing the Word, and the Liveliness of the Preacher is a means to stir up the Attention of the Hearers, and beget suitable Affection in them. Sermons that are Read are not delivered with Authority, they favour of the Sermons of the Scribes, *Mat.* 7.29. Experience shews that Sermons Read are not so Profitable as others. It may be Argued, that it is harder to remember Rhetorical Sermons, than meer Rational Discourses; but it may be Answered, that it is far more Profitable to Preach in the Demonstration of the Spirit, than with the enticing Words of mans wisdom.

USE, II. *See the Reason why there is so little Effect of Preaching.* There is much good Preaching, and yet there is want of good Preaching. There is very good Preaching in *Old England,* yet there is great want of good Preaching, especially among the Conformists: And there is very good Preaching in *New-England,* and yet there is some want of good Preaching; especially in some places: And this is one Reason that there is no more good done. There is a great fault in Hearers, they are not studious of the mind of God; they are Enemies to the gospel: And when Christ Himself Preached among them, many did not Profit by it. Yet some Preachers are much to blame, and tho' they do Preach profitably many times, yet they have

great cause to be Humbled for their Defects.

1. *For hence it is that there is so little Conversion.* There is great Complaint in one Country and in another, that there be few Converted; it is apparent by mens Unsanctified Lives and their unsavoury Discourses. This is one Reason, there is a great deal of Preaching that doth not much Promote it, but is an hindrance to it. To tell men that *they may be Converted tho' they don't know the time:* To teach that *there is no need of a work of Humiliation to prepare them for Christ;* and that *Faith is nothing else but a Perswasion that the Gospel is true,* is the very way to make many Carnal Men hope that they are Converted. It makes other Preaching very ineffectual: It makes them think that it is needless to strive for Conversion. Such Preaching hardens men in their Sins: The want of dealing plainly with men is the reason, why there is seldom a noise among the *Dry Bones.* In some Towns there is no such thing to be Observed for *Twenty Years together.* And men continue in a senseless condition, come to Meeting and hear Preaching, but are never the better for it. In some Towns godly men are very thin sown. Most of the People are in as bad a condition as if they had never heard the Gospel: Go on in a still way, following their worldly Designs, carry on somewhat of the Form of godliness, but mind little but the World and the Pleasures of this Life. The Scribes did not Preach with Authority, *Mat.* 7.29. And they *entred not into the Kingdom of God themselves, and they that were entring in they hindred.* Such Preaching is not mighty *to the pulling down of strong Holds.* Conversion-work will fail very much where there is not Sound Preaching.

2. *Hence many men that make an high Profession, lead Unsanctified Lives:* They are not dealt *Plainly with;*

and so tho' they Profess high, they Live very Low: They are not dealt *Roundly with;* and they believe they are in a good Estate, and Conscience suffers them to Live after a Corrupt Manner. Some of them live a Proud and Voluptuous Life, and they are not Searched as they should be. If they were told their own, that would keep them from saying that *they were Rich and increased in* *goods,* and had *need of nothing:* If they were *rebuked Sharply,* that might be a means *to make them Sound in the Faith,* Tit. 1.13. It might make them not only to Reform, but lay a better Foundation for Eternal Life, than ever yet was laid. *Paul* was very thorough in his work, and wherever he came he had the fulness of the blessing of the Gospel of Christ, *Rom.* 15.29.

3. Revival Preaching before the Awakening: Gilbert Tennent, *Solemn Warning,* 1735

[Gilbert Tennent, *Solemn Warning to the Secure World from The God of terrible Majesty* . . . (Boston, 1735), vii–ix, xi–xii]

Beloved Brethren, You have often heard your Danger describ'd, you have had many a Call, by the *Word,* and *Providence* of *God,* as well as by your own *Consciences,* and are you not awaken'd yet? O strange! O mournful! Others have been (through Grace) *convinc'd* and *chang'd* effectually by the Means you enjoy, and won't these be a Witness against you at the *Tribunal* of *Christ?* What will you be able to say in your own Vindication? Then won't *Blushing* and *Confusion* cover you, and *guilty Silence* be your Answer? What, does the Word prove a Savour of Life unto Life to others, and of Death unto Death to you? O dreadful! What do you intend to do *dear Brethren?* Will you sleep for ever? Will you sleep till *Death* and *Hell awake you?* Or do you think that you may go to *Heaven* in this *Slumber* of carnal *Security?* If you do you shall find your selves miserably mistaken! as is fully prov'd in the following Tract. Be not deceiv'd Brethren, *The Kingdom of Heaven suffers Violence, and the violent* (and they only) *take it by Force,* Matth. 11. 12. Let me address you as the *Prophet Elijah* did the People of *Israel,* 1 Kings 18. 21. *How long halt ye between two Opinions? If the* *Lord be God follow him: but if Baal then follow him.* Or as the *Shipmaster* to *Jonah,* who was fast asleep in the midst of a great Tempest, Jonah 1. 5. *What meanest thou, O Sleeper? Arise, call upon thy God, if so be he will think upon us that we perish not,* Verse 6. [———] just and pertinent Note of Mr. *Henry,* upon this Passage of Scripture, *"That those who sleep in a Storm may well be ask'd what they mean?"* Brethren, You sleep in a greater *Storm* than *Jonah* did; that only concern'd the *Body,* but this the precious *Soul;* that a *temporal,* but this an *eternal Death.* You are (whether you know it or not sensibly) every Moment ready to be *swallow'd* up by the *boisterous Billows* of *God's* justly *incensed Ire,* and the *Vessel* of your *Souls* like to be *broken* by a dreadful *Inundation* of his vindictive *Fury* and *Revenge:* Deut. 32. 41, 35. Rom. 12. 19. *"And yet will you sleep, what Metal are you made of? What God do you fear? Or are you deaf to all the Menaces of Heaven?"* Will not the *Terrors* of an *eternal God,* and an *eternal Hell* make you *afraid?* What mean you? Are you yet wholly lost to *Sense,* to *Reason,* and to *Conscience?* Are you *degenerated* into *Beasts?* Or *petrified* into

Stones? Are you cover'd with the *Levi-athan's Scales* that no *Arrow* from the *Bow* of God will *pierce* you! Mayn't the Example of *Jonas's* Fellow Mariners make you asham'd? Jonah 1. 5. *Then the Mariners were afraid, and cry'd every Man to his God, and cast forth the Wares that were in the Ship, into the Sea, to lighten it of them. But perhaps you mock at Fear, and are not af-frighted, though the Heavens look black, and God's Lightnings and Thun-ders,* from *blazing, trembling Sinai, flash and groan, and rore hideously!* Tho' *God's Law condemn* you, and your own *Consciences tell* you, that you shall surely perish, if ye die in the same State you are now in, yet you boldly, or rather shall I say impudently, or stupidly brave it out in the Face of an *angry Heaven!* And run upon the thick *Bosses* of *God's Bucklers,* and are not afraid when *God's* great *Ordnance* is *level'd* at your *naked Bosom.* You won't be perswaded by any *Importunity* to cast these *Goods* out of the Ship, (as the Mariners did) which will if retain'd sink it in *Death.* I mean your *darling Lusts* which you must *for-sake* or *perish.* Mat. 5. 29. Again, the affrighted Mariners *cry'd every one to his God,* Ver. 5. Why don't you awake poor Souls, and cry every one of you to *God,* with the utmost Vehemence, as the *Disciples of Christ* did in a *Storm,* when the Waves were like to overwhelm the Vessel, *Lord, save us we perish!* Mat. 8. 25. Or as *Peter's* Hearers, Acts 2. 37. *Men and Brethren, What shall we do to be saved? Sirs,* Suffer me to acost you in the Language of *Paul* to the *Ephesians,* Chap. 5. 14. *Awake thou that sleepest, and arise from the Dead, and Christ shall give thee Light; for the Time past of our Life may suffice us, to have wrought the Will of the Gentiles.* 1 Pet. 4. 3. *Awake to Righteousness and sin not: for some have not the Knowledge of God: I speak this to your Shame.* I Cor. 15. 34. *And especially knowing the*

Time, that now it is high Time to awake out of Sleep. But I can't in Re-gard of you add the Apostle's Reason, Rom. 13. 11. *For now is your Salvation nearer than when ye believed.* No Brethren! I am oblig'd in *Faithfulness* to *God,* and *Love* to you, to tell that inasmuch as you did not, and now do not *believe,* that your *Damnation* is nearer than when ye first *heard* the *Gos-pel* of *Christ,* and *Salvation* by his *Blood;* because of your *unbelieving Ob-stinacy* and *presumptuous Security.*

Awake, Awake Sinners, stand up and look where you are hastning, least *you drink of the Hand of the Lord, the Dregs of the Cup of his Fury; the Cup of trembling, and wring them out,* Isai. 51. 17. *Awake ye Drunkards,* and *weep and howl,* Joel 1. 5. For what can ye expect (so continuing) but to drink of that *Cup of Trembling* I but now mention'd.

Awake ye *prophane* Swearers, and re-member ye will not get a *drop of Water* to cool your cursing cursed Tongues in Hell, when they and you shall *flame* in the *broad burning Lake,* Luke 16. 24. *God has said he will not hold you Guilt-less, that take his Name in vain,* Exod 20. 7.

Awake ye *unclean Adulterers,* and *Whoremongers,* and remember that without a speedy Repentance, your dis-mal *abode* shall be ever with *unclean Devils, the Soul of a God* shall be *aveng'd* upon you, Jer. 5. 8, 29.

Awake ye *Sabbath-Breakers,* and *re-form;* or *God* will *break* you upon the *Wheels* of his *Vengeance,* and *torture* you eternally upon the *Rack* of his *Jus-tice,* Neham. 13. 16, 17, 18.

And let all other sorts of *prophane Sinners* be entreated to *awake* out of *Sleep* and consider their *Danger.*

Awake ye *covetous griping Nabals,* and read what the Apostle *James* says to you, Chap 5. 1 to 6. *Go to now, ye rich Men, weep and howl for the Miseries that shall come upon you. The Rust of your Gold and Silver shall be a Witness against you. Ye have lived in Pleasure upon Earth, and been wanton, you have nourished your Hearts as in a Day of Slaughter.* Here we may Note by the Way, that those who *live like Beasts here,* and will not be induc'd by any Perswasive to *repent, reform* and act like Men, shall *howl like Beasts hereafter,* without being *heard* or *pitied,* 1 Cor. 16. 13. Prov. 1. 26.

Awake ye *secure Moralists,* and *lifeless, sapless Formalists,* who are Strangers to the *Power of experimental Religion:* Remember your *shadowy Appearances,* can't *deceive* the *Rein trying God,* Gal. 6. 7. Nor your dry *Leaves* of husky spiritless *Duties, secure* your *guilty Souls,* from an astonishing overwhelming *Inundation* of his high and terrible *Displeasure,* Mat. 5. 20.

. . . .

Awake every of you that are yet in a *Christless unconvinced State!* Are you not asham'd to sleep all the Day in Sloth, while some are trembling, troubled and distress'd about their Souls, who are not greater Sinners than your selves? Nay, perhaps not near so great; what *sleep?* while others are crying Night and Day with *Tears,* and heavy *Groans* to God, for pardoning Mercy, who have no more precious Souls than you. *Sleep!* While others are *labouring* hard and taking *Heaven* by *Storm!* What *sleep!* While some are *travelling* fast to the *heavenly Jerusalem,* and re-

joycing in the *Way* with *Joy* unspeakable and glorious. What will ye draw the *Curtains* of a carnal *Security,* and false Hope about you, and *sleep to Death* and *Hell,* even when the *meridian Sun* of the *Gospel* shines full in your *Face,* and Life and Immortality is brought to Light, and *God,* and *Christ,* his *Ministers, Word, Providences,* and your own *Consciences,* are ringing a loud *Alarm,* a *Peal* of *Thunder* in your Ears to *awake* you: That you may consider your Ways, and turn your Feet to God's Testimonies. Will you sleep with *Fire* in your Bosoms? (the unpardon'd Guilt of Sin) with the *Curse* of God upon your *Souls,* the *Heavens frowning* upon you, and *shut* against you, the *burden'd Earth travelling* under you, and *Hell* yauning wide to *devour* and consume you! Mayn't I say to you as *Moses* to *Israel,* Deut. 29. 4. *Yet the Lord hath not given you a Heart to perceive, and Eyes to see, and Ears to hear, unto this Day.* O! Is it not to be fear'd that *God* in Justice has left you to a *Spirit* of *Slumber?* Because you shut your Eyes against the Light, John 3. That you should sleep and never awake. Jer. 51. 57. *And I will make drunk her Princes, and her wise Men, and her Rulers, and her mighty Men; and they shall sleep a perpetual Sleep, and not awake, saith the King, whose Name is the Lord of Hosts.* Prov. 6. 9. *How long wilt thou sleep, O Sluggard? when wilt thou arise out of thy Sleep?*

CHAPTER TWO

THE ITINERANTS

THE Great Awakening began in earnest with the tour of George Whitefield (1714–1770) through the colonies in 1740 and 1741. Whitefield (pronounced Whitfield) was not an unknown when he arrived in America. Although a young man who had only taken his degree at Oxford in 1736, he was already widely admired in England for his eloquent preaching of the new birth and also deeply resented for his abuse of less fervent ministers. At Oxford he had undergone conversion himself and became closely associated with the Wesleys, Charles and John, and the budding Methodist movement. At their instigation he spent a few months in America in 1738, when he decided to sponsor the orphanage in Georgia for which he raised money on his subsequent tour of the colonies. Upon his return to England, vast crowds thronged to hear him, and, since most pulpits were closed to him, he resorted to preaching in the fields, a practice which became his trademark. By the time he landed in Philadelphia in December of 1739, his reputation for good and ill had gone ahead of him. Ministers from all over the colonies came to hear him and reports of his triumphs, usually colored by the reporter's personal response, appeared in newspapers everywhere (No. 4).

For the most part the clergy welcomed him. Many urged him to visit their areas in the hope that his unusual powers might arouse their people (No. 5). Wherever he went huge crowds came to hear him. Often he took to the fields, not because of clerical inhospitability, but for lack of space inside the meetinghouses. His published journals invariably tell of weeping and anguish in the audiences he addressed (No. 6). After each meeting, concerned people crowded into his rooms for pastoral counsel. The printed versions of his simple and direct sermons convey only a small part of the majesty and deep passion of the man (No. 7). Whitefield says that Jonathan Edwards, a far more sophisticated and learned person than himself, wept through the entirety of one of these discourses.

For all his persuasiveness, Whitefield met opposition in the colonies as he had in England. The Anglican ministry accused him of disorderly conduct from the beginning, and the commissary in Charleston, Alexander Garden, went so far as to call Whitefield before an ecclesiastical court. The conservative Presbyterian and Congregational clergy suspected him of enthusiasm, the eighteenth-century word for the belief that impulses and intense feelings were to be followed as revelations from God. They also criticized him for calling the ministers unconverted and strangers to Christ.

His daily journals, published shortly after he left the colonies, created still more enemies. In them he lamented the absence of clerical piety and criticized Harvard for neglecting its students' souls. He rebuked the college for reading churchmen like Archbishop Tillotson and rationalist writers like Samuel Clarke rather than Solomon Stoddard and Thomas Shepard, one of the saintly founders of New England. In response to charges in the journals, William Brattle (1706–1776) stoutly defended Harvard, albeit without repudiating Whitefield (No. 8). The great evangelist's virtues were still widely admired. Only later, as events unfolded, did the college bluntly denounce him.

After Whitefield's departure and at his request, Gilbert Tennent toured New England to keep the flame alight. Local ministers caught up by the religious excitement began to itinerate as well. Preachers whose congregations had begun to revive were invited to visit churches which had not yet been touched. These itinerants spread the spirit of the revival with astounding results. Skeptics who came to scoff went away broken in spirit and pleading to God for mercy. Apparently hardened and dead congregations came to life. Effective preachers like Eleazar Wheelock (1711–1779) were in great demand. Invitations from all over New England came to his parsonage in Lebanon, Connecticut. Even Jonathan Edwards asked him to preach in East Windsor, the parish where Edwards's father was pastor. Wheelock's correspondence with ministers seeking his services, with other itinerants reporting their experiences, and with laymen like Captain John Lee, venting both religious feelings and hatred of the Old Light clergy, reveal not only the concerns of awakened men but their growing sense of common interests which transcended the limits of town and colony (No. 10). After the Awakening subsided, Wheelock opened a school for Indians, which in 1770 he moved to Hanover, New Hampshire, and named after the second earl of Dartmouth, one of the school's English benefactors.

James Davenport (1716–1757), one of the most powerful and certainly the most controversial of all the itinerants, followed Gilbert Tennent on the New England circuit. Wheelock and other New Lights had known of Davenport's unusual ability before the Awakening began, although they were also wary of his poor health and fragile emotional stability. Presaging his later extravagant gestures, Davenport, after he resolved to become an itinerant, called together his people at Southold, Long Island, and spoke to them for twenty-four hours. When he began to preach in southern Connecticut, Davenport confirmed all the worst fears of the Awakening's enemies. While he attracted huge crowds and won the hearts of many, he put himself at the disposal of enthusiastic impulses and impressions and freely censured the unconverted clergy whose unregenerate condition he claimed unerringly to perceive. In 1742 Connecticut found him guilty of disturbing the peace and, judging him unbalanced, deported him from the colony (No. 11). Unabashed, Davenport went on to Boston where the New Lights rebuked him for his censoriousness and closed their pulpits to him (No. 12). He preached in the streets and denounced the clergy anyway, until the authorities judged him insane and sent him home. A year later, back in New London to organize a group of converts into a church, Davenport fell into further excesses, but seemed to sense by this time that he had gone too far (No. 13). In 1744 he publicly confessed his mistakes (No. 15).

By that date the damage was done. To the dismay of the New Lights, Davenport was incontrovertible evidence of the danger of overweening religious zeal. His charges against the standing clergy, reinforced by outcries from local New Lights, divided congregations against their ministers and emboldened some to separate and form churches of their own. The itinerants' flaming passions incited audiences to intemperate emotional excesses. The revival appeared to many to harm religion more than promote it.

Many conservatives thought unrestrained itineracy was the fundamental cause of the difficulties. Theophilus Pickering (1700–1747) of Ipswich, Massachusetts, for example, complained that the unauthorized preaching of New Light ministers from neighboring parishes broke down the order of the churches and subverted his authority as minister (No. 16). The Connecticut clergy recommended to the General Assembly that itineracy be forbidden altogether, except where pastor and people agreed to invite a visiting preacher (No. 17A). While most New Lights acquiesced in the law, they believed it wrong.

A number actually disregarded it, and suffered the consequences, among them Benjamin Pomeroy (1704–1784), Davenport's companion on his visit to Connecticut (No. 17B). For some zealous New Lights, the government's opposition to God's purposes warranted a measure of civil disobedience.

When Whitefield visited the colonies again in 1744, many fewer ministers welcomed him. A number adamantly refused admission to their pulpits and urged others also to shut their doors (No. 18). Before Whitefield arrived in Boston, New Light leaders cautioned him against censures that would encourage separations, an ecclesiastical problem that was assuming major proportions (No. 19). Whitefield again was warmly received by the people and received sufficient encouragement to stay in the colonies until 1748. Not one to shrink before criticism, he returned four times more, dying in Newburyport, Massachusetts, in 1770. But he never again was to see a revival like the glorious Awakening of 1740 and 1741.

George Whitefield

4. A Report on Whitefield in New York: *The New England Weekly Journal*, 1739

[*The New England Weekly Journal*, December 4, 1739]

The Rev. Mr. *Whitefield* arrived at the City of *N. York* on Wednesday the 14th Inst. a little before Night. The next Morning he waited on the Rev. Mr. *Vesey*, and desired leave to preach in the English Church, but was refus'd: The Reason assigned for such Refusal was, because Mr. *Whitefield* had no Licence to Preach in any Parish but that for which he was ordained; and an old Canon was read. To this Mr. *Whitefield* reply'd, That that Canon was Obsolete, and had not been in Use for above 100 Years, That the whole Body of the Clergy, frequently preach out of the Bounds of their Parishes, without such Licence. These Arguments not prevailing, some Application was made to the Rev. Mr. *Boel,* for the Use of the *New Dutch Church,* but this also was refus'd. Then Mr. *Whitefield* had the offer of the *Presbyterian Church,* but did not care at first to accept it, not being willing to give any Offence to his Brethren of the Church of *England;* but said, *He chose rather to go without the Camp, bearing his Reproach, and Preach in the Fields.* At length being informed, that in some Parts of this Country, the Meeting Houses had been alternately us'd by the Ministers of the several Communions, and very often borrowed by the Church of the Dissenters, he consented to accept the Offer for the Evening. However, in the Afternoon he preached in the Fields to many Hundreds of People.

Among the Hearers, the Person who gives this Account, was one. I fear Curiosity was the Motive that led me and many others into that Assembly. I had read two or three of Mr. *Whitefield's*

Sermons and part of his Journal, and from thence had obtained a settled Opinion, that he was a Good Man. Thus far was I prejudiced in his Favour. But then having heard of much Opposition, and many Clamours against him, I tho't it possible that he might have carried Matters too far—That some *Enthusiasm* might have mix'd itself with his Piety, and that his Zeal might have exceeded his Knowledge. With these Prepossessions I went into the Fields; when I came there, I saw a great Number of People consisting of *Christians* of all Denominations, some *Jews,* and a few, I believe, that had no Religion at all. When Mr. *Whitefield* came to the Place before designed, which was a little Eminence on the side of a Hill, he stood still, and beckned with his Hand, and dispos'd the Multitude upon the Descent, before, and on each side of him. He then prayed most excellently, in the same manner (I guess) that the first Ministers of the *Christian Church* prayed, before they were shackled with Forms. The Assembly soon appeared to be divided into two Companies, the one of which I considered under the Name of GOD's *Church,* and the other the *Devil's Chappel.* The first were collected round the Minister, and were very serious and attentive. The last had placed themselves in the skirts of the Assembly, and spent most of their Time in Gigling, Scoffing, Talking and Laughing. I believe the Minister saw them, for in his Sermon, observing the Cowardice and Shamefacedness of *Christians* in Christ's Cause, he pointed towards this Assembly, and reproached the former with the boldness and Zeal with which the Devil's Vassals serve him. Towards the last Prayer, the whole Assembly appeared more united, and all became hush'd and still; a solemn Awe and Reverence appeared in the Faces of most, a mighty Energy attended the Word. I heard and felt something astonishing and surprizing, but, I confess; I was not at that Time fully rid of my Scruples. But as I tho't I saw a visible Presence of GOD with Mr. *Whitefield,* I kept my Doubts to my self.

Under this Frame of Mind, I went to hear him in the Evening at the *Presbyterian Church,* where he Expounded to above 2000 People within and without Doors. I never in my Life saw so attentive an Audience: Mr. *Whitefield* spake as one having Authority: All he said was *Demonstration, Life* and *Power!* The Peoples Eyes and Ears hung on his Lips. They greedily devour'd every Word. I came Home astonished! Every Scruple vanished. I never saw nor heard the like, and I said within my self, *Surely God is with this Man of a Truth.* He preach'd and expounded in this manner twice every Day for four Days, and this Evening Assemblies were continually increasing. On Sunday Morning at 8 o'Clock, his Congregation consisted of about 1500 People: But at Night several Thousands came together to hear him, and the Place being too strait for them, many were forced to go away, and some (tis said) with Tears lamented their Disappointment.

5. An Invitation from the Eastern Consociation, Fairfield County, Connecticut, 1740

[*Invitations To the Reverend Mr. Whitefield, From the Eastern Consociation of the County of Fairfield* . . . (Boston, 1745), 3–6]

At a Stated Meeting of the Eastern Consociation of the County of *Fairfield* at *Stratfield,* on Tuesday the 7th of *October* 1740.

Mr. COOKE chosen Moderator, and Mr. MINER chosen Scribe.

Voted, That, considering the wonderful Success that hath attended the Rev. Mr. *Whitefield's* Ministry in the Places where he hath preached, in awakening secure Sinners and the Promotion of Piety; the Moderator and Scribe do, in the Name of this Consociation, prepare a Letter and send it to the abovesaid Rev. Gentleman with all convenient Speed, intreating that he would make a Visit to the several Towns within our District, that if it may be the Will of GOD, he may be an Instrument of reviving decayed Religion in our Churches also.

A true Copy of Record,
Test. *Samuel Cooke,* Register.

To the Reverend Mr. WHITEFIELD.

Reverend and dearly beloved Brother,

In Pursuance of the Vote of our Consociation, in which was present every Pastor in our Circuit, and a Messenger from every Church, save one; an attested Copy of which Vote we have sent you subjoined: We do (as well in the Name of said Consociation as in our own Names) earnestly intreat you to make a ministerial Visit to us and our People in our several religious Societies. We in these Parts may be said in some Respects to have a Name to live, and to maintain something of the Form of Godliness. We are indoctrinated in the Christian Faith, conformable to the *Westminster Assembly's Shorter Catechism,* to which our People generally in Words assent, and which our Children drink in, as it were with their Mother's Milk, etc. But alas for us! it is too notorious to be denied or palliated, that the Life and Power of Godliness in our Parts is generally sunk to a Degree very lamentable. As far as we know our selves, we may say, that we sincerely bewail and mourn over dying Religion, and do heartily wish, pray for, and willingly endeavour its Revival in the Hearts and Lives of our selves and People, not without some affecting Sense of our own very criminal Indolence in Times past. God in Mercy forgive us, and inspire us and our Brethren in the Ministry with a renewed and warmer Zeal, and more assiduous Activity in pleading the Cause of languishing Piety, and erecting and building up the spiritual Kingdom of Christ in the Hearts and Lives of Professors! The good Lord cure us of our *Laodicean* Lukewarmness, that he spue us not out of his Mouth! Oh that we were more generally acquainted with the Necessity, Nature, Symptoms, and Effects of a divine, spiritual Regeneration, and more earnestly engaged in the Pursuit of it; without which, all Externals in Religion and Morality will leave us short of the heavenly Kingdom: And that there were neither Masters nor Disciples in our *Israel* that should ignorantly deride and ridicule such Doctrines! Our Eyes and our Hearts are lift up unto God in the Heavens, and our Dependance is wholly upon him as the Efficient, who hath the Hearts of all in his Hands, and turns them as the Rivers of Water, with whom is the Residue of the Spirit, that he would more plentifully pour out his Spirit upon us and our People of the risen and rising Generation, even a Spirit of Grace and Supplication, a Spirit of Conviction and Awakening, a Spirit of Conversion and Regeneration, a Spirit of progressive Sanctification and Consolation.

But for as much as God is wont to raise up, spirit, and improve some special Instruments for these great and good Designs towards a People for whom he hath Designs of Signal Grace and Favour, and hath distinguishingly animated and succeeded you, as an happy Instrument of the Spirit for these

Purposes; we can't but most affectionately wish that we may share in your personal Ministrations; and our daily Prayer is, that you may come to us in the Fulness of the Blessing of the Gospel of Christ, and that the Blessing of many among us who are ready to perish may come upon you; and likewise for you, that you may glorify God in the most becoming inward Frames and outward Conduct, under all the good and evil Report occurring, and not be on the one Hand exalted above Measure, nor on the other impatiently succumb under Discouragements arising from Male-treatment.

Sir, There are two Things more which we heartily wish, and shall take Leave to mention as Prudentials, *viz.*

1. That while you are zealously pleading what we, as well as you, look upon as the Cause of Christ and his Religion, you will not be free in personal Reflections to wound the Characters of others who have been generally well accepted among Christians for Piety; lest some be hereby occasionally so prejudiced as not to receive the Love of the Truth that they might be saved. We can't but think that Unsoundness in Principles, and Hypocrisy in Profession, may be far more advantageously impleaded, and the contrary Truths imprinted, without fixing personal Brands, tho' they were (absolutely considered) ever so just. How it is elsewhere we do not pretend to know, but are morally assured that such a Caution is necessary to be observed here in order to the more general Success of the Gospel-Ministry either stated or occasional.

2. That you expect not among us Collections for your *Orphan-House* in *Georgia:* For tho' we were our selves ever so far from entertaining a Thought so injurious to your Character, as to suspect that under that Name, you were pursuing a private, worldly Interest of your own; yet it will be exceeding hard, if not impossible for us, who are very little acquainted with that Affair, to dispossess others of hurtful Prejudices on that Score. And we sincerely believe that the glorious Design of reviving Religion among us by your occasional Ministry, will have probably a much better and more extensive Effect without such a Collection. *Sed Deus & Dies docebunt.*

To what has been offered, we shall only subjoin our Request, that you would write us by the first Opportunity, and let us know when we may expect you in our District, that we may notify our distant Brethren in the Ministry as well as others.

Thus, with our hearty Thanksgivings to God for the good Success which hath hitherto attended your painful Labours, and praying that God would yet abundantly add thereunto, and our Desires of a special Interest in your Prayers, for us, our Families and Flocks, we subscribe,   Sir,

Your Brethren and Fellow-Labourers in the Gospel,

SAMUEL COOKE,

RICHARDSON MINER.

Connecticut, ss.

Stratfield, Octob. 14. 1740. A true Copy of a Letter sent to the Rev. Mr. *George Whitefield* &c.

Test. *S. Cooke,* Register of the Consociation.

6. George Whitefield, *Journals*, 1740

[*George Whitefield's Journals: A new edition containing fuller material than any hitherto published* ([n.p.], 1960), 420–425, 457–458, 460–462, 469–470, 472–477]

PHILADELPHIA

Saturday, May 10. Though God has shewn me great things already in this place, yet to-day I have seen greater. I preached twice, and to larger congregations than ever. In the evening, I went to settle a Society of young women, who, I hope, will prove wise virgins. As soon as I entered the room, and heard them singing, my soul was delighted. When the hymn was over, I desired to pray before I began to converse; but, my soul was so carried out, that I had not time to talk at all. A wonderful power was in the room, and with one accord, they began to cry out and weep most bitterly for the space of half an hour. They seemed to be under the strongest convictions, and did indeed seek Jesus sorrowing. Their cries might be heard a great way off. When I had done, I thought proper to leave them at their devotions. They continued in prayer for above an hour, confessing their most secret faults; and, at length, the agonies of some were so strong, that five of them seemed affected as those who are in fits. The present Captain of our sloop going near the waterside, was called in to a company, almost in the same circumstances; and, at midnight, I was desired to come to one who was in strong agonies of body and mind, but felt somewhat of joy and peace, after I had prayed with her several times. Her case put me in mind of the young man whom the devil tore, when he was coming to Jesus. Such-like bodily agonies, I believe, are from the devil; and, now the work of

God is going on, he will, no doubt, endeavour by *these* to bring an evil report upon it. O Lord, for Thy mercy's sake, rebuke him; and, though he may be permitted to bite Thy people's heel, fulfil Thy promise, and let the Seed of the Woman bruise his head! Amen, Amen!

Sunday, May 11. Preached to about fifteen thousand people in the morning. Went twice to church, and heard myself taken to task by the Commissary, who preached from these words: "I bear them record, they have a zeal for God, but not according to knowledge." I could have wished he had considered the next words: "For they being ignorant of God's righteousness, have not submitted themselves to the righteousness of God." Had he considered these words, I might justly have said, "Speaketh Mr. Commissary of this false zeal in reference to himself, or of some other man?" He exclaimed loudly against me in the pulpit, and, I soon found, obliged many of his hearers to do what they were before inclined to do, *viz.*, resolve to leave me entirely. I bear him record, that experience will soon convince him, that whatever mine may be, his own zeal is by no means according to knowledge. After he had done, I preached my farewell sermon to very near twenty thousand hearers. Though the Commissary's sermon was chiefly of personal reflections, I thought it not proper to render railing for railing. However, I considered it my duty, in an especial manner to recommend the Messrs. Tennents and their associates, being most worthy preachers of our Lord Jesus. One passage out of the Second Lesson for the morning, much affected me: "And the Lord had compassion on the multitude, because they were scattered, as sheep having no shepherd." I then reminded them of our Lord's command, "Pray ye therefore the Lord of the harvest that He may send out labourers into His harvest." For though "the harvest is plenteous, the labourers are few."

The poor people were much concerned at my bidding them farewell; and, after I had taken my leave, many came to my lodgings, sorrowing that they were to see my face no more for a long season. Near fifty negroes came to give me thanks for what God had done to their souls. How heartily did those poor creatures throw in their mites for my poor orphans. Some of them have been effectually wrought upon, and in an uncommon manner. Many of them have begun to learn to read. One, who was free, said she would give me her two children, whenever I settle my school. I believe masters and mistresses will shortly see that Christianity will not make their negroes worse slaves. I intended, had time permitted, to have settled a Society for negro men and negro women; but that must be deferred till it shall please God to bring me to Philadelphia again. I have been much drawn out in prayer for them, and have seen them exceedingly wrought upon under the Word preached. I cannot well express how many others, of all sorts, came to give me a last farewell. I never saw a more general awakening in any place.

Religion is all the talk; and, I think I can say, the Lord Jesus hath gotten Himself the victory in many hearts. I have scarce had time to eat bread from morning to evening; some one or other was generally applying to me under deep soul-concern, and others continually pressing upon me to baptise their infants. I did comply with as many as I could; but I was obliged sometimes to say, "The Lord sent me not to baptise, but to preach the Gospel."

Many of the Quakers have been convinced of the righteousness of Jesus Christ, and openly confess the truth as it is in Jesus; for which, I believe, they will shortly be put out of their synagogues. Some of their head men are zealous against me, and are much afraid their foundation will be sadly shaken. Great numbers of the inhabitants would have built me immediately a very large church, if I would have consented; but the Lord, I am persuaded, would have His Gospel preached in the fields; and building a church would, I fear, insensibly lead the people into bigotry, and make them place the Church again, as they have done for a long time, in the church walls. For these reasons I declined it; though notwithstanding, I believe they will build some place. What I mostly fear is, now there is such a general awakening, the people will not know where to go for proper food, and thereby fall into different sects and parties. Lord Jesus, look upon them, and let not Satan divide them again; but raise them up pastors after Thy own heart. Amen and amen.

. . . .

NOTTINGHAM

Wednesday, May 14. Got to a Quaker's house, which lay in our way to Nottingham, about midnight [May 13], and met with a hospitable reception. Preached at Nottingham both morning and evening, with such demonstration of the Spirit, and such a wonderful movement amongst the hearers, as few ever saw before. I was invited thither, by some of the inhabitants, who had a good work begun amongst them, some time ago, by the ministry of Mr. Blair, the Messrs. Tennents, and Mr. Cross, the last of which had been denied the use of the pulpit by one of his own brethren, and was obliged to preach in the woods, where the Lord manifested forth His glory, and caused many to cry out, "What shall we do to be saved?" It surprised me to see such a multitude gathered together, at so short a warning, and in such a desert place. I believe there were near twelve thousand. I had not spoken long before I perceived numbers melting. As I proceeded, the influence increased, till, at last (both in the morning and the afternoon), thousands cried out, so that they almost drowned my voice. Never did I see a more glorious sight. Oh what tears were shed and poured forth after the Lord Jesus. Some fainted; and when they had got a little strength, they would hear and faint again. Others cried out in a manner as if they were in the sharpest agonies of death. Oh what thoughts and words did God put into my heart! After I had finished my last discourse, I was so pierced, as it were, and overpowered with a sense of God's love, that some thought, I believe, I was about to give up the ghost. How sweetly did I lie at the feet of Jesus! With what power did a sense of His all-constraining, free, and everlasting love flow in upon my soul! It almost took away my life. At length, I revived, and was strengthened to go with Messrs. Blair, Tennent, and some other friends to Mr. Blair's house, twenty miles from Nottingham. In the way, we refreshed our souls by singing psalms and hymns. We got to our journey's end at midnight. Oh Lord, was ever love like Thine!

.   .   .   .

BOSTON

Friday, September 19. I was visited by several gentlemen and ministers, and went to the Governor's with Esquire Willard, the Secretary of the Province, a man fearing God, and with whom I have corresponded some time, though before unknown in person. The Governor received me with the utmost respect, and desired me to see him as often as I could. At eleven, I went to public worship at the Church of England, and afterwards went home with the Commissary, who had read prayers. He received me very courteously; and, it being a day whereon the clergy of the Established Church met, I had an opportunity of conversing with five of them together. I think, one of them began with me for calling "that Tennent and his brethren *faithful* ministers of Jesus Christ." I answered, "I believed they were." They then questioned me about "the validity of the Presbyterian ordination." I replied, "I believed it was valid." They then urged against me a passage in my first *Journal*, where I said, "That a Baptist minister at Deal did not give a satisfactory answer concerning his mission." I answered, "Perhaps my sentiments were altered." "And is Mr. Wesley altered in his sentiments?" said one; "for he was very strenuous for the Church, and rigorous against all other forms of government when he was at Boston." I answered, "He was then a great bigot, but God has since enlarged his heart, and I believed he was now like-minded with me in this particular." I then urged, "That a catholic spirit was best, and that a Baptist minister had communicated lately with me at Savannah." "I suppose," said another, "you would do him as good a turn, and would communicate with him." I answered, "Yes," and urged "that it was best to preach the new birth, and the power of godliness, and not to insist so much on the form: for people would never be brought to one mind as to that; nor did Jesus Christ ever intend it." "Yes, but He did," said Dr. Cutler. "How do you prove it?" "Because Christ prayed, 'That all might be one, even as Thou Father and I are One.'" I replied, "That was spoken of the inward union of the souls of believers with Jesus Christ, and not of the outward Church." "That cannot be," said Dr. Cutler, "for how then could it be said, 'that the world might know that Thou hast sent Me?'" He then (taking it for granted that the Church of England was the only true apostolical Church) drew a parallel between the Jewish and our Church, urging how God required all things to be made according to the pattern given in the Mount. I answered, "That before the parallel could be just, it must be proved, that every thing enjoined in our Church was as much of a Divine institution as any rite or ceremony under the Jewish dispensation." I added further, "That I saw regenerate souls among the Baptists, among the Presbyterians, among the Independents, and among the Church folks,—all children of God, and yet all born again in a different way of worship: and who can tell which is the most evangelical?"

. . . .

Monday, September 22. Preached this morning at the Rev. Mr. Webb's meeting-house, to six thousand hearers in the house, besides great numbers standing about the doors. Most wept for a considerable time. Sometime after, I received a letter, wherein were these words:

"But what I must give the preference to was that gracious season at the New North, the Monday following, where there was more of the presence of God through the whole visitation, than ever I had known through the whole course of my life. Justly might it have been said of that place, 'it was no other than the House of God and the Gate of Heaven!' O how dreadful was the place, and yet how delightful! The Lord Jesus seemed to be visibly walking in that His golden candlestick, to try some of the many thousands who were prepared for so holy an inquisition! I am sure I know none who could not but be humble at the thoughts of it. And who, indeed, could help crying out, 'Woe is me, for I am undone, because I am a man of unclean lips for mine eyes have seen the King, the Lord of Hosts.' The Spirit of God, indeed, seemed to be moving upon the face of the waters at that time, and who knows, but that to a great many souls, God was pleased to say, 'Let there be light, and there was light.'"

In the afternoon I went to preach at the Rev. Mr. Checkley's meeting-house; but God was pleased to humble us by a very awful providence. The meeting-house being filled, though there was no real danger, on a sudden all the people were in an uproar, and so unaccountably surprised, that some threw themselves out of the windows, others threw themselves out of the gallery, and others trampled upon one another; so that five were actually killed, and others dangerously wounded. I happened to come in the midst of the uproar, and saw two or three lying on the ground in a pitiable condition. God was pleased to give me presence of mind; so that I gave notice I would immediately preach upon the common. The weather was wet, but many thousands followed in the field, to whom I preached from these words, "Go out into the highways and hedges, and compel them to come in." I endeavoured, as God enabled me, to improve what had befallen us. Lord, Thy judgments are like the great deep. Thy footsteps are not known. Just and Holy art Thou, O King of saints!

In the evening, I was weak in body, so that I could not say much at the house where I supped; but God, by His Blessed Spirit, greatly refreshed and comforted my soul. I drank of God's pleasure as out of a river. Oh that all were made partakers of this living water: they would never thirst after the sensual pleasures of this wicked world.

. . . .

Wednesday, September 24. Went this morning to see and preach at Cambridge, the chief college for training the sons of the prophets in New England. It has one president, four tutors, and about a hundred students. The college is scarce as big as one of our least colleges at Oxford; and, as far as I could gather from some who knew the state of it, not far superior to our Universities in piety. Discipline is at a low ebb. Bad books are become fashionable among the tutors and students. Tillotson and Clark are read, instead of Shepard, Stoddard, and such-like evangelical writers; and, therefore, I chose to preach from these words,—"We are not as many, who corrupt the Word of God." A great number of neighbouring ministers attended. God gave me great boldness and freedom of speech. The President of the college and minister of the parish treated me very civilly. In the afternoon, I preached again, in the court, when, I believe, there were about seven thousand hearers. The Holy Spirit melted many hearts. A minister soon after wrote me word, "that one of his daughters was savingly wrought upon at that time." Lord, add daily to the Church, such as shall be saved! Paid my respects to the Lieutenant-Governor, who lives at Cambridge; and returned in the evening to Boston, and prayed with and exhorted many people who were waiting round the door for a spiritual morsel. I believe our Lord did not send them empty away. O Blessed Jesus, feed them with that Bread of Life Which cometh down from Heaven.

. . . .

Thursday, October 9. Every morning, since my return, I have been applied to by many souls under deep distress, and was grieved that I could not have more time with them. Gave, this morning, the public lecture at Dr. Sewall's meeting-house, which was very much crowded. When I came near the meeting-house, I found it much impressed upon my heart, that I should preach upon our Lord's conference with Nicodemus. When I got into the pulpit, I saw a great number of ministers sitting around and before me. Coming to these words, "art thou a master in Israel, and knowest not these things?" the Lord enabled me to open my mouth boldly against unconverted ministers; for, I am persuaded, the generality of preachers talk of an unknown and unfelt Christ. The reason why congregations have been so dead is, because they had dead men preaching to them. O that the Lord may quicken and revive them! How can dead men beget living children? It is true, indeed, that God may convert people by the devil, if He chooses; and so He may by unconverted ministers; but I believe, He seldom makes use of either of them for this purpose. No: He chooses vessels made meet by the operations of His Blessed Spirit. For my own part, I would not lay hands on an unconverted man for ten thousand worlds. Unspeakable freedom God gave me while treating on this head.

After sermon, I dined with the Governor, who seemed more kindly affected than ever. He told one of the ministers, who has lately begun to preach *extempore*, "that he was glad he had found out a way to save his eyes." Oh that others would follow him. I believe, they would find God ready to help and assist them.

. . . .

Sunday, October 12. Spoke to as many as I could, who came for spiritual advice. Preached, with great power, at Dr. Sewall's meeting-house, which was so exceedingly thronged, that I was obliged to get in at one of the windows. Dined with the Governor, who came to me, after dinner, when I had retired, and earnestly desired my prayers. The Lord be with and in him, for time and eternity! Heard Dr. Sewall preach, in the afternoon. Was sick at meeting, and, also, after it was over. Went with the Governor, in his coach, to the common, where I preached my farewell sermon to near twenty thousand people—a sight I have not seen since I left Blackheath—and a sight, perhaps never seen before in America. It being nearly dusk before I had done, the sight was more solemn. Numbers, great numbers, melted into tears, when I talked of leaving them. I was very particular in my application, both to rulers, ministers, and people, and exhorted my hearers steadily to imitate the piety of their forefathers; so that I might hear, that with one heart and mind, they were striving together for the faith of the Gospel. After sermon, the Governor went with me to my lodgings. I stood in the passage, and spoke to a great company, both within and without doors; but they were so deeply affected, and cried so loud, that I was obliged to leave off praying. The Governor took his leave in the most affectionate manner, and said he would come and take me in his coach to Charleston ferry the next morning.

The remainder of the evening was almost entirely spent in speaking to persons under great distress of soul. I believe, the poor girl that followed me from Roxbury, got a saving knowledge of Christ this morning; for when I preached on these words, "The Lord our Righteousness," she was enabled to say, "The Lord *my* Righteousness," and that she was not afraid to die. I found upon enquiry, she could not read, which

shews the sovereignty of God's electing love, and confirms what the Apostle says, "that the Lord chooses the foolish things of this world to confound the wise." Charity will incline me to take her to Georgia; for she is cast out already, in effect, for Christ's sake. Blessed be God! for what He has done in Boston. I hope a glorious work is now begun, and that the Lord will stir up some faithful labourers to carry it on.

Boston is a large, populous place, and very wealthy. It has the form of religion kept up, but has lost much of its power. I have not heard of any remarkable stir for many years. Ministers and people are obliged to confess, that the love of many is waxed cold. Both seem to be too much conformed to the world. There is much of the pride of life to be seen in their assemblies. Jewels, patches, and gay apparel are commonly worn by the female sex. The little infants who were brought to baptism, were wrapped up in such fine things, and so much pains taken to dress them, that one would think they were brought thither to be initiated into, rather than to renounce, the pomps and vanities of this wicked world. There are nine meeting-houses of the Congregational persuasion, one Baptist, one French, and one belonging to the Scots-Irish. There are two monthly, and one weekly lectures; and those, too, but poorly attended. I mentioned it in my sermons, and I trust God will stir up the people to tread more frequently the courts of His house. One thing Boston is very remarkable for, viz., the external observance of the Sabbath. Men in civil offices have a regard for religion. The Governor encourages them; and the ministers and magistrates seem to be more united than in any other place where I have been. Both were exceedingly civil during my stay. I never saw so little scoffing, and never had so little opposition. Still, I fear, many rest in a head-knowledge, are close Pharisees, and have only a name to live.

It must needs be so, when the power of godliness is dwindled away, where the form only of religion is become fashionable amongst people. However, there are "a few names left in Sardis, which have not defiled their garments." Many letters came to me from pious people, in which they complained of the degeneracy of the times, and hoped that God was about to revive His work in their midst. Even so, Lord Jesus, Amen and Amen. Yet Boston people are dear to my soul. They were greatly affected by the Word, followed night and day, and were very liberal to my dear orphans. I promised, God willing, to visit them again when it shall please Him to bring me again from my native country. The Lord be with thy ministers and people, and grant that the remnant, which is still left according to the election of grace, may take root and bear fruit, and fill the land!

. . . .

HADLEY AND NORTHAMPTON

Friday, October 17. Set out as soon as it was light, and reached Hadley, a place where a great work was carried on some years ago; but lately the people of God have complained of deadness and losing their first love. As soon as I mentioned what God had done for their souls formerly, it was like putting fire to tinder. The remembrance of it caused many to weep sorely. After a little refreshment, we crossed the ferry to Northampton, where no less than three hundred souls were saved about five years ago. Their pastor's name is Edwards, successor and grandson to the great Stoddard, whose memory will be always precious to my soul, and whose books entitled "A Guide to Christ," and "Safety of appearing in Christ's Righteousness," I would recommend to all. Mr. Edwards is a solid, excellent Christian, but, at present, weak in body. I think I have not seen his fellow in all New England. When I came into his pulpit, I found my heart drawn out to talk of scarce anything besides the consolations and privileges of saints, and the plentiful effusion of the Spirit upon believers. When I came to remind them of their former experiences, and how zealous and lively they were at that time, both minister and people wept much. In the evening, I gave a word of exhortation to several who came to Mr. Edwards' house. My body was weak, and my appetite almost gone; but my Lord gave me meat, which the world knows nothing of. Lord, evermore give me this bread! Amen and Amen.

. . . .

Sunday, October 19. Felt great satisfaction in being at the house of Mr. Edwards. A sweeter couple I have not yet seen. Their children were not dressed in silks and satins, but plain, as become the children of those who, in all things, ought to be examples of Christian simplicity. Mrs. Edwards is adorned with a meek and quiet spirit; she talked solidly of the things of God, and seemed to be such a helpmeet for her husband, that she caused me to renew those prayers, which, for some months, I have put up to God, that He would be pleased to send me a daughter of Abraham to be my wife. Lord, I desire to have no choice of my own. Thou knowest my circumstances; Thou knowest I only desire to marry in and for Thee. Thou didst choose a Rebecca for Isaac, choose one to be a helpmeet for me, in carrying on that great work which is committed to my charge. Preached this morning, and good Mr. Edwards wept during the whole time of exercise. The people were equally affected; and, in the afternoon, the power increased yet more. Our Lord seemed to keep the good wine till the last. I have not seen four such gracious meetings together since my arrival. Oh, that my soul may be refreshed with the joyful news, that Northampton people have recovered their first love; that the Lord has revived His work in their souls, and caused them to do their first works!

7. A Whitefield Sermon: *Marriage of Cana*, 1742

[George Whitefield, *The Marriage of Cana. A Sermon Preached at Black-Heath and Philadelphia* (Philadelphia, 1742), 31–40]

Did I come to preach myself, and not *Christ Jesus* my Lord, I would come to you, not in this Plainness of Speech, but with the enticing Words of Man's Wisdom. Did I desire to please natural Men, I need not preach here in the Wilderness. I hope my Heart aims at nothing else than what our Lord's great Fore-runner aim'd at, and which ought to be the Business of every Gospel Minister, that is, to point out to you the God-Man *Christ-Jesus.—Behold* then, by Faith behold, *the Lamb of God, who taketh away the Sins of the World.—* Look unto him, and be saved. You have heard how he has manifested, and will yet manifest his Glory to true Believers; and why then, O Sinners, will you not believe in him? I say, O Sinners, for now I have spoken to the Saints; I have many Things to speak to you. And Oh! may God give you all an hearing Ear, and an obedient Heart!

My Lord, even the Lord *Jesus,* who shewed forth his Glory above 1700 Years ago, has made a Marriage Feast, and offers to espouse all Sinners to himself, and to make them Flesh of his Flesh, and Bone of his Bone. He is willing to be united to you by one Spirit. In every Age, at sundry Times, and after divers Manners, he hath sent forth his Servants, and they have bid many, but yet, my Brethren, there is Room.—The Lord therefore now has given a Commission in these last Days to other of his Servants even to compel poor Sinners by the Cords of Love to come in.—For our Master's House must and shall be filled. —He will not shed his precious Blood in vain.—Come then, my Brethren, come to the Marriage.—Do not play the Harlot any longer.—Let this be the Day of your Espousals with *Jesus Christ,*—he only is your lawful Husband,—he is willing to receive you, tho' other Lords have had Dominion over you, Come to the Marriage.—Behold the Oxen and Fatlings are killed, and all Things are ready, let me hear you say, as *Rebecca* did, when they asked her, whether she would go and be a Wife to *Isaac;* Oh let me hear you say, We will come. Indeed you will not repent it. The Lord shall turn your Water into Wine. He shall fill your Souls with Marrow and Fatness, and cause you to praise him with joyful Lips. Do not say, you are miserable, and poor, and blind and naked, and therefore ashamed to come, for it is to such that this Invitation is now sent. The Polite, the Rich, the Busy, Self-righteous Pharisees of this Generation have been bidden already, but they have rejected the Counsel of God against themselves. They are too deeply engaged in going, one to his Country House, another to his Merchandize. They are so deeply wedded to the Pomps and Vanities of this wicked World, that they, as it were with one Consent, have made Excuse. And tho' they have been often called in their own Synagogues, yet all the Return they make is to thrust us out, and thereby in Effect say, they will not come. But God forbid, my Brethren, that you should learn of them; no, since our Lord condescends to call first, (because if left to yourselves you would never call after him) let me beseech you to answer him, as he answered for you, when called upon by infinite offended Justice to die for your Sins, that is, *Lo! I come to do thy Will, O God!* What if you are miserable, and poor, and blind, and naked, that is no Excuse;—Faith is the only wedding Garment *Christ* requires; he does not call you because you are already, but because he intends to *make you Saints.* No, it pities him to see you naked. He wants to cover you with his Righteousness. In short, he desires to shew forth his Glory, that is, his free Love thro' your Faith in him. Not but that he will be glorified, whether you believe in him or not; for the infinitely free Love of *Jesus Christ* will be ever the same, whether you believe it, and *so* receive it, or not. But our Lord will not send out his Servants in vain, to call you always. The Time will come when he will say, None of those which were bidden, and would not come, shall taste of my Supper.—Our Lord is a God of Justice, as well as a God of Love; and if Sinners will not take hold of his Golden Sceptre, verily he will bruise them with his Iron Rod. It is for your Sakes, O Sinners, and not his own, that he thus condescends to invite you. Oh suffer him then to shew forth his Glory, even the Glory of the exceeding Riches of his free Grace, by believing on him. *For we are saved by Grace thro' Faith.* It was Grace, free Grace, that moved the Father so to love the World, as *to give his only begotten Son, that whosoever believeth in him should not perish, but have everlasting Life!* It was Grace that made the Son come down and dye. It was Grace, free Grace, that moved the

Holy Ghost to undertake to sanctify the Elect People of God; and it was Grace, free Grace that moved our Lord *Jesus Christ* to send forth his Ministers to call all poor Sinners this Day. Let me not then, my Brethren, go without my Errand. Why will you not believe in him? will the Devil do such great and good Things for you as *Christ* will? No indeed, he will not. Perhaps he may give you to drink at first of a little brutish Pleasure, But what will he give you to drink at last? a Cup of Fury, and of trembling; a never dying Worm, a self condemning Conscience, and the bitter Pains of eternal Death. But as for the Servants of *Jesus Christ,* it is not so with them. No he keeps his best Wine till the last. And tho' he may cause you to drink of the Brook in the Way to Heaven, and of the Cup of Affliction, yet he sweetens that with a Sense of his Goodness, and makes it pleasant Drink, such as their Souls do love. I appeal to the Experience of any Saint here present, (as I doubt not but there are many such in this Place) whether *Christ* has not proved faithful to his, ever since you have been espoused to him? Has he not shew'd forth his Glory ever since you have believed on him? And now, Sinners, what have you to object? I see you are all silent, and well you may.—For if you will not be drawn by the Cords of Infinite and everlasting Love, what will draw you? I could urge many Terrors of the Lord to perswade you; but if the Love of *Jesus Christ* will not constrain you, your Case is desparate. Remember then this Day I have invited all, even the worst of Sinners, the most abandon'd Adulterers and Adulteresses to the Lord *Jesus.* If you perish remember you do not perish for lack of Invitation—You yourselves shall stand forth at the last Day, and I here give you a Summons to meet me at the Judgment Seat of *Christ,* and to clear both my Master and me.—Would weeping, would Tears prevail on you, I could wish my Head Waters, and my Eyes Fountains of Tears, that I might weep our every Argument, and melt you into Love.—Would any Thing I could do or suffer influence your Hearts, I think I could bear to pluck out my Eyes, or even to lay down my Life for your Sakes. Or was I sure to prevail on you by Importunity, I could continue my Discourse till Midnight, I would wrestle with you even till the Morning Watch, as *Jacob* did with the Angel, and would not go away till I had overcome.—But such Power only belongeth unto the Lord,—I can only invite; it is He only can work in you both to Will and to Do after his good Pleasure; It is his Property to take away the Heart of Stone, and give you a Heart of Flesh; It is his Spirit that must convince you of unbelief, and of the everlasting Righteousness of his dear Son.—'Tis he alone must give Faith to apply his Righteousness to your Hearts, It is He alone can give you a wedding Garment, and cause you to sit down and drink New Wine in his Kingdom.—Whatever others may boast of Man's Free-will, I know of no Free-will any one hath, except a Free-will to do Evil continually—As to Spirituals we are quite dead, and have no more Power to turn to God of ourselves than *Lazarus* had to raise him self, after he had lain stinking in the Grave four Days.—If thou canst go, Oh Man, and breathe upon all the dry Bones that lye in the Graves, and bid them live, if thou canst take thy Mantle and divide yonder River as *Elijah* did the River *Jordan* [then] will we believe thou hast a Po[wer] to turn to God of thyself: But [as] thou must despair of the one, so thou must despair of the other, without Christ's preventing and quickning Grace; In him is thy only Help;—Fly to him then by Faith; Say unto him, as the poor Leper did, *Lord if thou wilt, thou canst make us willing;* and he will stretch forth the Right-Hand of his Power to afflict and relieve you: He will sweetly guide you by his Wis[do]m on Earth, and afterwards take you up to partake of his Glory in Heaven.

8. A Reply to Whitefield's Criticism of Harvard: *Boston Gazette*, 1741

[*Boston Gazette*, April 20, 1741]

To the Reader,
The Author of the following Remarks is a true and hearty Lover of the Rev. Mr Whitefield, thinks that he has been Instrumental in awakening and stirring up People to a serious Concern for the Salvation of their precious Souls; and it is the Author's daily Prayer that the Convictions and Awak'nings among us, may terminate in a sound Conversion, evidenced by newness of Life and new Obedience; but still he is not so blinded as to think that worthy Gentleman is infallible; and whoever reads his last Journal must be of the same Mind; there being many Things therein contained, and particularly with Relation to the College *in* Cambridge, *and the Ministers of* New England, *without Foundation: And least this partial Account of the former, and his uncharitable Thoughts of the latter, should do as much Hurt to Religion as his Preaching did Good, the following Remarks are made.*

Mr. Whitefield observes, that on the 24th of *September,* he preached at the *College:* that it has one President, and four Tutors—Here his Account is partial, for he ought to have said that there are two Professors; one of Divinity, the other of the Mathematicks; as also an Hebrew Instructor; and he had added that these three Gentlemen were as well qualified for their respective Trusts, as any he ever conversed with, he would have spoke the Truth, and done the College but Justice.

He observes, that Discipline is at a low Ebb there; in which he is intirely mistaken. I lived at the College in two Presidents Time, both very excellent Men; the first particularly remarked for being a Man of Authority; and I am perfectly acquainted with the Government of the College at this Time, and so am as capable of knowing the Truth of that Matter as Mr. *Whitefield,* who never was at College but once in his Life, and then not a quarter of an Hour (except whilst a Preaching) and I do solemnly declare that I never saw the Authority of Government more maintained than at this Time, and I believe no one ever thought the contrary, saving this Reverend Stranger.

Again, he observes that the Tutors neglect to pray with and examine the Hearts of their Pupils; by which Account any one must necessarily suppose that they are in a worse State at College than the Heathens; for they have their publick Prayers: but here is a Society that call themselves Christians, consisting of above an Hundred Persons, and yet there are no publick Prayers offered up to Almighty GOD for them, by those unto whose Care they are committed. But now is this the Case at College; no, the President prays twenty-eight Times a Week in the College-Hall, and the Professor of Divinity four Times; so that there are thirty-two Prayers offered up to GOD by the President and Professors every Week with and for the Students, who by Law are obliged to attend the same. *David,* a Man after God's own Heart, prayed Evening and Morning, and at Noon; which makes twenty-one Times in a Week: these Gentlemen pray two and thirty Times in a Week with the Students; and yet, there are no Prayers at College. Again, are not the Holy Scriptures read by the President twice every Day in publick, and often expounded by him? Hath not the Professor of Divinity three Lectures every Week upon the best and most important Subjects? Again, I do not see how it can be called a *Neglect* in the Tutors should they not pray with their Pupils; it was what was never done in good Mr. *Shepard's* Day, nor since the College had an Existence; they are not obliged by the Laws of the College to do it, which if it was tho't necessary, undoubtedly it would have been injoined them by the Corporation and Overseers; b[ut] if it is necessary, and yet not injoined them, the Legislative Power in the College are more to blame than the Tutors. Again, the Tutors praying with the Pupils is what I believe was never known in any University, especially where there are so many Prayers every Day as at the College in *Cambridge.*

But then how does Mr. *Whitefield* know that the Tutors do not privately talk with their Pupils, with respect to their Souls. I know the Tutors never told him they did not, I know he never had it from the Pupils, how then came he by his Knowledge; I conclude he argues it from this, he finds no Journal printed giving an Account of these Things, and therefore these Things cannot be. Private and personal Instructions, Examinations, Advice, and the like in their own Nature ought to be kept secret; and because I do not know that a Man does this or the other Thing, shall I therefore infer he doth not do it. I never heard any Man pray in secret, must I therefore conclude and report abroad that no Man makes Conscience of that Duty, because he doth not publish it. But in Truth I believe the Tutors do talk with their Pupils about their Souls as Occasion requires: I was when at College under Mr. *Flynt,* who to my certain Knowledge was very faithful as to that Particular, as well as all other.

Again, Mr. *Whitefield* is pleased to observe that bad Books are read, *Tillotson* and *Clark,* instead of *Shepard* and *Stoddard.* If he means by the Undergraduates, it is a Mistake, they do not read them; if he means the Graduates, I believe they do read *Tillotson,* and I hope they will, but not in the room and stead of Bishop *Hopkins,* Bishop *Peirson,* Dr. *Bates,* Mr. *How,* Dr. *Owen,* Mr. *Baxter,* and Dr. *Wates,* who were as Great and as Good Men as Mr. *Shepard* and Mr. *Stoddard;* these they could not read till lately, because out of print; and therefore if they read other Books as good, I hope they will be forgiven; and if they should read Dr. *Tillotson* also, I do not know that it would be a Crime. Those that censure him undoubtedly have read him; pray then allow others the same Liberty you take yourselves. There are a great many excellent good Things in Dr. *Tillotson,* that the Enemies to Dr. *Tillotson,* as I have heard some of them acknowledge, have got a great deal of Good by, and so may others. It certainly would have been better for Mr. *Whitefield* to have treated Dr. *Tillotson,* unto whom the Protestant Religion, and the Dissenters are so vastly indebted, as he has done the great Mr. *Stoddard:* He speaks very honourable and justly of him, and his Works, and recommends them; but then he thinking differently from Mr. *Whitefield* in some Things, about unconverted Ministers (where by the way Mr. *Stoddard* was perfectly right in my Opinion, as also in his Thoughts about unconverted Persons going to the Sacrament) is pleased to say of him thus— 'That he honours the Memory of that great and good Man, yet he thinks he is much to be blamed for endeavouring to prove that unconverted Men may be admitted into the Ministry.' So I think Mr. *Whitefield* might have spoke of Dr. *Tillotson;* might have recommended his Works in General, and cautioned the Scholars against his Errors, none of which were more destructive to Christianity (allowing Mr. *Whitefield's* Thoughts to be just about unconverted Ministers) then are Mr. *Stoddard's* Tho'ts and Writings upon that Subject. But again, there are in Dr. *Tillotson's* Writings Things fundamentally wrong (in Mr. *Whitefield's* Opinion) or there are not, if there are not, then no such Crime to read them; if there are, still they ought to be read by those capable of making a Judgment: Because Mr. *Whitefield* may be mistaken in these Things as well as Mr. *Stoddard* in other Fundamentals. And upon Supposition Mr. *Whitefield* should be mistaken, and Dr. *Tillotson* in the right, what will become of those that have neglected reading him, upon Mr. *Whitefield's* Prohibition; will that plead their Excuse in the Great Day? And as to the Students reading Dr. *Clark* and other Arian Writers, I believe they never did. True it is, that about the Year 1735, Dr. *Clark* and many Books much worse than his were read, and some were then given up to strong Delusions, and began to deny the God that bought them; immediately upon which the Divinity Professor laboured more abundantly in asserting and proving the important Truths then denied; and by the Blessing of God upon his learned and faithful Endeavours, a Stop was soon put thereto.

In short, Mr. *Whitefield* had no Advantages of knowing the true State of the College; never had any Account about the College from any Persons of Truth, and that were acquainted with it; provided he had no other Account, than what he has given in his Journal; and therefore what Regard can be had to it.

But before I leave the College, I beg leave to observe that by Mr. *Whitefield's* and *Tennent's* Preaching, there, the Scholars in general, have been wonderfully wrought upon, and their En-quiry now is, *What shall we do to be saved?* Some I believe have lately been savingly brought home to God: These Gentlemen have planted, Mr. *Appleton* hath watered; and a blessed watering it hath been: but after all, it was GOD who gave the Increase.

9. Whitefield Responds: *Boston Gazette*, 1742

[*Boston Gazette*, March 16, 1742]

The following Letter from the Reverend Mr. Whitefield, to the Students of *Harvard College* in *Cambridge,* and *Yale College* in *New-Haven,* we are desired to insert in this Paper; and which is as follows, *viz.*

> *On Board* the Mary Ann,
> *bound from* London *to* Scotland,
> *July* 25th 1741.

Dear Gentlemen,

With unspeakable Pleasure have I heard that there seems to be a general Concern amongst you about the Things of God. It was no small Grief to me that I was obliged to say of your Colleges that your Light was become Darkness. Blessed be God that I can now say, that tho' you were Darkness, yet are ye becoming Light in the Lord. I heartily thank God, even the Father of our glorious Redeemer, for sending dear Mr. *Tennent* among you. What great Things may we now expect to see in *New England,* since it has pleased God to work so remarkably among the Sons of the Prophets? Now we may expect a Reformation indeed, since it is beginning at the House of God. A dead Ministry will always make a dead People. Whereas if Ministers are warmed with the Love of God themselves, they cannot but be Instruments of diffusing that Love amongst others. This, This is the best Preparation for the Work whereunto you are to be called. Learning without Piety will only render you more capable of promoting the Kingdom of the Devil. Henceforward therefore I hope you will enter into your Studies, not to get a Parish, not to be a polite Preacher, but to be a great Saint. This indeed is the most compendious Way to true Learning; for an Understanding enlightned by the Spirit of God is more susceptible of divine Truths; and I am certain is the best Way to prove useful to Mankind: for the more holy you are, the more will God delight to Honour you. He loves to make use of Instruments like himself. I hope the good old Divinity will now be precious to your Souls, and you will think it an Honour to tread in the Steps of your pious Forefathers. They were acquainted with their Hearts. They knew what it was to be tempted themselves, and therefore from their own Experience knew how to succour others. Oh may you follow them, as they followed Christ. Great then, very great will be your Reward in Heaven. I am sure you can never serve a better Master than Jesus Christ or be engaged in a higher Employ, than in calling home Souls to him. I trust, *Dear Gentlemen,* you will not be offended with me for sending you these few Lines. I wrote out of the fulness of my Heart. I make mention of you always in my Prayers: O forget me not in yours. I am a poor weak Worm. I am the chief of Sinners. And yet, Oh stupendous Love, the Lord's Work still prospers in my unworthy Hands. Fail not to give Thanks as well as pray for,

Your affectionate Brother and Servant in our common Lord,

G. WHITEFIELD.

Eleazar Wheelock

10. Correspondence of a Connecticut Itinerant, 1740–1745

A. WILLIAM GAYLORD, NOVEMBER 1740

[William Gaylord to Eleazar Wheelock, Norwalk, Conn., Nov. 24, 1740, Dartmouth College Archives, Hanover, N.H.]

REVD. AND DEAR BROTHER

Since we can See one another but Seldom, I am glad to do my part toward Supplying that Defect by a frequent Exchange of Letters, Tho having many Things to Say, which the narrow Limits of a Letter won't allow of, it can be done, but imperfectly—I heartily rejoyce that Mr. Whitfld has been thro the Countrey preaching the Gospel in every Place with Such Life and Zeal as are rarely to be Seen in this Dead and frozen Age. I think he was Received by the Generality of the Ministers in these Parts with Sincere Respect Love and Joy, tho Some of the best of them, think he has a Touch of Enthusiasm, but that they can easily forgive at Such a Time as this, when the Generality are gone So far into the contrery and more Dangerous Extream of Lukewarmness. For my own Part however indifferent my Opinion has been of him heretofore I realy desired his Coming and was heartily glad to See him, because I believe he excells in that which we (especially in these Parts) want most, I mean Zeal for God and compassion for immortal Souls. For tho I believe in his extemporery Manner of Preaching he frequently drops such Expressions as are liable to [———] Exception, yet I believe it is well adapted, (even beyond what is common) to rouse Stupid and thotless Sinners, which abound so among us. And I think he preached considerably better here than when we heard Him at

N.Y. In a word I bless God that he has been among us, my Opinion and Hopes of him are better than heretofore—but I must Say, I am not perfectly free from all fears concerning him—and I find Some whose Character is much better than mine, have much greater Fears and Jealousies than I have—and Some, you know despise him. But I realy believe, thro Divine Blessing, he has been an Instrument of much Good among us, as well as in other Places, Especially by stirring up Ministers, (even Such as in other respects may excell him) to a holy emulation of his zeal. I have been lately much refresh'd by a Letter from a Minister in one of the Principal Towns in the Government (nearer to you than to me, and younger than either of us) of prime Note for Learning and Good Sense, and of good Character in all Respects and very free from all suspicion of Enthusiasm even among the gretest pretenders to Reason etc. who seems much animated by what he has Seen and heard in Mr. W. of Whom he says "I have now heard that Miracle of a man Mr. W. blessed be God for it: You Said righ[t], Sir when you told me Sometime Since, that he was not a very polite or correct preacher, but what then? Does he not urge men to come to Christ with astonishing Power and Authority, does he not Speak plainly and boldly in the Name of his and our Divine Lord and Master, is he not an admirable orator? etc. I cannot but think that a Silley

Affectation of polite Ease and Elegance in Preaching to ignorant and Stupid Congregations is one of the Judgments of God on the present Age, for what is the Effect of Such Preaching, the whole Congregation Stands agape they wonder they Stare, but every Soul is unmoved and every Conscience unalarmed. On the Contrary Mr. W Speaks to the Understanding etc. In Short I believe God is with him of a Truth, and that his preaching is admirably adapted to rouse and awaken a Stupid world"—thus far He—I was heartily glad to hear him Speak thus. But dear Brother let us not call any man Father or Master on Earth —and Since the Days of infalible Inspiration are ceased, let us not Set up any man more as a perfect Pattern. Without Exception, You know there is a Mixture of Wisdom and Folly Good and Evil in best men we meet with. As Much as I love and Respect the name of Mr. W, I think he is by no means to be commended nor imitated without exception ——tho I believe unconverted Ministers

taken in the Lump have been the bane of the christian World, yet I believe in Some Instances as the Case may be an unconverted minister otherwise qualified may be much better than none at all—and I think he lays vastly too much Weight upon the Affection, Tears and Meltings etc. that appear in the Face of the Assembly, as an Argument of his success—for you know, Dear Sir that there is a vast Difference between mens being affected and their being converted—other things might be mentioned— but I have exceeded the Limits of the letter. What is excellent in him let us praise and follow, what is otherwise let us—and never cease praying and laboring for more light, and never think our Selves perfect till we come to the regions of [————] light above, where God of his Infinite Mercy Grant that you and I may meet attended with a Numerous Spiritual Offspring—these with heartiest Affection from your Loving

Brother and Humble servant,

WILLIAM GAYLORD

B. JOHN LEE, DECEMBER 1740

[Captain John Lee to Eleazar Wheelock, East Lyme, Conn., Dec. 5, 1740, Dartmouth College Archives, Hanover, N.H.]

DEAR SIR

Take it not amiss that one to you almost unKnown takes the boldness to trouble you with a few lines. I have heard of you by the hearing Oposer[s]. Yea I have heard of the Defaming of many. You are not unacquainted that you for Christs Sake have been Counted an Enthusiast, mad man and Dunce but Lett not these things move you for they that will live godly in Christ Jesus must Suffer persecution. It Amazes me to hear how many of the Great Doctors and Letter Larned teachers, of this Day, talk as Ignorantly of the New birth as their Great Patron, Nicodemus Did,

some making it Consist in Nothing more than being a moralist; I am much Surprised to see that among our own teachers that profess to be Calvinist yet Seem to Stand mute when any thing is Said about inward feelings and of being Led by the Spirit Praying by the spirit etc. They Seem hardly to understand the meaning of Such words and Phraises and among those few that is Left in our Isreal that have not bowed the knee to Baell the Idol of Salvation by the Law Oh how few is their that like Elijah Dirst be bold for god and Say to, and of the Great Doctors of this age tis you that Trouble our Isreal but the most are preaching Smoth things Sewing [————] Daubing with untemperate Morter and healing the Daughter of my people Slightily but god hath not Left him Self without a witness. In almost Every place Some faithfull Sons of the Prophets he Strengthens with Zeal and Courage to tell to Jacob their sin and to Isreal their transgressions. Tho tis true we have generally a name to live but alas I would to god that were not all that in a Generall way it can be said of most. What a Sad Condition must a people be in when the Prophets prophesie Lies, and the preists bare rule by these means; and the people Love to have it So, then how easeyley and pleasently Do the blind lead the blind till they all fall into the Ditch of Everlasting torments togather but when God Stirs up any to Stand in the way and tell both preists and People their Danger in the Dreadful End of such blind Guids and their followers, how will the Divel and blind Preists his Prime Ministers rage and roar. They'll Represent such men as the turners of the world upside Down. Common mischief makes men not fit to Live. They will follow them with the most base calumnies load them with the vilest Reproaches dress them in the skins of the most hatful Animals in order to Set the Popoluss on them as so many hell hounds to Devour them but God who will Carry on his own work against all opposition when ever he Pleases turns all there Council into foolishness bring[s] paleness upon all faces Stops Confounds yea Converts the most virulent and hardy opposers when Ever he pleases. He puts such Courage into his Dear Children that like the meek man Moses they Care not for Pharoh and all his Magicians nor a David be Dismayed att the huge bulky stature of a feirce and Dominearing Goliah nor an Elijah Regard the violent threatining of an Ahab and Jesebell. He can send fourth a John Baptist to

preach and to pronounce woes against the most potent and most conceited Self righteous Pharisees. A Dozen poor Illiterate fishermen Can Subdue Kingdoms, not with carnall weapons but with the Pure word of God, preach in a Spirit of meekness, and Dare be bold for god. They feared not the faces of the Great the king of Terrores was no terror to them; So when god Called Luther a poor fryer out of his Cell, to bear wittness for his name and bring many Sons to Glory. All the Power of [Rome] and Hell Can't Dismay him; and in our time may we not Say that God hath raised up Some men as burning and shining Lights to Restore the Church to the Purity that she professt at the Dawn of the Reformation, but how are such Precious sons of Zion (Compareable to fine Gold) set at nought; but of all that god hath stired up that falls under our view the most to be admired is the Revd. Mr. Whitefield a valiant young David that fears not the faces of all the uncircumcised Goliahs. How does god [direct] the Stone (which he hurls at such,) into their foreheads. They fall Down to their own Confusion. I have had the hapyness, (God be praised) to hear this sun of thunder 7 times and have been Greatly Impresst thereby, more Especially by a Sermon on the words of our Saviour Except your righteousness Exceeds the righteousness of the Scribes and Pharisee ye shall in no Case Enter into the Kingdom of heaven; it was a most Awakening Sermon to formal Professors and Self Righteous pharisees, and God hath not Left himself without a witness amongst us. We have in this town three faithfull ministers but what is Remarkable is Mr. Parsons who when first Settled was a Strong yea a furious Arminian in Principle but for about two or three years hath been Humbled and bro't to Christs foot and made Experimently to See that by the Deeds of the Law shall

No flesh Living be Justified. He having had opportunity to See and Converse with Mr W—f—d, his Spirit Seems to be knit to his, like the spirit of Jonathan to David. His Preaching and Common Conversation is much Altered. He is now a sun of thunder breaking the peace and Disturbing the Carnall Security of formall professors. This I see brings an odium upon him in the opinion of Some of his Self righteous hearers and Carnall brethern and acquaintances but Surely he in the Eyes of his master is most precious. I lately had the opportunity to hear him three Sermons. More awakening heart Searching Sermons I Never heard (except Mr. W—f—ds). His Zeal fervency and Great Concearn for Souls makes some ready to Call him a hot Zealot a mad fellow etc. —and so 'twill be with all Such as Dare be So bold as to break the Peace of the Carnally Secure. I have often tho't that ministers will ordinarally do but litle Good with light without heat. Like the moon they may Give us Some faint Rays of Light but no heat. The people Generally Speaking don't So much want to be taught to Know as be made willing to do their Duty; then that minister, that can make his way into the hearts and move the Passions of his hearers will in this Country Do the most Good. Suerly the Creator did not furnish men with Passions for Nothing. No Surely they are to be wrought upon by Setting before them, that Every moment they are in an unconverted Condition they hang over hell by the thread of Life which they are Every moment Provokeing god by their Sins (Especially of unbeli[ef]) to cut assunder. Who Knows but they may then Cry in good Earnest what must we do to be saved; and then to Set before them the Death and Sufferings of Christ his active and passive obedence as the only mean[s] of Security against the Dainger that they are

in, and that by which they may obtain heaven and So make both fear and hope Subservant to the Stirring men up to flee from the wrath to Come. This week hath been att N London Mr. Gilbert Tennant and Preached two Sermons. I have had this Day the oppertunity to Converse with Some of the most Serious and Intelleagble persons that heard him and they Say never man Speak like him, but the Church Party Rage and Roar like So many furies Just broke loose. They call him [romish] Preist and his Sermons Hellfire Sermons and Say all manner of Evel falsely of him a Great deceiver etc. I Happened to hear one Petty Pigmire belching out his vennom against him. I asked wherein he was to blame. He told me he preached false Doctrine. In what perticulers said I. Why he Said he Could not tell he did not hear him but he was told that he Said in his Sermon that man's good works was not that for which god would justifye him, and if So then the consequences was said he to open a Dore to all licenciousness but for his part he would hear no Such Decivers, and indeed he Cast about firebrands arrows and Death Like a mad man and in that Condition I Left him. I would to God he was the only one that thus please the father of lyes, by Defameing the worthy Servants of Jesus Christ—Now sir you may be Sure (that if you are singularly good) to meet with Scoffers. Expect to meet with persecution and tryalls of cruell mocking but lett none of these things move you but go on to Conquer. I pray God that hell may tremble before you, and all the Powers of Darkness be shaken. You wrestle not with flesh and blood only but with the rulers of Darkness etc. I intend to wait upon you as soon as my business will permit. I am sir your Sincere friend and harty well wisher etc.

[JOHN LEE]

C. Daniel Russell, January 1741

[Daniel Russell to Eleazar Wheelock, Wethersfield, Conn., Jan. 7, 1741, Dartmouth College Archives, Hanover, N.H.]

Revd. Sir:

My indisposition of body has been such since I saw you at Wethersfield that I have been Scarce able to move abroad since was not able to go out the Last Sabbath and yet remain very poorly or I should have been up to have waited on you this day: I rejoyce greatly to hear that God is in Such a wonderfull extraordinary and powerful manner carrying on his own work in this town which hath for so long a time layn as it were in a dead sleep: and as I am perswaded it cannot but be matter of great rejoycing to you to see such happy fruits and effects of your labour desire and endeavours that the work of God is carried on in such a powerfull manner: so I cannot but think that it gives matter of encouragment to you to preach wherever you are called to preach the Gospel: and it gives incouragment to me to renew my request to you that you would come and preach to my people which I should be glad might be tomorrow however request it might be before you return home my people as well as myself being very desirous thereof—and desire that you would send me an answer by the bearer: now that you may enjoy the constant presence strength and assistance of the great Lord of the harvest that you may yet see to your rejoycing the happy fruits and effects of your labours and travels and as God has been pleased to honour and distinguish you here in making you a special instrument in carrying on this blessed and glorious work so may you be distinguished in the rewards of his faithfull servants in his eternall kingdom is the herty desire and earnest request of your friend and fellow labourer in the Gospel of Christ—

Daniel Russel

D. Peter Thatcher, November 1741

[Peter Thatcher to Eleazar Wheelock, Middleborough, Conn., Nov. 2, 1741, Dartmouth College Archives, Hanover, N.H.]

Revd. and Dear Sir

I Desire to bless God who hath brou't You Into our Neighbourhood, On that good design of Serving Souls In their Eternall Interests—Dear Sir I do with Utmost Importunity Intreat You to allott Some Considerable portion of Your time and Labours with this poor secure people. Sir I Can't be denyed of you. I wont take A denyal from You, for I Ask for Christs sake, and the sake of the souls of my family and Charge. Now Sir I perswade and Assure myself could I lay open Our Case, You would readily Comply. Oh Sir I Ask not silver and Gold of you, but since I have heard there is such A Converting power Attending Your Ministry from the soverain pleasure of God, putting His Hand Upon You—this Moves me Oh that God would Incline your heart to spend some days with Us. I wish I could have been the bearer. I Intreat your Answer your prayers for and blessing on, the meanest of your fellow laborers

In the Gospel Service

Peter Thacher

E. Samuel Buell, April 1742

[Samuel Buell to Eleazar Wheelock, Boston, Mass., Apr. 20, 1742, Dartmouth College Archives, Hanover, N.H.]

REVD. AND DEAR SIR

After my Duty to Yourself, and Prayer to God that Grace mercy and Peace may Bee multiplied to Your Church, and the houshold of faith, these to inform that Since I Last wrote to Yourself, the Lord has I Charitably hope giving all Glory to his name made me instrumentall in the conversion of a hundred or Ten Score Souls—the Lord Surely is making use of the most Vile Poluted Lump of Clay, that Could Bee found to open Blind eyes, that he may Show his Soveraingty, how the potter hath power over the Clay, and that the excellency of the Power may be Seen to Bee of God, and not of man. I have no time to give a Very Perticular account of things—I have Preach'd 5 times in Boston Publickly to Vast assemblies— my Labours have Been attended with Great Success throu the Blessing of God, . . . and in Several adjacent towns —on the morrow the Lord willing I Set out for old York. I expect to Preach Daily, as I have done for a long time, if the Lord gives Strength—I have Letters and invitations to Preach from all Parts —an effectual Door is open Daily for my Preaching, But there are many adversaries—the world rages, hell trembles heaven Rejoyces—while the Lord is with me owning my Labours Confounding the wisdome of the mighty by a Child—many refuse to Let me into there Pulpits But my hands are full. Great numbers are Daily hanging about me for Some Spirittual morsle—and Did not the Lord remarkably assist me I Could not Perform what I Do Daily— But I am ashamed when I hear of Mr. Whitefield['s] indefatagable Labours. . . . We fear it will Bee Some time before he comes to New-England—and it is Privately Said by his friend here, that he will have But a Cold reception by too many when he comes—or Mr. Tennant [ei]ther—opposition increases So fast here in Boston, that what the event of it will Bee we know not—and tremble to think, . . . I hope the Lord will give his Ministers the Subtlety of the Serpent intermixt with the harmless nature of the Dove—and make em as a flam of fier—

I am your unworthy Brother in Christ and humble Servant

SAMUELL BUELL

F. Eleazar Wheelock, February 1745

[Eleazar Wheelock to Stephen Williams, Lebanon, Conn., Feb. 18, 1745, Dartmouth College Archives, Hanover, N.H.]

REVD. SIR AND VERY DEAR BROTHER

I've had no opportunity Since I Came home to Convey a Line to You Nor Do I know of any Now, however hope it May fall into some hand that will Convey it. I Got home Safe, and Seasonably the Day I Left You, and found My family Much as I Left it, and So they S[t]ill Continue, . . . The Confusions at Windham etc. Yet Continue. I preachd there the Sabath before Last but the Separatists would Not Come to hear Me. I See no appearance of the Like Difficulties Yet Among My Own people, but hear we are [———] With a Visit Speedily from them. Whether they will have any [———] among us or not I can't tell. I Wish that Mr. Edwards or some other Gentleman that has an interest in Mr. Whitfield Would Give him A faithful account of the State of things in these parts before he Comes Among us. I have Done it in short already, and I Cant but think it Would be of Service if Some Good Friend of his at some Distance should Do the Same. He has doubtless heard Many reports and What his Apprehensions are I Cant tell but we Dread the Consequences of his Coming here and not Discountenancing and Discouraging these things. We Salute You and Yours Most affectionately. Pray for us.

Your Affectionate tho' unworthy Brother

ELEAZAR WHEELOCK

James Davenport

11. Connecticut Expels James Davenport: *Boston Weekly News-Letter*, 1742

[*Boston Weekly News-Letter*, July 1, 1742]

Extract of a Letter from Hartford, *dated* June 15th 1742.

SIR,

Inclos'd is a faithful Account of the Trial of Mr. Davenport, *which I have been desired to transmit to some Friend in order to make it publick in the News-Papers: The Gentleman that drew it up, has, I believe, been desired to do it by the most considerable in the Government. Yours, etc.*

Hartford, June 10, 1742.

SIR,

As well to gratify your own and the curiosity of many others, as to prevent such misrepresentations as is more than probable will be made, touching the late proceedings with Mr. *Davenport* here, I shall, as an eye-witness to the greater part of it, give you the account as follows, *viz.*

On the 27th of *May* last came certain Gentlemen of the parish of *Ripton* in the town of *Stratford,* and against said Mr. *Davenport* and one Mr. *Pomroy* under their Hands, filed their complaint with the secretary, (the general assembly then sitting) importing and setting forth, That about ten days before, came said Mr. *Davenport* to said *Stratford,* and soon after him said Mr. *Pomroy,* and that they, together with certain illiterate persons, under colour of preaching, praying and religious exhortations, and frequently congregating great numbers of persons, chiefly children and youth, did by sundry unwarrantable things, by them in an indecent and unjustifiable manner uttered and inculcated, put the said town, and especially said parish, into great confusion and disorder, and so for many days continued in a grievous manner to disturb the peace and quiet of his majesty's good subjects there, and thereupon praying relief in the premises.

On which representation, the question being put, Whether the things complained of were worthy the special notice and care of the assembly? was, by the concurrence of both houses, resolved in the affirmative. And thereupon, in the words following, Ordered, 'That the secretary of this colony make out a precept, directed to the sheriff of the county of *Hartford* or his deputy, to arrest the bodies of *James Davenport* and *Benjamin Pomroy* wheresoever they may be in this colony, and them forthwith to bring before the general assembly now setting, to answer to such matters and things as are objected and complained of against them before this assembly, and also to summon such evidences as may have any knowledge of said matters complained of as aforesaid.'

Whereupon by vertue of a precept, pursuant to said order, issued forth, they the said messr. *Davenport* and *Pomroy* being both found and taken at *New-Haven*, were on the first instant bro't before the general assembly, to answer their misdemeanour, And upon a large and full hearing (which lasted considerable part of two days) the assembly on the 3d instant came into the following resolve, *viz.*

'Forasmuch as Capt. *Blacklatch* and Mr. *Samuel Adams*, both of *Stratford*, have made complaint to this assembly of great disorders, etc. which have lately happened in *Stratford* by occasion of one *James Davenport* and others convening great numbers of people together in several parts of said town; which complaint this assembly tho't proper to enquire into, thereby to prevent any growing disorders in this colony.

'Thereupon having heard the evidences produced by the king's attorney to prove said complaint, and also the witnesses produced by the said *Davenport* in his behalf, and the matters conceded by him, and the things alledged in his own defence; and this court further observing the behaviour, conduct, language and deportment of said *Davenport* in the time of his trial and what happen'd in the evening after the matter was in hearing and not gone thro' with; after consideration of which, this assembly is of opinion, that the things alledged, and the behaviour, conduct and doctrines advanced and taught by the said *James Davenport* do and have

a natural tendency to disturb and destroy the peace and order of this government.

'Yet it further appears to this assembly, that the said *Davenport* is *under the influences of enthusiastical impressions and impulses, and thereby disturb'd in the rational faculties of his mind,* and therefore to be pittied and compassionated, and not to be treated as otherwise he might be.

'And this assembly considering that the settled place of his abode is in the town of *Southold on Long Island,* whereto it is best he should be removed. thereupon it is ordered by this assembly, that the said *Davenport* be forthwith transported out of this colony to *Long-Island* to the place from whence he came and wherein he is settled. And the governour and council are desired to take effectual care that this order be duly executed.' The above-recited orders or resolves of assembly are true copies of record.

Examin'd per GEORGE WYLLYS, Secr.

And accordingly by a special warrant by the governour and council issued forth, and to the sheriff directed to that purpose, he said *Davenport* having first heard the assembly's said resolve and order openly read to him, was then about 4 o'clock afternoon, by the sheriff, under the protection of two files of muscatiers, aided down to the great river, and committed to the especial care and custody of one Mr. *Whitmore* on board his vessel then at anchor there; by him to be transported to his own place as abovesaid, and during his passage thither to be treated with all proper care, tenderness and humanity, which said *Whitmore* being also authorized and impowered to command all necessary occasional assistance to the effectual discharge and fulfilment of said order and undertaking; then immediately weigh'd anchor and proceeded down the river with the said *Davenport* on his voyage to the intended haven, where we hope he may be safe arrived; and under the care of those whom we hope by this time will be convinced that he is not under circumstances to go abroad from under the inspection and guidance of his friends; for by the same evidences by which it is possible to know that any one ever was disturb'd in the exercise of his intellectual faculties, *viz.* by his looks, words and behaviour, by these same evidences we know this *Mr. Davenport* frequently to be so; for tho' one *sober* may mimic a *mad man,* as once did *David;* yet not *vice versa:* And we must charitably think his to be in reality a degree of what in *David* was only feign'd.

Mr. *Pomroy's* demeanour tho' by it self wild and extravagant, yet comparing with the other gentleman, seeming almost orderly and regular, he was thereupon dismist.

And now *Sir,* As the matters complain'd of and the grounds of these proceedings are in but general terms exprest, and to gratify your curiosity as to the circumstances, etc. of the above affair, I shall proceed to give you in substance from minutes taken at the time; 1. The *principal* and more *particular things* either evidenced or conceded to. And, 2 His *behaviour* and treatment during, and sundry *circumstances* attending, the agitation of these things.

I. The *particular and principal things* either evidenced or conceded to, were,

1. That speaking of his, and his adherents *conduct* and *doctrines* and the effects thereof in the land, and under the general character of, This good work; and speaking also of the *laws of the government* made, or about to be made, to regulate or restrain the same, he declared and insisted, that *all such laws ought to be disregarded,* and were *against the laws of GOD.*

2. That he earnestly inculcated it upon the minds of children and youth, that this work was the work of God, which they also were engaged in carrying on; and that all *prohibitions* and *commands* of *parents and masters* not to adhere to them, and attend their religious exercises, meetings, etc. were in *no wise to be obeyed.*

3. That he declared that *people ought not to regard or attend the preaching of unconverted ministers;* and that *he was well-assured the greater part of the ministers in the country* were such.

And. 4. That he endeavoured by *unwarrantable means to terrify* and *affect* his hearers. And that,

(1.) By pretending some *extraordinary discovery and assurance* of the very near approach of the *end of the world;* and that tho' he didn't assign the *very day,* yet that he then lately had it *clearly open'd to him,* and *strongly imprest upon his mind,* that in a very *short time* all these things will be involv'd in devouring flames. And also that on supposition and pretence of *extraordinary intercourse with heaven,* he frequently pray'd for direction and acted in his undertakings.

(2.) By an *indecent and affected imitation* of the agony and passion of our blessed SAVIOUR; and also, by *voice* and *gesture,* of the surprize, horror and amazement of persons suppos'd to be sentenc'd to eternal misery. And,

(3.) By a *too peremptory and unconditioned* denouncing damnation against such of his auditory he look'd upon as opposers; vehemently crying out, That *he saw hell-flames slashing in their faces;* and that *they were now! now! dropping down to hell;* and also added, *Lord! Thou knowest that there are many in that gallery and in these seats, that are now dropping down to Hell!* etc.

5. It appeared also, That sundry of these things happened *unseasonably* and *late at night*.

II. Touching his *behaviour* and *treatment* during, and the *circumstances* attending, the agitation of these things, take as follows, *viz*—On notice first given him by the sheriff of the will of the assembly, he shew'd himself thereto resign'd, tho' just before, it seems had been determined to a different course by the special guidance of a superior authority.

On his arrival at *Hartford*, by the indulgence of the sheriff (who from first to last, treated and entertain'd at his own house, him and Mr. *Pomroy*, with unexceptionable tenderness and civility) he spent the first night, and the greater part of the next day, among his special friends of followers, uninterrupted in religious Devotions; in his way: by no means therein forgetting to vent the most virulent invectives against both ministers and magistrates, especially the general assembly, representing them as opposers of the work of God, and doing the work of the devil, etc.

Nextly, view him at the barr of the assembly: his approach to which, his air and posture there; that inflexibility of body, that affectatious oblique reclining of the head, that elevation, or rather inversion of the eyes, that forced negligence and retirement of soul, and that uncouth shew, that motly mixture of pride and gravity wrought up to sullenness, is not easily to be described. In this Posture view him invariable as a statue, 'till the adjournment and withdrawing of the assembly that evening; when, amid the thronging multitude (on that occasion very numerous) remov'd and moving out of the meeting-house, he and Mr *Pomroy* took their stand upon the assent to the front door, and there exhibited a lively specimen of their flaming zeal, or rather enthusiastic fury; many of the members of the general assembly then by. With vehement stentorian voice, and wild distortions of body, said *Davenport* began an exhortation; on which the sheriff, by speaking and gently taking him by the sleeve, endeavouring to silence and remove him, he instantly fell a praying, crying out, *Lord! thou knowest somebody's got hold of my sleeve, strike them! Lord, strike them*—which said *Pumroy* also observing cry'd out to the sheriff and his assistants, *Take heed how you do that heaven daring action! 'tis heaven-daring presumption, to take him away! and the God of Heaven will assuredly avenge it on you! strike them, Lord, strike them!* many of the concourse beginning to sigh, groan, beat their breasts, cry out, and to be put into strange agitations of body. Others of their adherents rushing in violently interposed to prevent and resist the sheriff; while others refused their assistance when commanded, saying, *they were serving the devil*, etc. 'til the tumult rose even to an uproar, which at length a little subsiding, the Sheriff, with the two ministers, being about to retire to a gentleman's house hard by, a multitude flock'd after, some giving out and threatning, that the next day they should have five to one on their side, etc.

But being gotten into said gentleman's house, and thither followed by a considerable number of their admirers, he, said *Davenport*, fell immediately to exhorting, and together with the rest, a praying, singing, etc. with much noise and vehemence; in which persisting, notwithstanding the repeated intreaties and prohibition of the master of the house, remonstrating it was a great Disturbance to his Family, some of them then a bed, and ill able to endure the tumult.

Notwithstanding also the requests and the authoritative commands of the sheriff to forbear, still the hubbub increased; and in about two hours time was scarcely suppress'd and dispers'd by the interposition and authority of sundry of his majesty's council, with the assistance of the sheriff, who, 'til then, had in vain attempted it.

In the mean time, almost all night, in other parts of the town, were such shocking scenes of horror and confusion, under the name and pretext of religious devotion, as language can't describe. Which wild ungovernable efforts of enthusiastic zeal and fury, being regarded as a bold and threatening insult upon the whole legislative body of the government, then on the spot; orders were forthwith given out to one of the commanding officers of the town, with about forty men in arms the next morning to wait upon the assembly; and so 'til the conclusion of these affairs: to prevent further insolencies, which seem'd to be threatening. Which orders were accordingly observed 'til the rising of the assembly.

But to return: Next morning being again bro't before the assembly, and seeming more on a level with his fellow-mortals, and to act something in resemblance of a man, being put on his defence, he on motion, had the witnesses which the night before had given in their evidence, interrogated anew: The import of which interrogation was, Whether when they had heard him express himself as abovesaid, touching obedience to laws, etc. and the end of the world, etc. he didn't thereto annex some qualifying words from whence different construction might be put upon what he delivered? To which they all answer'd in the negative. Nextly, His own witnesses being sworn and interrogated, and especially touching such qualifications, answered generally, affirmatively, that he did so qualify such of said expressions as they heard, full to their satisfaction and understanding; but on more particular inquiry what any of those qualifying expressions were, were not able to tell one word.

Then on his defence proceeding with a demeanour wholly his own, insisted, That the apparent effects of his ministry might well authenticate his conduct —That the greater part of the ministers in the land were undoubtedly unconverted; and that four or five of them had lately own'd to him *they* were such —That he had lately had clear discoveries and strong impressions made on his mind touching these things, etc.— And in a word, in the face of the assembly spake and acted so like himself, as to render in a measure useless all other evidence of his extravagancies. And the pleadings being concluded, the assembly adjourned to consider the matter; the result of which is the resolve above recited.

The next day being again brought to the barr, and said resolve and order publickly read to him—reply'd—*Tho' I must go, I hope* CHRIST *will not, but tarry and carry on his work in this government, in spight of all the power and malice of earth or hell.* Then turn'd and went off.

I am Sir, Yours, etc.
ANTI-ENTHUSIASTICUS.

12. Davenport Rebuked in Boston: *The Declaration of A Number of the associated Pastors of Boston and Charles-Town, 1742*

[*The Declaration of A Number of the associated Pastors of Boston and Charles-Town relating to the Rev. Mr. James Davenport, and his Conduct* (Boston, 1742), 3–7]

WE the associated Pastors in the Towns of *Boston* and *Charles-Town* in the Province of the *Massachusetts-Bay* in *New-England,* being assembled *June* 28. in our stated Course of Meeting, and being then inform'd that the Reverend Mr. *James Davenport,* Pastor of the Church of Christ in *Southhold Long-Island* was come to Town, sent two of our Brethren to inform the said Mr. *Davenport,* that we were then assembled, and should be glad to see him.

Whereupon he presently came to us; and after a respectful Greeting, we desir'd him to inform us of the Reasons of his leaving his Flock so often, and for such Length of Times as we had heard of; as also concerning his assuming Behaviour in the Places whether he had gone; more especially in judging the spiritual State of Pastors and People, and too positively and suddenly declaring concerning one and another, that they were in a converted or unconverted Estate; thereby stumbling the Minds of many, and alienating the Hearts of others from their Ministers and Brethren, even to such a Degree that some had withdrawn from the Ministry and Communion to which they belong'd.

Whereupon Mr. *Davenport* in a free and ready Manner gave us such an Account of the Manner of God's working upon him from his early Days, and his effectual Calling in riper Years, as that he appear'd to us to be a Man truly pious; and we hope that God has us'd him as an Instrument of Good unto many Souls.

Nevertheless also it appears to us that he is a Gentleman acted much by sudden Impulses, upon such Applications of the Holy Scriptures to himself, and his particular Friends, Desires and Purposes, as we can by no Means approve of or justify, but must needs think very dangerous and hurtful to the Interests of Religion.

And in particular, by the Account he gave us of his judging some Reverend Ministers of the Gospel on *Long-Island,* and in *New-England,* to be in an unconverted State, it did by no Means appear to us that he had Reason and Righteousness on his Side in so doing— Nor do we see into his Scripture Warrant for thinking himself called of God to demand from his Brethren from Place to Place, an Account of their regenerate State, when or in what Manner the Holy Spirit of God wrought upon and renew'd them.

We judge also that the Reverend Mr. *Davenport* has not acted prudently, but to the Disservice of Religion, by going with his Friends singing thro' the Streets and High-Ways, to and from the Houses of Worship on Lord's-Days, and other Days; and by encouraging private Brethren to pray and exhort in larger or smaller Assemblies of People gather'd together for that Purpose: A Practice which we fear may be found big with Errors, Irregularities and Mischiefs.

We judge it therefore to be our present Duty not to invite Mr. *Davenport* into our Places of publick Worship, as otherwise we might have readily done, that so we may not appear to give Countenance to the forementioned Errors and Disorders; against which we bear this Testimony, both in Faithfulness Love and Care to the Churches of Christ, and also to our said Brother, whose Usefulness in the Church is likely to be still more obstructed by his being deeply tinctur'd with a Spirit of Enthusiasm.

And tho' we are not satisfied that the Rev. Mr. *Davenport* has a Call to preach in the Fields from Day to Day as he has done of late, yet we think it our Duty to bear a Testimony against all those Disorders and that Prophaneness which have been promoted by any who have lately gone forth to hear him.

Upon the whole, we humbly beseech the great Lord and Head of the Church, to lead us, and all his Ministers and Churches, into all the Paths of Truth, Righteousness, Peace and spiritual Edification, for his Name's Sake. And we take this Opportunity to repeat our Testimony to the great and glorious Work of GOD, which of his free Grace he has begun and is carrying on in many Parts of this and the neighbouring Provinces; beseeching him to preserve, defend, maintain and propagate it, in Spite of all the Devices of Satan against it of one Kind or other; that however it may suffer by the Imprudence of it's Friends, or by the virulent Opposition of it's Enemies, yet it may stand as on the Rock, and the Gates of Hell may never prevail against it.

Boston, July 1.

1742.

BENJAMIN COLMAN
JOSEPH SEWALL
THOMAS PRINCE
JOHN WEBB
WILLIAM COOPER
THOMAS FOXCROFT
SAMUEL CHECKLEY
WILLIAM WELSTEED
JOSHUA GEE
HULL ABBOT
MATHER BYLES
THOMAS PRENTICE
ELLIS GRAY
ANDREW ELIOT.

13. Religious Excess at New London: *Boston Weekly Post-Boy*, 1743

[*The Boston Weekly Post-Boy*, March 28, 1743]

New-London, March 14th 1742, 3.
To the Publisher of the *Boston Post-Boy*.

SIR,

The Conduct of some of the People call'd N Lights, or Christians, as they please to call themselves, has been so extraordinary here the last Week, that 'tis desired by some that an Account of their wild, frantick and extravagant Management may be inserted in one of your next Prints; and therefore send you the following Sketch of some of their Transactions;

At the Beginning of the present Month came to this Place the famous Mr *Davenport,* accompanied with Three Armour-Bearers, and some others; upon his Arrival, the Christians, or dear Children, gather'd round about him in Crouds, who paid him such profound Respect, Reverence and Homage, that his well-known great Modesty and Humility oblig'd him to check their Devotion, by telling them, he was not a God, but a Man. However this did not abate their Veneration for him so much, but that even the Chief of them ('tis credibly said) made auricular Confessions to him; and this being over, (and it may be reasonably suppos'd ample

Absolution, and proper Indulgences were given thereupon,) they might judge themselves to be in a good Condition to do some memorable Exploits, to the lasting Honour of their Sect, and the Establishment of their Religion; and having by Fasting and Prayer sought for Direction to do something, one of them declar'd, he had a Revelation; which was, that they should root out Heresy and pull down Idolatry: The Motion was well approved by the Assembly, who soon resolv'd to make a bold and vigorous Attempt to effect it; and accordingly on the 6th Instant, it being the Lord's Day, just before the Conclusion of the Publick Worship, and also as the People were returning from the House of GOD, they were surpriz'd with a great Noise and Out-cry; Multitudes hasten'd toward the Place of Rendezvous, directing themselves by the Clamor and Shouting, which together, with the ascending Smoak bro't them to one of the most public Places in the Town, and there found these good People encompassing a Fire which they had built up in the Street, into which they were casting Numbers of Books, principally on Divinity, and those that were well-approved by *Protestant* Divines, viz. Bp. *Beveridge's* Thoughts, Mr. *Russel's* Seven Sermons, one of Dr. *Colman's*, and one of Dr. *Chauncy's* Books, and many others. Nothing can be more astonishing than their insolent Behaviour was during the Time of their Sacrifice, as 'tis said they call'd it; whilst the Books were in the Flames they cry'd out, *Thus the Souls of the Authors of those Books, those of them that are dead, are roasting in the Flames of Hell;* and that *the Fate of those surviving, would be the same, unless speedy Repentance prevented:* On the next Day they had at the same Place a second Bonfire of the like Materials, and manag'd in the same manner. Having given this fatal Stroke to *Heresy,* they made

ready to attack *Idolatry,* and sought for Direction, as in the Case before; and then Mr. *D—p—t* told them to look at Home first, and that they themselves were guilty of idolizing their Apparel, and should therefore divest themselves of those Things especially which were for Ornament, and let them be burnt: Some of them in the heighth of their Zeal, conferred not with Flesh and Blood, but fell to stripping and cast their Cloaths down at their Apostle's Feet; one or two hesitated about the Matter, and were so bold as to tell him they had nothing on which they idoliz'd: He reply'd, that such and such a Thing was an Offence to him; and they must down with them: One of these being a Gentleman of Learning and Parts ventur'd to tell Mr. *D—p—t,* that he could scarce see how his disliking the Night-Gown that he had on his Back, should render him, guilty of Idolatry. However, This carnal Reasoning avail'd nothing; strip he must, and strip he did: By this Time the Pile had grown to a large Bulk, and almost ripe for Sacrifice; and that they might be clear and well-warranted in the Enterprize, Mr. *D —p—t* order'd one of his Armour-Bearers to pray for a full Discovery of the Mind—in the Affair; he did accordingly, but had no Answer: Another also at his Direction pray'd, but no Answer yet: Next Mr. *D—p—t* pray'd himself; and now the Oracle spake clear to the Point, without Ambiguity, and utter'd that *the Things must be burnt;* and to confirm the Truth of the Revelation, took his wearing Breeches, and hove them with Violence into the Pile, saying, *Go you with the Rest.* A young Sister, whose Modesty could not bear to see the Mixture of Cloaks, Petty Coats and Breeches, snatch'd up his Breeches, and sent them at him, with as much Indignation, as tho' they had been the Hire of a Wh—— or the Price of a Dog: At this Juncture came in a Brother from a neighbouring Town; a Man of more Sense than most of them have; and apply'd warmly to Mr. *D—p—t,* told him, He was *making a Calf,* and that he thot', *the D——l was in him:* Mr. *D—p —t* said, He *tho't so too;* and added, That he *was under the Influence of an evil Spirit, and that God had left Him.* His most famous Armour Bearer has had bitter Reflections on their late odd Transactions; and declar'd, That *altho' he had for three Years past* believ'd (and why not *known*) *himself to be a Child of God,* he now tho't *he was a Child of the D——l, and a* Judas; *and* *thought he should be hang'd between Heaven and Earth, and have his Bowels gush out.* Another poor young Man of *Boston,* (whom I wish with his Friends) said the same Things (save that he did not foresee the same dismal Fate) at that Time, in the same Company, and all in the Presence of Mr. *D—p—t,* who is now indispos'd in Body, but better compos'd in Mind: I wish him nothing worse than, *Mens sane, in Corpore sano.*

Who am, Sir,
Your humble Servant.

14. Davenport Deserted: A Letter, 1743

[Sarah Pierpont to Eleazar Wheelock (New Haven, Conn.), May 30, 1743, Dartmouth College Archives, Hanover, N.H.]

REVD. AND DEAR SIR

. . . I hear by Dr Smith and others who have latly seen dear Mr. Davenport (at Stanford) that he lyes in the dark before God for his conduct at N. London. Your aunt Howel who has been the most bitter against him is latly come from Stanford and is now so turned in favour of him that She can't bear to hear a reflecting Word against him. I perceive by the Doctor that Mr. Davenport is very much alone in the world. His friends forsake him. He rides from town to town without any attendance. But by what I can learn he enjoys a great deal of Soul Satisfaction from that God who is an unchangable and never failing friend and feels the truth of that promise *which* is *more worth than a mountain of Gold. viz—I will never leave you nor forsake you.* . . .

I subscribe my self your affectionate freind and unworthy Servant

SARAH PEIRPOINT

15. James Davenport, *Confession and Retractions,* 1744

[James Davenport, *The Reverend Mr. James Davenport's Confession and Retractions* (Boston, 1744), 3–8]

ALTHO' I don't question at all, but there is great Reason to bless God for a *glorious and wonderful Work of his Power and Grace* in the *Edification* of his Children, and the *Conviction* and *Conversion* of Numbers in *New-England,* in the *neighbouring Governments* and *several other Parts,* within a few Years past; and believe that the Lord hath favoured me, tho' most unworthy, with several others of his Servants, in granting special Assistance and Success; the Glory of all which be given to JEHOVAH, to whom alone it belongs:

Yet after frequent Meditation and Desires that I might be enabled to apprehend Things justly, and, I hope I may say, mature Consideration; I am now fully convinced and persuaded that *several Appendages to this glorious Work* are no essential Parts thereof, but of a *different* and *contrary* Nature and Tendency; *which Appendages* I have been in the Time of the Work very industrious in and instrumental of promoting, by a misguided Zeal: being further much influenced in the Affair by the *false Spirit;* which, unobserved by me, did (as I have been brought to see since) prompt me to *unjust Apprehensions* and *Misconduct* in *several Articles;* which have been great Blemishes to the Work of God, very grievous to some of God's Children, no less ensnaring and corrupting to others of them, a sad Means of many Persons questioning the Work of God, concluding and appearing against it, and of the hardening of Multitudes in their Sins, and an awful Occasion of the Enemies blaspheming the right Ways of the Lord; and withal very offensive to that God, before whom I would lie in the Dust, prostrate in deep Humility and Repentance on this Account, imploring Pardon for the Mediator's Sake, and thankfully accepting the Tokens thereof.

The *Articles,* which I especially refer to, and would in the most public Manner *retract,* and *warn others against,* are these which follow, *viz.*

I. The Method I us'd for a considerable Time, with Respect to some, yea many *Ministers* in several Parts, in openly *exposing such as I fear'd or thought unconverted, in public Prayer or otherwise:* herein making my private Judgment, (in which also I much suspect I was mistaken in several Instances, and I believe also that my Judgment concerning several, was formed rashly and upon very slender Grounds.) I say making my private Judgment, the Ground of public Actions or Conduct; offending, as I apprehend (altho' in the Time of it ignorantly) against the *ninth Commandment,* and such other

Passages of Scripture, as are similar; yea, I may say, offending against the Laws both of Justice and Charity: Which Laws were further broken,

II. By my *advising and urging to such Separations* from *those Ministers,* whom I treated as above, as I believe may justly be called rash, unwarrantable, and of sad and awful Tendency and Consequence. And here I would ask the Forgiveness of those Ministers, whom I have injured in both these Articles.

III. I confess I have been much led astray by *following Impulses* or Impressions as a Rule of Conduct, whether they came with or without a Text of Scripture; and my neglecting also duly to observe the Analogy of Scripture: I am persuaded this was a great Means of corrupting my Experiences and carrying me off from the Word of God, and a great Handle, which the *false Spirit* has made use of with Respect to a Number, and me especially.

IV. I believe further that I have done much Hurt to Religion by *encouraging private Persons to a ministerial and authoritative Kind or Method of exhorting;* which is particularly observable in many such being much puft up and *falling into the Snare of the Devil,* while many others are thus directly prejudic'd against the Work.

V. I have Reason to be deeply humbled that I have not been duly careful to endeavour to remove or prevent Prejudice, (where I now believe I might then have done it consistently with Duty) which appear'd remarkable in the Method I practis'd, of *singing with others in the Streets* in Societies frequently.

I would also penitently confess and bewail my *great Stiffness* in retaining these *aforesaid Errors* a great while, and Unwillingness to examine into them with any Jealousy of their being Errors, notwithstanding the friendly Counsels and Cautions of real Friends, especially in the Ministry.

Here may properly be added a Paragraph or two, taken out of a *Letter from me* to Mr. *Barber* at *Georgia;* a *true Copy* of which I gave Consent should be publish'd lately at *Philadelphia:* "—I would add to what Brother T—— hath written on the awful Affair of Books and Cloaths at *New-London,* which affords Grounds of deep and lasting Humiliation; I was to my Shame be it spoken, the Ringleader in *that horrid Action;* I was, my dear Brother, under the powerful Influence of the *false Spirit* almost one whole Day together, and Part of several Days. The Lord shewed me afterwards that the Spirit I was then acted by was in it's Operations void of true inward Peace, laying the greatest Stress on Externals, neglecting the Heart, full of Impatience, Pride and Arrogance; altho' I thought in the Time of it, that 'twas the Spirit of God in an high Degree; awful indeed! my Body especially my Leg much disorder'd at the same Time,* which Satan and my evil Heart might make some Handle of."

And now may the holy wise and good God, be pleas'd to guard and secure me against *such Errors* for the future, and stop the Progress of those, whether Ministers or People, who have been corrupted by my Words or Example in any of the above mention'd Particulars; and if it be his holy Will, *bless this public Recantation* to this Purpose. And Oh!

* I had the *long Fever* on me and the cankry Humour raging at once.

may he grant withal, that such as by Reason of the aforesaid *Errors and Misconduct* have entertained unhappy Prejudices against Christianity in general, or the late glorious Work of God in particular, may be this Account learn to distinguish the *Appendage* from the *Substance* or *Essence,* that which is *vile* and *odious* from that which is *precious, glorious* and *divine,* and thus be entirely and happily freed from all those Prejudices refer'd to, and this in infinite Mercy through Jesus Christ; and to these Requests may all God's Children, whether Ministers or others say, *Amen.*

July 28. 1744.

JAMES DAVENPORT.

P.S. In as much as a Number, who have fallen in with and promoted the *aforesaid Errors* and *Misconduct,* and are not alter'd in their Minds, may be prejudic'd against this *Recantation,* by a Supposition or Belief, that I came into it by Reason of Desertion or Dulness and Deadness in Religion: It seems needful therefore to signify, what I hope I may say without boasting, and what I am able thro' pure rich Grace to speak with Truth and Freedom; that for *some Months* in the Time of my coming to the *abovesaid Conclusions* and *Retractations,* and since I have come through Grace to them; I have been favoured a great Part of the Time, with a sweet *Calm and Serenity of Soul and Rest in God,* and sometimes with special and remarkable Refreshments of Soul, and these more free from corrupt Mixtures than formerly: *Glory to God alone.*

J. D.

Opposition to Itineracy

16. The Subversion of Church Order: Theophilus Pickering, *Letters*, 1742

[Theophilus Pickering, *The Rev. Mr. Pickering's Letters To the Rev. N. Rogers and Mr. D. Rogers of Ipswich* . . . (Boston, 1742), 7–10]

To the Reverend Mr. *Nathanael Rogers, Junior*-Pastor of the First Church in *Ipswich*.

Rev. Sr.

INASMUCH as the LORD JESUS by his Providence and Grace has called me to the work of the *Ministry* and cast my Lot into the same Town with you, it may be reasonably suppos'd that I have not been altogether unobservant of the Methods by which you and your Brother (Mr. *Daniel*) have lately signaliz'd yourselves. And fearing that you were building upon the Foundation, *Wood Hay Stubble,* as well as *Gold Silver* and *precious Stones;* I conceiv'd it behooved me to inquire into the Design of some Things that lookt to be of *doubtful Meaning* and of *dangerous Tendency:* To which End, I wrote you my *Letter* of the 3rd of *Feb.* last: expecting such Reply to the reasonable Request therein contained, as might be some way satisfactory.

But the *Answer* you sent me, seem'd to be *superficial* and *evasive.*

Therefore I wrote you a *second Letter* dated the 15th of *Feb.* hoping that upon further Consideration you would endeavour to give me *better Light and Satisfaction:* But instead of that; you and your Brother [without advising with me, or any Consent of mine first obtained,] came last *March* into my Parish, and held several Meetings in the House for public Worship: and have moreover been pleas'd to pray for me in your Assemblies—*That God would open mine Eyes*—and *that the Scales*

might fall from 'em: yea one of you tho't fit, publickly in the Hearing of my People, to call me, their *Blind Minister.*

And therefore when you came Hither (alone) on the 26th of *May,* I was so far dispos'd to *magnify mine Office,* as, instead of favouring your Preaching among us, to send you *a Message of Denial;* with an Intimation *that I dislikt your Conduct;* and desir'd you *to forbear coming to preach to my People, either in the Meeting-house or any where within the Limits of my Parish, unless I was foreacquainted with your Design and consenting thereunto.* Upon which you show'd so much Complaisance, as not to go into the Parish-House: But yet you saw meet to hold an Assembly *abroad:* as if *this* alter'd the case; which serv'd only to palliate the matter, and make the People believe that you did not infringe upon my Pastoral Charge, because your Service was not perform'd within the Meeting-house Walls: When indeed it was much the same Thing (both in the Nature and Consequents of it,) whether you officiated in the Meeting-house or elsewhere in the Parish: And accordingly in discourse with you (a few Minutes) on *May* 31, you acknowledged that *truly it made no great odds;* but seem'd to excuse the Matter, as if *you were so urg'd to preach that you could not well avoid it:* Whereupon I reply'd, *That I hop'd you endeavour'd to satisfy your self, that your Conduct was right:* To which you gave an *affirmative Answer,* and said *that you was clear in it:* Whereby I understood you as acting from *Principle* notwithstanding your *colourable Excuse.*

Nevertheless, I have Charity for you, that you *aim at the Glory of God* in your Ministrations; and am willing to make due Allowance for *humane Infirmities,* being conscious of my own Imperfections.

But yet, as your Carriage in some respects appear'd so exceptionable that I thought my self oblig'd to discountenance your *itinerant Labours,* so I was in hopes that you wou'd be cautious of giving me further Molestation. But by what I have lately heard, I learn that you entertain some Thoughts of renewing your *Visits;* and am confirm'd in it, by some Discourse that I had *last Tuesday,* with your Harbinger Mr. *John Rogers* the younger, who *then* exercis'd his Gifts among us without my Leave, but conformable to your Example.

Wherefore I now send intreating as a *Minister* a *Neighbour* a *Brother,* that you wou'd seriously review the Steps you have taken, that you may be sensible of your Misconduct *in coming to minister in my Parish without my Consent or Allowance.* If any that have *itching Ears* applaud your Zeal herein, yet their Weakness can never justify your Measures. For you know that even in the *Apostle's Day,* care was taken that the Churches might be furnisht with *ordinary Pastors* appointed to their *several Charges,* and that both *You* and *I* have our *respective Flocks* of which the HOLY GHOST hath made us *Overseers.* And therefore for you to invade my *Peculiar* (without open Council and fair Trial) is evidently subversive of *the Order of the Gospel and Peace of the Churches.*

If the Place where you dwell be too strait for you, and you affect to be *a Minister at large* (like your Brother Mr. *Daniel*) ; then I pray that you would *go at large among the ungospelized Heathen,* and not trespass upon your Neighbours Rights, by breaking into *Christ's Inclosures* put under the Care of *other Husbandmen.*

Or if you think that some Parishes call for your Pity, in being so unhappy as to have such Men for their Teachers that are *sadly in the Dark;* why are not you so *kind* and *faithful* as to shew such Ministers their *great Mistakes,* and to labour to convince 'em of their Errors *by the Word of* GOD?—and not to assume such despotick Power as to go within *Another's Line,* either of your own Head, or upon any Invitations or Complaints the grounds whereof may be controverted. I can hardly believe that you wou'd like to be dealt with in such Sort: at least I'm perswaded it would not be well-pleasing to the *Great* LORD and HEAD of the Church; the Laws of whose Kingdom provide for the well-ordering of his House; without leaving it to poor imperfect Men (as the Best of his ministers are,) to manage in an arbitrary way—which would tend to destroy the Interests of Christianity through Strifes and Divisions. Judge then what is right: *For God is not the Author of Confusion but of Peace as in all Churches of the Saints.*

But what aggravates the Matter, is the Liberty taken to vent your Zeal in forward Expressions tending to render me suspected and bring my Ministry into Contempt, after I had earnestly sought to you, and you had put me off with some general Intimations and frivilous Shifts, instead of endeavouring by the *Divine Oracles* to enlighten my Darkness.

17. Connecticut Inhibits Itinerants: *The Public Records of Connecticut*

A. AN ACT FOR REGULATING ABUSES, 1742

[Charles J. Hoadly, ed., *The Public Records of the Colony of Connecticut*, VIII (Hartford, 1874), 454–457]

An Act for regulating Abuses and correcting Disorders in Ecclesiastical Affairs.

Whereas this Assembly did, by their act made in the seventh year of the reign of her late Majesty Queen Anne, establish and confirm a confession of faith, and an agreement for ecclesiastical discipline, made at Saybrook, *anno Dom.* 1708, by the reverend elders and the messengers delegated by the churches in this Colony for that purpose, under which establishment his Majesty's subjects inhabiting in this Colony have enjoyed great peace and quietness, till of late sundry persons have been guilty of disorderly and irregular practices: whereupon this Assembly, in October last, did direct to the calling of a general consociation, to sit at Guilford in November last, which said consociation was convened accordingly; at which convention it was endeavoured to prevent the growing disorders amongst the ministers that have been ordained or licenced by the associations in this government to preach, and likewise to prevent divisions and disorder among the churches and ecclesiastical societies settled by order of this Assembly: Notwithstanding which, divers of the ministers, ordained as aforesaid, and others licenced to preach by some of the associations allowed by law, have taken upon them, without any lawful call, to go into parishes immediately under the care of other ministers, and there to preach to and teach the people; and also sundry persons, some of whom are very illiterate, and have no ecclesiastical character or any authority whatsoever to preach or teach, have taken upon them publickly to teach and exhort the people in matters of religion, both as to doctrine and practice; which practices have a tendency to make divisions and contentions among the people in this Colony, and to destroy the ecclesiastical constitution established by the laws of this government, and likewise to hinder the growth and increase of vital piety and godliness in these churches, and also to introduce unqualified persons into the ministry, and more especially where one association doth intermeddle with the affairs that by the platform and agreement abovesaid, made at Saybrook aforesaid, are properly within the province and jurisdiction of another association, as to the licencing persons to preach, and ordaining ministers: Therefore,

1. *Be it enacted by the Governor, Council and Representatives, in General Court assembled, and by the authority of the same,* That if any ordained minister, or other person licenced as aforesaid to preach, shall enter into any parish not immediately under his charge, and shall there preach or exhort the people, shall be denied and secluded the benefit of any law of this Colony made for the support and

encouragement of the gospel ministry, except such ordained minister or licenced person shall be expressly invited and desired so to enter into such other parish and there to preach and exhort the people, either by the settled minister and the major part of the church of said parish, or, in case there be no settled minister, then by the church or society within such parish.

2. *And it is further enacted by the authority aforesaid,* That if any association of ministers shall undertake to examine or licence any candidate for the gospel ministry, or assume to themselves the decision of any controversy, or as an association to counsel and advise in any affair that by the platform or agreement abovementioned, made at Saybrook aforesaid, is properly within the province and jurisdiction of any other association, then and in such case, every member that shall be present in such association so licencing, deciding or counselling, shall be, each and every of them, denied and secluded the benefit of any law in this Colony made for the support and encouragement of the gospel ministry.

3. *And it is further enacted by the authority aforesaid,* That if any minister or ministers, contrary to the true intent and meaning of this act, shall presume to preach in any parish not under his immediate care and charge, the minister of the parish where he shall so offend, or the civil authority, or any two of the committee of such parish, shall give information thereof in writing, under their hands, to the clerk of the parish or society where such offending minister doth belong, which clerk shall receive such information, and lodge and keep the same on file in his office; and no assistant or justice of the peace in this Colony shall sign any warrant for the collecting any minister's rate, without first receiving a certificate from the clerk of the society or parish

where such rate is to be collected, that no such information as is abovementioned hath been received by him or lodged in his office.

4. *And it is further enacted by the authority aforesaid,* That if any person whatsoever, that is not a settled and ordained minister, shall go into any parish and (without the express desire and invitation of the settled minister of such parish (if any there be) and the major part of the church, or if there be no such settled minister, without the express desire of the church or congregation within such parish,) publickly preach and exhort the people, shall for every, such offence, upon complaint made thereof to any assistant or justice of the peace, be bound to his peaceable and good behaviour until the next county court in that county where the offence shall be committed, by said assistant or justice of the peace, in the penal sum of one hundred pounds lawful money, that he or they will not again offend in the like kind; and the said county court may, if they see meet, further bind the person or persons offending as aforesaid to their peaceable and good behaviour during the pleasure of said court.

5. *And it is further enacted by the authority aforesaid,* That if any foreigner, or stranger that is not an inhabitant within this Colony, including as well such persons that have no ecclesiastical character or licence to preach as such as have received ordination or licence to preach by any association or presbytery, shall presume to preach, teach or publickly to exhort, in any town or society within this Colony, without the desire and licence of the settled minister and the major part of the church of such town or society, or at the call and desire of the church and inhabitants of such town or society, provided that it so happen that there is no settled minister there, that every such

preacher, teacher or exhorter, shall be sent (as a vagrant person) by warrant from any one assistant or justice of the peace, from constable to constable, out of the bounds of this Colony.

B. THE ARREST OF BENJAMIN POMEROY, 1744

[Charles J. Hoadly, ed., *The Public Records of the Colony of Connecticut*, IX (Hartford, 1876), 28, 29].

Whereas, Elihu Hall, Esq., King's Attorney for the county of New Haven, at the sessions of this Assembly at said New Haven, in October, exhibited and filed one certain bill of indictment or information against Mr. Benjamin Pomroy, of Hebron in the county of Hartford, pastor of the church there, complaining and setting forth that said Benjamin Pumroy had, about the 1st of September then last past, publickly declared and said, that the late law of this Colony, made concerning ecclesiastical affairs, was a great foundation to encourage persecution and to encourage wicked men to break their covenants, and that if wicked men did not take the advantage of it, it was no thanks to the Court; and that he further said, that the law that was made to stop ministers from going about to preach in other towns was made without reason and contrary to the word of God; with design to bring said laws into contempt, etc.; and thereupon moved said Pumroy should be proceeded against, as to law and justice appertains: And whereas said bill, filed as abovesaid, was continued, and the prosecution thereof put off to this time, and the said Pumroy ordered to be brought before this Assembly in its present session, to answer in the premises: And whereas Daniel Edwards, Attorney to our Lord the King, against the said Mr. Benjamin Pumroy one other bill of indictment now exhibited representing that on the publick fast day in this Colony in April last, he, said Pumroy, did publickly declare and say, that the great men had fallen in and joyned with those that are on the devil's side and enemies to the kingdom of Christ, and raised such persecution in the land that if there be a faithful minister of the Lord Jesus he must lose his estate, and if there be but a faithful man in civil authority he must lose his honor and usefulness; and further, in the after part of said day, said, there is no Colony so privileged as Connecticut was, and now there is no Colony so bad as Connecticut for persecuting laws, I never heard nor read of such persecuting laws as is in Connecticut, nay there is no such thing among the heathen, and the very heathen are a shame to them, or words to that effect. . . .

And this Assembly having thereon duly considered, as touching the said first indictment, are of opinion that the things in special justification thereof offered are insufficient; and also having duly weighed and considered the pleas and evidences on the said plea of not guilty, either in behalf of the King or by the counsel for said Pumroy exhibited and produced, do find that the said Benjamin Pumroy is thereof guilty. Whereupon, it is considered and resolved by this Assembly, that the said Benjamin Pumroy become bound in the sum of fifty pounds money, payable to the publick Treasurer of this Colony, with condition that if he, the said Benjamin Pumroy, do at all times hereafter, from this day until the sessions of this Assembly in May next, both in word and deed, use, bear and behave himself well, faithfully and peaceably towards all this Majesty's liege subjects, and especially towards the Legislature and all the civil authority of this Colony, in such wise as that by any act, speech or thing by the said Benjamin Pumroy committed, done, reported, spoken or published, they, the said Legislature or any of the civil authority of said Col-

ony, be not at any time hereafter in any manner injured, troubled, villified or defamed, or in their name, office, honour or authority, anyway impeached, slandered or taken away, then the said bond to become void, otherwise to be in force and virtue; and that he at this Assembly in May next appear to take up such bond. . . .

Whitefield Returns

18. Close the Pulpits: *A Letter . . . to the Associated Ministers of Boston and Charlestown,* 1745

> [*A Letter from Two Neighboring Associations of Ministers in the Country, to the Associated Ministers of Boston and Charlestown, relating to the Admission of Mr. Whitefield into their Pulpits* (Boston, 1745), 2–7]

Reverend and dear Brethren,

The Return of the Rev. Mr. *Whitefield* to *New-England,* and the Reception he may meet with from Ministers in our most populous Towns, being (as we apprehend) of Consequence to *these Churches;* we think we should be neither just to *ourselves* and the *particular Flocks* committed to our *pastoral Care,* nor appear to be influenced by that affectionate Regard to the Interests of our *Redeemer* in this *Land,* which becomes our Character as Ministers of the Gospel, if we were silent upon the *hasty Admission,* which we perceive he hath already obtained into some of your Pulpits, and is, we fear, about to find into others. We are far from pretending to dictate what Preachers you shall receive, and whom you shall reject: This would be such arrogant Assuming as we would neither injuriously practice, nor patiently bear. And if the Consequences of admitting Mr. *Whitefield* were of a lower and more private Nature, confined within the Limits of your own Walls, though we should have been very

willing to assist any Brother in the Ministry with our best Advice, to prevent, or rectify his Mistakes, we should not have thought it our Duty to have done it in so publick a Manner. But as we are convinced the Consequences of this Action are no less *extensive* than *hurtful,* pardon us, *dear Brethren,* if, upon what we apprehend so melancholly an Occasion, we cannot but complain.

We think we are writing to Gentlemen who, what high Apprehensions soever they may have had of the Glory of the Times, and how much soever they may differ from our Sentiments upon this Matter, are yet sensible many undesireable Things, and of dangerous Consequence to the Interests of Religion and of Peace, have prevailed, and been promoted by ITINERANTS of far less Name than Mr. *Whitefield.* Some *enthusiastical* Teachers you have formerly born a publick Testimony against; the present Separations, so disagreeable to the Rules of the Gospel, we presume you discountenance, together with various Kinds of Disorders, which, to the great Scandal of Religion and Grief of good Men, have very ignorantly, not to say profanely, been attributed to the Divine *Spirit*. It is not our Design to enumerate the various Evils which, in these Times of Misunderstanding in Matters of Religion, have overspread the Land; the Relation of which will please none but our Enemies, whose greatest Advantages arise from the Divisions of Protestants. It is enough that *such Evils* have prevailed, and that some *Itinerants,* highly extolled and incessantly followed by many People, and eagerly set upon preaching *out of their Line,* have been the *Instruments* in promoting them.

Now, *Brethren,* are you satisfied Mr. *Whitefield* approves not of these *Disorders?* Is he against *Separations?* Is he an Enemy to *Enthusiasm?* Have you enquired to your Satisfaction, and found that you agree with him in affixing the same Ideas to the same Terms, and in your Sentiments upon the same Questions? Have you taken this Care with Respect to *All* the Evils, which your selves acknowledge have prevailed, by Means of other *Itinerants* in these Times? And why have you not imparted the Grounds of your Satisfaction, if you have received any, to the Publick, both to justify your own Conduct, and calm the Minds, and dissipate the Fears of many godly People, who dreaded the Return of *these Mischiefs* with their *original Author.*

Do you find in him a Disposition to the *most plain Christian Duty of humbly confessing and publickly retracting his wicked and slanderous Suggestions concerning the Ministry, and concerning our Colleges, so much our Glory?* Have you prevailed with him to make *full Satisfaction to the Injured?* Has he done, or is he doing it?

Do you find him inclined to heal the unhappy *Divisions* occasioned by his *former Visit?* Can you learn whether we are to be united in Affection and Christian Communion, tho' of different Sentiments about Things of the present Day, or whether some one Party, and perhaps *that* at the Head of which a few Ministers have appeared, whose *enthusiastic* Conduct you have not yet approved, is not, if possible, to prevail upon the Ruin of the Rest? And if this be his Design, can you doubt of his Success, if, besides the Assistance you give him, you consider his *peculiar Faculty* by his *Address* and *sanctimonious* Pretences, to recommend with little Proof what he pleaseth to many People?

Pray *Brethren,* What Good do you propose to *yourselves* or your *Country,* that shall countervail the many Evils already sprung up, and the many more of the like, or different Kinds, which we have Reason to fear? Was there ever such an Alienation of Affections amongst Brethren in the Ministry, or Divisions in our Churches, within the Memory of Man? Such an unchristian Spirit, and uncharitable Expressions? Hath the visible Good of his *former Visit,* by any Means equalled the *visible* Mischiefs that followed? Or are we to be told of much *secret* Good, of which no Mortal, no, nor Angel can determine; it being the Prerogative of the omniscient *God* to search the Heart and try the Reins?

Have you such Grounds to hope for the Good you seem to expect from the Preaching of Mr. *Whitefield* amongst us, in our present divided Situation, as will justify you in doing what may probably involve some of your *Brethren* in the Ministry, of Sentiments differing from your's in these Matters, in Difficulties almost inextricable? Could you be unapprehensive of these Difficulties, or that your inviting him into your Pulpits would have a direct Tendency to bring them on? Pray, *Brethren,* consider what you have done. Have you not by opening your Pulpit Doors to this

Gentleman, encouraged and spirited up the *weaker* Sort of People to expect the like of their Ministers? And have you not then brought many of your *Brethren* into this unhappy Dilemma; if they refuse to invite him, they fear their Serviceableness in the Church of Christ is at an End, and perhaps their Families, most of them poor enough, and in no Way to get their Bread, cast upon the wide World. If they admit him, are not their Consciences lamentably wounded? And can it be expected but that they must go mourning all their Days for their Weakness and Want of Courage, since they could not help being convinced (whether mistaken or not) that his *Preaching* tended to promote, not the *Interests of Religion* but, *Enthusiasm*—which, though sometimes mistaken for it, will ever be found its effectual Destroyer?

Or, if no Regard must be had for those, who have been reputed *Opposers* from the Beginning, should you have entertained no Concern for many of your worthy *Brethren* in the Ministry, of *distinguishing Abilities* and *eminent Sanctity,* who, at the first, hoped such happy Times, as they had wished and prayed for, were coming on; but afterwards became sensible that very much of what had appeared to be pure *Gold* was a Mixture of *baser Metals,* and they had mistaken in many Instances *Evil for Good,* and *Darkness for Light?* And tho' they are of Opinion, Good hath been done; yet upon the Whole fear, *much more Hurt than Good?* Some Gentlemen of this Character committed unhappy Mistakes at first, whereby a Door was opened, thro' which many Evils rushed into the Churches, which have occasioned them since, much Trouble and Grief; but are the more excusable in that their earnest Desire to see the Kingdom of Christ prevail, prejudiced them in Favour of Things resembling in *their first Appearance,* but very different in *Nature* from *true Conversion* and *Godliness.* What they earnestly wished, *that* they too easily believed— And have any Ministers been in more unhappy Circumstances than some of these? And can any Thing perplex *their* Conduct more than *yours* in asking Mr. *Whitefield* to preach, as it must undoubtedly create much Dis-affection to them, in many of their People for refusing him?

If you believed your countenancing *this Gentleman,* as some of you have already done, to be of *extensive Influence,* and likely to *affect very greatly Ministers and Churches, throughout the Land,* did it not become you to have consulted, in some general Meeting, or Method, those that must be affected with it? Have you not, *Brethren,* in a Sense determin'd for them *all,* in a Case of *common* and *universal* Concern, and upon which therefore one would think they had a Right, at least, to be heard? And if at such a general Consultation, the Ministers of the Country should appear to be greatly divided, and many of their Churches represented as in Danger of being thrown into the most *violent Convulsions,* is not the Blessing of *Peace* of inexpressibly *greater Importance* than the *Reception of any Man living?* Much less of one no better qualified to serve the Interests of true Religion, than we apprehend Mr. *Whitefield* to be?

Lastly, How much is it to be lamented that when Ministers, alienated in their Affections from each other, by Reason of different Apprehensions, and opposite Measures, too warmly pursued, perhaps, on both Sides, began again to look towards one another, and feel the pleasing Returns of brotherly Love, the delightful Prospects, by this Means presented to us, should all be made to vanish in a Moment, by this unhappy Step of setting the *Author* of *our Divisions* to *preach* among us again?

And now, *dear Brethren,* What Effect this *Letter* will produce, is impossible for us to determine. But what we earnestly wish is, that, by the Blessing of *God,* it may be a Means of convincing those, who have taken it, that this *hasty Step* of admitting Mr. *Whitefield* into their Pulpits, opens, in these Churches, a *Scene of Confusion and wild Disorder,* by disaffecting and disuniting both *Ministers* and *People:* And that they, who have not yet taken it, may be induced seriously to consider the *consequent Dangers* and *Mischiefs;* and, as they *pray for the Peace of Jerusalem,* may manifest their Sincerity by a *stedfast* Adherence to their *Principles* in so important a Point of Conduct, and by an unshaken Opposition to the Sollici-tations of those, who urge them into it. And as for *our selves,* though we see a *gloomy Cloud* overspreading these Churches, and have melancholly Prospects of what, we fear, is to befall them, if the ITINERANCY of *this Gentleman,* and *others,* be encouraged, it will be no small Comfort to us to reflect upon the Sincerity, Courage and Constancy by which *God* enables us to plead for his Cause, and bear a *Testimony* to our *Brethren in the Ministry,* to *all these Churches,* and *to the whole World,* against the Evils which threaten its Subversion.

We subscribe our selves, *Rev. Gentlemen,*

Your Brethren in the Service of *Jesus Christ,*

First *Association.*

CALEB CUSHING, Pastor of the First Church in *Salisbury*

JOSEPH WHIPPLE	*Hampton-Falls*
JOHN LOWELL	*Newbury*
PAIN WINGATE	*Amesbury*
JEREMIAH FOGG	*Kensington*
NATHANIEL GOOKIN	*North-Hampton, New-Hampshire*
ELISHA ODLIN	*Amesbury*
PETER COFFIN	*Kingston*
WILLIAM PARSONS	*South-Hampton, New-Hampshire*
SAMUEL WEBSTER	*Salisbury.*

Second *Association.*

JOHN BARNARD, Pastor of the First Church in *Andover.*

JOSEPH PARSONS	*Bradford*
WILLIAM BALCH	*Bradford*
JAMES CUSHING	*Haverhill*
CHRISTOPHER SERGEANT	*Methuen*
WILLIAM JOHNSON	*Newbury*
JOHN CUSHING	*Boxford*
THOMAS BARNARD	*Newbury*
EDWARD BARNARD	*Haverhill.*

Dec. 26, 1744.

19. George Whitefield, *Journals,* 1744

[*George Whitefield's Journals: A new edition
containing fuller materials than any hitherto
published* ([n.p.], 1960), 528–530]

Tuesday, November 27th

Had the pleasure of dining today at my lodging with the Rev. Dr. Sewell, Doctor Coleman, Mr. Foxcroft, and Mr. Prince, four of the Seniour Ministers in Boston and very worthy men.

Before dinner we had some free conversation together in relation to some passages in my journals and the present posture of religious affairs in New England.

I found by what they said and by what I had heard by letters that the work of God had went on in a most glorious manner for near two Years after my departure from New England, but then a chill came over the [churches] work, through the imprudence of some Ministers who had been promoters and private persons who had been happy subjects of it.

They were apprehensive, I found too, that I would promote or encourage separations, and that some would have been encouraged to separate by my saying in my journal that I found the generality of Preachers preached an Unknown Christ, that the Colleges had darkness in them, even darkness that might be felt, and that speaking of the danger of an Unconverted Ministry, I said, How can a Dead man beget a living Child?

But I told them that these words were not wrote to imply that it was absolutely impossible but that it was highly improbable that an Unconverted man should be made instrumental to beget souls to Christ.

I said, I was sorry if anything I wrote had been a means of promoting separations for I was of no separating principles, but came to New England to preach the Gospel of peace [to all that were willing to hear] in my way to Georgia, and promote charity and love among all.

We talked freely and friendly [upon] about several other things, [and dined very comfortably] by which their jealousies they had entertained concerning me seemed to be in a great measure ended, and Dr. Coleman invited me to preach the next day at his Meeting house.

Oh the benefit of free and open dealing! How wise is the Saviour's advice, If thou hast aught against thy Brother go and tell him of it between him and thee. How much mischief, noise, and division would have been prevented through the Christian world, was this one precept but observed. Bind it O Lord as a frontlet about my head. Write it O my God in the table of my heart!

Wednesday, November 28th

Opened my public administration at Boston this afternoon at Dr. Coleman's meeting house from Rom. 1st, 16th. I am not ashamed of the Gospel of Christ for it is the power of God unto salvation to everyone that believeth. The congregation was very large, several ministers were present and the word was attended with sweet power.

CHAPTER THREE

THE NEW BIRTH

AT the heart of the Awakening was the new birth. It was the culmination of the revival preacher's efforts, the point toward which he drove his listeners, the moment of release for those awakened to the terrors of the Lord. Not narrowly religious by any means, conversion released deep psychological and social forces which understandably affected colonial life at many levels. The disturbances in the churches, the theological controversies in the press, and spates of social turmoil all followed from the vision of life opened in conversion.

The Spiritual Travels of Nathan Cole (b. 1711), the guileless autobiography of a common farmer in Farmington, Connecticut, shows the shattering effects of the direct confrontation with guilt and the gratifying peace that faith ultimately afforded (No. 20). Cole had heard of Whitefield well before the evangelist arrived in Connecticut. When word came one morning that he was to preach at nearby Middletown, Cole dropped his work in the fields and hurried off with his wife to listen. From that moment his confidence was gone, and he wrestled with crushing despair until at last assurance came. Moderate New Lights would have considered Cole's vision of God at the moment of rebirth as a form of enthusiasm. Visions and specific revelations had led the Muenster Anabaptists to horrid excesses that still haunted Calvinists. The majority of New Lights condemned enthusiasm as vigorously as reliance on works. Cole set himself off from the main body of reborn men in claiming so much for his conversion, just as he was to set himself off from the congregation in Kensington parish in 1747. At least into the 1770s when his journals end, he mainly worshipped alone in his house or with a few friends.

Cole's lonely religious life was not characteristic. More often people received strong communal support from the moment of their first awakening, through conversion, and in their worship thereafter. Samuel Blair (1712–1751), one of the graduates of William Tennent's Log College, prepared for Prince's *Christian History* an account of the revival of an entire church at Fagg's Manor (New Londonderry), Pennsylvania (No. 21). In this more typical situation, each person took courage from the minister urging him to acknowledge his guilt and from others who felt the same anguish. The despair, the humiliation, and the subsequent assurance, besides being a personal experience, were components of an identity recognized and valued in the community. One reason why the revivals once begun spread like an epidemic is that common concern in the group pulled religious emotions to the surface.

All along the way, the clergy directed, prodded, and comforted. In 1741 Jonathan Dickinson (1688–1747), the distinguished pastor at Elizabethtown, New Jersey, and a leader in the Presbyterian synod, laid out the classical steps in conversion (No. 22). Theological descriptions like his put the raw emotional data of the new birth into a cosmic setting. It was the interplay of personal and social forces within a commanding intellectual structure which gave such power to the Awakening.

Dickinson was only one of a large company who explained the significance of the Awakening and were devoted to its advancement. In 1746 a number of them founded the College of New Jersey after the Log College closed with the passing of William Tennent. Dickinson was the first president, and Jonathan Edwards was one of his successors. After Harvard and Yale showed their colors by repudiating Whitefield, the new college, soon to move to Princeton, became the center of evangelistic Calvinism in America.

20. Conversion: The Spiritual Travels of Nathan Cole, 1741

[The Spiritual Travels of Nathan Cole, Manuscript, Connecticut Historical Society, Hartford, Conn., 2, 5–14]

When I was young I had very early Convictions; but after I grew up, I was an Arminian untill I was near 30 years of age; I intended to be saved by my own works such as prayers and good deeds. . . .

When I saw Mr Whitfield come upon the Scaffold he lookt almost Angelical; a young, Slim, slender, Youth before some thousands of people with a bold undaunted Countenance, and my hearing how God was with him every where as he came along it Solemnized my mind; and put me into a trembling fear before he began to preach; for he looked as if he was Cloathed with Authority from the Great God; . . . and a sweet sollome solemnity sat upon his brow And my hearing him preach, gave me a heart wound; By Gods blessing: my old Foundation was broken up, and I saw that my righteousness would not save me; then I was convinced of the doctrine of Election: and went right to quarrelling with God about it; because that all I could do would not save me; and he had decreed from Eternity who should be saved and who not: I began to think I was not Elected, and that God made some for heaven and me for hell. And I thought God was not Just in so doing, I thought I did not stand on even Ground with others, if as I thought; I was made to be damned; My heart then rose against God exceedingly, for his making me for hell; Now this distress lasted Almost two years—Poor—Me— Miserable me. It pleased God to bring on my Convictions more and more, and I was loaded with the guilt of Sin, I saw I was undone for ever; I carried Such a weight of Sin in my breast or mind, that it seemed to me as if I should sink into the ground every step; and I kept all to my self as much as I could; I went month after month mourning and begging for mercy, I tryed every way I could think to help my self but all ways failed—Poor me it took away most all my Comfort of eating, drinking, Sleeping, or working. Hell fire was most always in my mind; and I have hundreds of times put my fingers into my pipe when I have been smoking to feel how fire felt: And to see how my Body could bear to lye in Hell fire for ever and ever. Now my countenance was sad so that others took notice of it; Sometimes I had some secret hope in the mercy of God; that some time or other he would have mercy on me; And so I took some hopes, and thought I would do all that I could do, and remove all things out of the way that might possibly be an hindrance; And I thought I must go to my Honoured Father and Mother and ask their forgiveness for every thing I had

done amiss toward them in all my life: if they had any thing against me; I went and when I came near the house one of my Brothers was there, and asked me what was the matter with me: I told him I did not feel well, and passed by; But he followed and asked again what was the matter. I gave him the same answer, but said he something is the matter more than Ordinary for I see it in your Countenance: I refused to tell at present—Poor me—I went to my Father and Mother and told them what I came for: and asked them to forgive me every think they had against me concerning my disobedience or whatsoever else it might be; they said that had not any thing against me, and both fell aweeping like Children for Joy to see me so concerned for my Soul. Now when I went away I made great Resolutions that I would forsake every thing that was Sinfull; And do to my uttermost every thing that was good; And at once I felt a calm in my mind, and I had no desire to any thing that was sin as I thought; But here the Devil thought to Catch me on a false hope, for I began to think that I was converted, for I thought I felt a real Change in me. But God in his mercy did not leave me here to perish; but in the space of ten days I was made to see that I was yet in the Gall of bitterness; my Convictions came on again more smart than ever—poor me—Oh then I long'd to be in the Condition of some good Man; there was then a very Mortal disease in the land, the fever and bloody flux; And I was possest with a notion that if I had it I should die and goe right to hell, but I presently had it and very hard too: then my heart rose against God again for making me for hell, when he might as well have made me for heaven; or not made me at all—Poor me—Oh that I could be a Dog or a toad or any Creature but Man: I thought that would be a happy Change for they had no Souls and I had. Oh what will become of me was the language of my mind; for now I was worse than ever, my heart was as hard as a Stone; my Eyes were dry, once I could weep for my Self but now cannot shed one tear; I was as it were in the very mouth of hell: The very flashes of hell fire were in my Mind; Eternity before me, and my time short here. Now when all ways failed me then I longed to be annihilated; or to have my Soul die with my body; but that way failed too. Hell fire hell fire ran Swift in my mind and my distemper grew harder and harder upon me, and my nature was just wore out—Poor me—poor Soul —One night my brother Elisha came in to see me, and I spake to him and said I should certainly die within two or three days at the out Side for my Nature cannot possibly hold it any longer; and I shall certainly goe right to hell: And do you always remember that your poor brother is in hell; don't you never think that I am in heaven, but take care of your self and always remember every day that your poor brother is in hell fire —Misery—Miserable me; my brother got out of his Chair and went to speak to me, but he could not for weeping and went out of the house; and went away home and told my Father and Mother what I had said to him, and they were greatly distressed for me, and thought in the morning they would come and see me; but their distress grew so great for me that they could not stay but Came in the night. And when they came into the house Mother seem'd to bring heaven into the house; but there was no heaven for me: She said Oh Nathan will you despair of the mercy of God, do not for a thousand of worlds, don't despair of the mercy of God, for he can have mercy at the very last gasp; I told her there was no mercy for me, I was going right down to hell, for I cannot feel grieved for my self, I can't relent, I can't weep for my self, I cannot

shed one tear for my Sins; I am a gone Creature: Oh Nathan says she I have been so my self that I could not shed one tear if I might have had all the world for it; And the next moment I could cry as freely for Joy as ever I could for any thing in the world: Oh said she I know how you feel now, O if God should Shine into your Soul now it would almost take away your life, it would almost part soul and body; I beg of you not to despair of the mercy of God. I told her I could not bear to hear her talk so; for I cannot pray, my heart is as hard as a stone, do be gone, let me alone: do go home; you cannot do me any good, I am past all help of men or means, either for soul or Body, and after some time I perswaded them to go away; and there I lay all night in such a Condition untill sometime the next day with pining thoughts in my mind that my Soul might die with my Body; and there came some body in with a great Arm full of dry wood and laid it on the fire, . . . and went out. It burnt up very briskly as I lay on my Bed with my face toward the fire looking on, with these thoughts in my mind, Oh that I might creep into that fire and lye there and burn to death and die for ever Soul and Body; Oh that God would suffer it—Oh that God would suffer it—Poor Soul— And while these thoughts were in my mind God appeared unto me and made me Skringe: before whose face the heavens and the earth fled away; and I was Shrinked into nothing; I knew not whether I was in the body or out, I seemed to hang in open Air before God, and he seemed to Speak to me in an angry and Sovereign way what won't you trust your Soul with God; My heart answered O yes, yes, yes; before I could stir my tongue or lips, And then He seemed to speak again, and say, may not God make one Vessel to honour and another to dishonour and not let you know it; My heart answered again O yes

yes before I cou'd stir my tongue or lips. Now while my Soul was viewing God, my fleshly part was working imaginations and saw many things which I will omitt to tell at this time. When God appeared to me every thing vanished and was gone in the twinkling of an Eye, as quick as A flash of lightning; But when God disappeared or in some measure withdrew, every thing was in its place again and I was on my Bed. My heart was broken; my burden was fallen of my mind; I was set free, my distress was gone, and I was filled with a pineing desire to see Christs own words in the bible; and I got up off my bed being alone; And by the help of Chairs I got along to the window where my bible was and I opened it and the first place I saw was the 15th Chap: John—on Christs own words and they spake to my very heart and every doubt and scruple that rose in my heart about the truth of Gods word was took right off; and I saw the whole train of Scriptures all in A Connection, and I believe I felt just as the Apostles felt the truth of the word when they writ it, every leas[t] line and letter smiled in my face; I got the bible up under my Chin and hugged it; it was sweet and lovely; the word was nigh me in my hand, then I began to pray and to praise God; I could say Oh my God, and then I could think of no expression good enough to speak to Him, he was altogether—lovely and then I wou'd fall down into A muse and look back into my past life to see how I had lived and it seemed as if my very heart strings would break with sorrow and grief, to see how I had lived in abuse to this God I saw; then I began to pray and to praise God again, and I could say Oh my God and then I could not find words good enough to speak to his praise; then I fell into a muse and look'd back on my past life; and saw what an abominable unbeliever I had been, O now I could weep for joy and

Sorrow, now I had true mourning for sin and never before now I saw sin to be right against God; now my heart and Soul were filled as full as they Could hold with Joy and sorrow; now I perfectly felt truth: now my heart talked with God; now every thing praised God; the trees, the stone, the walls of the house and every thing I could set my eyes on, they all praised God; and while I was weeping, Sobing and Sighing, as if my heart wou'd break; there came somebody and opened the Door and spake to me, but I made no Answer nor turned to see who it was: but I remember I knew the voice but soon forgat who it was: presently my Wife came into the room and asked me what I cryed for; I gave her little or no answer, she stood a while and went out again; for I was swallowed up in God. Now I had for some years a bitter prejudice against three scornfull men that had wronged me, but now all that was gone away Clear, and my Soul longed for them and loved them; there was nothing that was sinfull that could any wise abide the presence of God; And all the Air was love, now I saw that every thing that was sin fled from the presence of God. As far as darkness is gone from light or beams of the Sun for where ever the Sun can be seen clear there is no Darkness. I saw that Darkness could as well be in the Clear light of the Sun, as well as Sin in the presence of God; who is so holy and Sovereign; now I saw that I must Suffer as well as do for Christ, now I saw that I must for sake all and follow Christ; now I saw with new eyes; all things became new, A new God; new thoughts and new heart; Now I began to hope I should be converted some time or other, for I was sure that God had done some great thing for my soul; I knew that God had subdued my stubborn heart: I knew my heart would never rise so against God as it had done; here I saw in the aforesaid 15

Chap: of John where I opened the bible first that Christ says to his disciples if ye love me keep my Commandments and then says he this is my Commandment that ye love one another. Oh I thought I could die A thousand deaths for Christ, I thought I could have been trodden under foot of man, be mocked or any thing for Christ—Glory be to God.

21. A Revival: Samuel Blair, *A Short and Faithful Narrative*, 1744

[Samuel Blair, *A Short and Faithful Narrative, Of the late Remarkable Revival of Religion In the Congregation of New-Londonderry, and other Parts of Pennsylvania. As the same was sent in a Letter to the Rev. Mr. PRINCE of Boston* (Philadelphia, [1744]), 7-28]

That it may the more clearly appear that the Lord has indeed carried on a Work of true real Religion among us of late Years, I conceive it will be useful to give a brief general View of the State of Religion in these Parts before this remarkable Season. I doubt not then, but there were still some sincerely religious People up and down; and there were, I believe, a considerable Number in the several Congregations pretty exact, according to their Education, in the Observance of the external Forms of Religion, not only as to Attendance upon publick Ordinances on the Sabbaths, but also, as the Practice of Family Worship, and perhaps secret Prayer too; but, with these Things the most Part seem'd to all Appearance to rest contented; and to satisfy their Consciences just with a dead Formality in Religion. If they perform'd these Duties pretty punctually in their Seasons, and, as they thought with a good Meaning, out of Conscience, and not just to obtain a Name for Religion among Men, then they were ready to conclude that they were truly and sincerely religious. A very lamentable Ignorance of the main essentials of true practical Religion, and the Doctrines nextly relating thereunto very generally prevail'd. The Nature and Necessity of the *New-Birth* was but little known or thought of, the Necessity of a Conviction of Sin and Misery, by the Holy Spirits opening and applying the Law to the Conscience, in order to a saving Closure with Christ was hardly known at all to the most. It was thought that if there was any need of a Heart-distressing Sight of the Souls Danger, and Fear of divine Wrath. It was only needful for the grosser Sort of Sinners, and for any others to be deeply exercis'd this Way (as there might sometimes be some rare Instances observable) this was generally look'd upon to be a great Evil and Temptation that had befallen those Persons. The common Names for such Soul-Concern were, *Melancholy, Trouble of Mind, or Despair.* These Terms were in common, so far as I have been acquainted, indifferently used as Synonimous; and *Trouble of Mind,* was look'd upon as a great Evil, which all Persons that made any sober Profession and Practice of Religion ought carefully to avoid. There was scarcely any Suspicion at all in general, of any Danger of depending upon Self-Righteousness, and not upon the Righteousness of CHRIST alone for Salvation: *Papists* and *Quakers* wou'd be readily acknowledged guilty of this Crime, but hardly any professed *Presbyterian.* The Necessity of being first in CHRIST by a vital Union, and in a justified State before our Religious Services can be well pleasing and acceptable to God, was very little understood or tho't of; but the common Notion seem'd to be, that if People were aiming to be in the Way of Duty as well as they could, as they imagin'd, there was no Reason to be much afraid.

According to these Principles, and this ignorance of some of the most Soul-concerning Truths of the Gospel, People were very generally thro' the Land careless at Heart, and stupidly indifferent about the great Concerns of Eternity. There was very little Appearance of any hearty Engagedness in Religion: And indeed the Wise, for the most Part, were in a great Degree asleep with the Foolish. 'Twas sad to see with what a careless Behaviour the publick Ordinances were attended, and how People were given to unsuitable worldly Discourse on the Lord's Holy Day. In publick Companies, especially at Weddings, a vain and frothy Lightness was apparent in the Deportment of many Professors; and in some Places very extravagant Follies, as Horse Running, Fiddling and Dancing, pretty much obtain'd on those Occasions.

Thus Religion lay as it were a dying, and ready to expire its last Breath of Life in this Part of the visible Church: And it was in the Spring *Anno Domini* 1740, when the God of Salvation was pleased to visit us with the blessed Effusions of his Holy Spirit in an eminent Manner. The first very open and Publick Appearance of this gracious Visitations in these Parts, was in the Congregation which God has committed to my Charge. The Congregation has not been erected above Fourteen or Fifteen Years from this Time: The Place is a new Settlement, generally settled with People from Ireland. (as all our Congregations in *Pennsylvania*, except two or three, chiefly are made up of People from that Kingdom) I am the first Minister they have ever had settled in the

Place. Having been regularly liberated from my former Charge in *East-Jersey*, above an hundred Miles North-Eastward from Hence (the Rev. Presbytery of *New-Brunswick* (of which I had the Comfort of being a Member) judging it to be my Duty, for sundry Reasons, to remove from thence) at the earnest Invitation of the People here I came to them in the beginning of *November* 1739, accepted of a Call from them that Winter, and was formally install'd and settled amongst them as their Minister in *April* following. There were some hopefully pious People here at my first coming, which was a great Encouragement and Comfort to me. I had some View and Sense of the deplorable Condition of the Land in general; and accordingly the Scope of my Preaching thro' that first Winter after I came here, was mainly calculated for Persons in a natural unregenerate Estate. I endeavour'd, as the Lord enabled me, to open up and prove from his Word, the Truths which I judged most necessary for such as were in that State to know and believe in order to their Conviction and Conversion. I endeavour'd to deal searchingly and solemnly with them; and thro' the concurring Blessing of God, I had knowledge of four or five brought under deep Convictions that Winter. In the beginning of *March* I took a Journey into *East-Jersey*, and was abroad for two or three Sabbaths. A neighbouring Minister, who seemed to be earnest for the Awakening and Conversion of secure Sinners, and whom I had obtained to preach a Sabbath to my People in my Absence, preached to them, I think, on the first Sabbath after I left Home. His Subject was the dangerous and awful Case of such as continue unregenerate and unfruitful under the Means of Grace. The Text was *Luk.* 13.7. *Then said he to the Dresser of his Vineyard, behold, these three Years I come seeking Fruit on this Fig Tree,*

and find none, cut it down, why cumbereth it the Ground? Under that Sermon there was a visible Appearance of
much Soul-Concern among the Hearers,
so that some burst out with an audible
Noise into bitter crying (a Thing not
known in those Parts before.) After I
had come Home there came a young
Man to my House under deep Trouble
about the State of his Soul, whom I had
look'd upon as a pretty light merry sort
of a Youth: He told me that he was not
any Thing concerned about himself in
the Time of hearing the above mentioned Sermon, nor afterwards, till the
next Day that he went to his Labour,
which was grubbing, in order to clear
some New-Ground; the first Grub he set
about was a pretty large one with a high
Top, and when he had cut the Roots, as
it fell down those Words came instantly
to his Remembrance, and as a Spear to
his Heart, *cut it down why cumbereth it
the Ground?* So thought he, *must I be
cut down by the Justice of God, for the
Burning of Hell, unless I get into another State than I am now in.* He thus
came into very great and abiding Distress, which, to all Appearance has had
a happy issue: His Conversation being
to this Day as becomes the Gospel of
Christ.

The News of this very publick Appearance of deep Soul-concern among
my People met me an Hundred Miles
from Home: I was very joyful to hear of
it, in Hopes that God was about to
carry on an extensive Work of converting Grace amongst them And the first
Sermon I preached after my Return to
them, was from *Mat. 6 33. Seek ye first
the Kingdom of God, and his Righteousness.* After opening up and ex-
plaining the Parts of the Text, when in
the Improvement, I came to press the
Injunction in the Text upon the Unconverted and Ungodly, and offer'd this
as one Reason among others, why they
should now henceforth first of all *seek*

*the Kingdom and Righteousness of
God,* viz. That they had neglected too
too long to do so already. This Consideration seem'd to come and cut like a
Sword upon several in the Congregation, so that while I was speaking upon
it they could no longer contain, but
burst out in the most bitter Mourning.
I desir'd them, as much as possible, to
restrain themselves from making a
Noise that would hinder themselves or
others from hearing what was spoken:
And often afterwards I had Occasion to
repeat the same Council. I still advised
People to endeavour to moderate and
bound their Passions, but not so as to
resist or stifle their Convictions. The
Number of the Awakened encreased
very fast, frequently under Sermons
there were some newly convicted, and
brought into deep Distress of Soul
about their perishing Estate. Our Sabbath Assemblies soon became vastly
large; many People from almost all
Parts around inclining very much to
come where there was such Appearance
of the divine Power and Presence. I
think there was scarcely a Sermon or
Lecture preached here thro' that whole
Summer, but there were manifest Evidences of Impressions on the Hearers;
and many Times the Impressions were
very great and general: Several would
be overcome and fainting; others deeply
sobbing, hardly able to contain, others
crying in a most dolorous Manner,
many others more silently Weeping,
and a solemn Concern appearing in the
Countenance of many others. And
sometimes the Soul Exercises of some
(tho' comparatively but very few)
would so far affect their Bodies, as to
Occasion some strange unusual Bodily
Motions. I had Opportunities of speaking particularly with a great many of
those who afforded such outward Tokens of inward Soul-Concern in the
Time of publick Worship and hearing
of the Word; indeed many came to me

of themselves in their Distress for private Instruction and Council; and I found, so far as I can remember, that with by far the greater Part, their apparent Concern in Publick was not just a transient Qualm of Conscience, or meerly a floating Commotion of the Affections; but a rational fix'd Conviction of their dangerous perishing Estate. They could generally offer as a convictive Evidence of their being in an unconverted miserable Estate, that they were utter Strangers to those Dispositions, Exercises and Experiences of Soul in Religion, which they heard laid down from God's Word as the inseparable Characters of the truly regenerate People of God; even such as before had something of the Form of Religion; and I think the greater Number were of this Sort, and several had been pretty exact and punctual in the Performance of outward Duties. They saw that they had been contenting themselves with the Form, without the Life and Power of Godliness; and that they had been taking Peace to their Consciences from, and depending upon their own Righteousness, and not the Righteousness of JESUS CHRIST. In a Word, they saw that true practical Religion was quite another Thing than they had conceiv'd it to be, or had any true Experience of. There were likewise many up and down the Land brought under deep distressing Convictions that Summer, who had lived very loose Lives, regardless of the very Externals of Religion. In this Congregation I believe there were very few that were not stirred up to some solemn Thoughtfulness and Concern more than usual about their Souls. The general Carriage and Behaviour of People was soon very visibly alter'd. Those awakened were much given to reading in the Holy Scriptures and other good Books. Excellent Books that had lain by much neglected, were then much perus'd, and lent from one to another; and it was a

peculiar Satisfaction to People to find how exactly the Doctrines they heard daily preached, harmonize with the Doctrines maintain'd and taught by great and Godly Men in other Parts and former Times. The Subjects of Discourse almost always when any of them were together, were the Matters of Religion and great Concerns of their Souls. All unsuitable, Worldly, vain Discourse on the Lord's Day seem'd to be laid aside among them: Indeed, for any Thing that appear'd, there seem'd to be an almost universal Reformation in this Respect in our Publick Assemblies on the Lord's Day. There was an earnest Desire in People after Opportunities for publick Worship and hearing the Word. I appointed in the Spring to preach every Friday thro' the Summer when I was at Home, and those Meetings were well attended, and at several of them the Power of the Lord was remarkably with us. The main scope of my Preaching thro' that Summer was, laying open the deplorable State of Man by Nature since the Fall, our ruin'd expos'd Case by the Breach of the first Covenant, and the awful Condition of such as were not in CHRIST, giving the Marks and Characters, of such as were in that Condition: And moreover, laying open the Way of Recovery in the New Covenant thro' a Mediator, with the Nature and Necessity of Faith in CHRIST the Mediator etc. I labour'd much on the last mentioned Heads; that People might have right Apprehensions of the Gospel-Method of Life and Salvation. I treated much on the Way of a Sinner's closing with CHRIST by Faith, and obtaining a right Peace to an awakened wounded Conscience; shewing, that Persons were not to take Peace to themselves on Account of their Repentings, Sorrows, Prayers, and Reformations, nor to make these Things the Grounds of their adventuring themselves upon CHRIST and his

Righteousness, and of their Expectations of Life by him: And, that neither were they to obtain or seek Peace in Extraordinary Ways, by Visions, Dreams, or immediate Inspirations; but by an understanding View and believing Persuasion of the Way of Life, as reveal'd in the Gospel, thro' the Suretyship, Obedience and Sufferings of JESUS CHRIST, with a View of the Suitableness and Sufficiency of that mediatory Righteousness of CHRIST for the Justification and Life of Law-condemned Sinners; and thereupon freely accepting him for their Saviour, heartily consenting to, and being well pleased with that Way of Salvation; and venturing their all upon his Mediation, from the Warrant and Encouragement afforded of God thereunto in his Word, by his free Offer, authorative Command, and sure Promise to those that so believe. I endeavour'd to shew the Fruits and Evidences of a true Faith, etc.

In some Time many of the convinced and distressed afforded very hopeful satisfying Evidence that the Lord had brought them to a true closure with Jesus Christ, and that their Distresses and Fears had been in a great Measure remov'd in a right Gospel-Way by believing in the Son of God, several of them had very remarkable and sweet Deliverances this Way. It was very agreeable to hear their Accounts, how that when they were in the deepest Perplexity and Darkness, Distress and Difficulty, seeking God as poor condemned Hell-deserving Sinners the Scene of the recovering Grace, thro' a Redeemer, has been open'd to their Understandings, with a surprizing Beauty and Glory, so that they were enabled to believe in Christ with Joy unspeakable and full of Glory. It appear'd that most generally the Holy Spirit improv'd for this Purpose and made use of some one Particular Passage or another of the Holy Scripture that came to their Remembrance in their Distress, some Gospel-Offer or Promise, or some Declaration of God directly refering to the Recovery and Salvation of undone Sinners by the New-Covenant: But with some it was otherwise, they had not any one particular Place of Scripture more than another in their View at the Time. Those who meet with such remarkable Relief, as their Account of it was Rational and Scriptural, so they appear'd to have had at the Time the Attendants and Fruits of a true Faith, particularly Humility, Love, and an affectionate Regard to the Will and Honour of God. Much of their Exercise was in self-abasing and self-loathing, and admiring the astonishing Condescention and Grace of God toward such vile and despicable Creatures that had been so full of Enmity and Disaffection to him. Then they freely and sweetly with all their Hearts chose the Way of his Commandments; their enflam'd desire was to live to him for ever, according to his Will and to the Glory of his Name. There were others that had not had such remarkable Relief and Comfort, who yet I cou'd not but think were savingly renew'd and brought truly to accept of, and rest upon Jesus Christ, tho' not with such a Degree of Liveliness and Liberty, Strength and Joy; and some of these continued for a considerable Time after, for the most Part under a very distressing Suspicion and Jealousy of their Case. I was all along very cautious of expressing to People my Judgment of the Goodness of their States, excepting where I had pretty clear Evidences from them, of their being savingly changed, and yet they continu'd in deep Distress, casting off all their Evidences: Sometimes in such Cases I have thought it needful to use greater Freedom that Way than ordinary, but otherwise I judged that it could be of little Use, and might readily be hurtful.

Beside these above spoke of, whose

Experience of a Work of Grace was in a good Degree clear and satisfying, there were some others (tho' but very few in this Congregation that I know of) who, having very little Knowledge or Capacity, had a very obscure and improper Way of representing their Case. In relating how they had been exercis'd, they would chiefly speak of such Things as were only the Effects of their Souls Exercise upon their Bodies from time to time, and some Things that were just Imaginary, which obliged me to be at much Pains in my Enquiries before I cou'd get any just Ideas of their Case. I would ask them, what were the Thoughts, the Views, and Apprehensions of their Minds, and Exercise of their Affections at such Times when they felt, perhaps, a quivering over come them, as they had been saying, or a Faintness, thought they saw their Hearts full of some nautious Filthiness, or when they felt a heavy Weight and Load at their Hearts, or felt the Weight again taken off, and a pleasant Warmness rising from their Hearts, as they would probably express themselves, which might be the Occasions or Causes of these Things they spoke of? And then, when with some Difficulty I cou'd get them to understand me, some of them wou'd give a pretty rational Account of solemn Spiritual Exercises. And upon a thorough careful Examination this Way, I cou'd not but conceive good Hopes of some such Persons.

But there were moreover several others, who seem'd to think concerning themselves that they were under some good Work, of whom yet I cou'd have no reasonable Ground to think that they were under any hopeful Work of the Spirit of God. As near as I could judge of their Case from all my Acquaintance and Conversation with them, it was much to this Purpose: They beleived there was a good Work going on, that People were convinced, and brought into a converted State, and they desir'd to be converted too; they saw others weeping and fainting, and heard People mourning and lamenting, and they thought if they could be like those it would be very hopeful with them: Hence they endeavour'd just to get themselves affected by Sermons, and if they could come to weeping, or get their Passions so raised as to encline them to vent themselves by Cries. Now they hoped they were got under Convictions, and were in a very hopeful Way; and afterwards they would speak of their being in Trouble, and aim at complaining of themselves, but seem'd as if they knew not well how to do it, nor what to say against themselves, and then they would be looking and expecting to get some Texts of Scripture apply'd to them for their Comfort, and when any Scripture Text, which they thought was suitable for that Purpose, came to their Minds, they were in Hopes it was brought to them by the Spirit of God, that they might take Comfort from it. And thus much in such a Way as this some appear'd to be pleasing themselves just with an imaginary Conversion of their own making. I endeavour'd to correct and guard against all such Mistakes so far as I discover'd them in the Course of my Ministry; and to open up the Nature of a true Conviction by the Spirit of God, and of a saving Conversion.

Thus have I given a very brief Account of the State and Progress of Religion here, thro' that first Summer after the remarkable Revival of it among us. Towards the End of that Summer there seem'd to be a Stop put to the farther Progress of the Work, as to the Conviction and awakening of Sinners; and ever since there have been very few Instances of Persons convinced. It remains then, that I speak something of the abiding Effects and After-fruits of those Awakenings, and other Religious

Exercises which People were under during the above mention'd Period. Such as were only under some slight Impressions and superficial Awakenings, seem in General to have lost them all again, without any abiding hopeful Alteration upon them: They seem to have fallen back again into their former Carelessness and Stupidity: And some that were under pretty great Awakenings, and considerable deep Convictions of their miserable Estate, seem also to have got Peace again to their Consciences without geting it by a true Faith in the Lord Jesus, affording no satisfying Evidence of their being savingly renew'd: But, thro' the infinite rich Grace of God, (and blessed be his Glorious Name!) there is a considerable Number who afford all the Evidence that can reasonably by expected and requir'd for our Satisfaction in the Case of their having been the Subjects of a thorough saving Change; except in some singular Instances of Behaviour (alas for them) which proceed from, and shew the sad Remains of Original Corruption even in the regenerate Childen of God while in this Imperfect State. Their Walk is habitually Tender and Conscientious; their Carriage towards their Neighbour Just and Kind; and they appear to have an agreeable peculiar Love one for another, and for all in whom appears the Image of God. Their Discourses of Religion, their Engagedness and Dispositions of Soul in the Practice of the immediate Duties and Ordinances of Religion, all appear quite otherwise than formerly. Indeed the Liveliness of their Affections in the Ways of Religion is much abated in General, and they are in some Measure humbly sensible of this and grieved for it, and are carefully endeavouring still to live unto God, much grieved with their Imperfections, and the Plagues they find in their own Hearts; and frequently they meet with some delightful Enlivenings of Soul, and particularly our sacramental Solemnities for communicating in the Lords Supper, have generally been very Blessed Seasons of enlivening and enlargement to the People of God. There is a very evident and great Increase of Christian Knowledge with many of them. We enjoy in this Congregation the happiness of a great Degree of Harmony and Concord: Scarcely any have appear'd to open Opposition and Bitterness against the Work of God among us, and else where up and down the Land, tho' there are pretty many such in several other Places thro' the Country. Some indeed in this Congregation, but very few, have separated from us, and join'd with the Ministers who have unhappily oppos'd this Blessed Work.

22. The Theology of New Birth: Jonathan Dickinson, *True Scripture-Doctrine*, 1741

[Jonathan Dickinson, *The True Scripture-Doctrine Concerning Some Important Points of Christian Faith* . . . (Boston, 1741), 137–151]

I'm then to consider,

In what Manner *the Spirit of God quickens dead Sinners, and brings them into a State of spiritual Life.*

To this I shall in general observe, that the principal Method, by which this great Change is wrought in the Heart of a Sinner by the Spirit of God, is *his giving him a realizing View of the great Truths revealed in the Word of God, and enabling him to see Things as they are.* It may be some Prejudice against the Doctrine of our Sanctification by the special Influences of the

Spirit of God upon our Hearts, that Men may imagine, there is hereby intended the Infusion of some new *Faculty* into the Soul, which it had not before; and that the new Creation implies our becoming a new Sort of Being, with Respect to the *natural* Powers and Properties of the Soul, which we were not before. But let it be consider'd that the Spirit of God does no more in the Conversion of a Sinner, than bring him to the right Exercise of those rational Powers, with which he was born; give him a *just View* of his greatest Concerns; and *enable* him to act worthy of a *reasonable* Being. Observe this, and all the Prejudices against the Doctrine before us are obviated, and vanish away. Now that this is the Case, I shall endeavour to shew, by taking some particular notice of the usual *progressive Steps* by which a Sinner is brought out of a State of carnal Security, to the Possession and Exercise of the divine Life; And I think it will appear that the whole Change is wrought in him by spiritual *Illumination,* by impressing a *right View* of Things upon his Mind, or by enabling him to act *reasonably.*

1. Then, if we consider the *first Change* wrought in a Sinner by the Spirit of God, it will appear to be no more than his bringing him to *realize his own miserable Condition, and see it as it is.* It is awfully certain from the Word of God, that every impenitent Sinner is an Enemy to God, under a Sentence of Condemnation, and an Heir of Hell and eternal Misery. And it is equally certain, that the most of the World are easy and quiet, careless and secure in this dreadful State. No Means that can possibly be used, will put the most of Mankind upon a proper Sollicitude about their eternal Welfare. The most awakening Addresses, that can be made them in the Name of the Lord, the most surprizing Alarms of God's

Providence, the most pathetick and compassionate Intreaties of their godly Friends, have no Effect upon them, to stop their Carreer for Hell and Damnation. They will yet sleep upon the Brink of the Pit. They will yet *run upon the thick Bosses of God's Bucklers.* They will yet indulge their Lusts, though they perish forever. And what is the Source of this Indolence, Thoughtlessness, and Security; but their want of a *just View* of their State and Danger? Could they but realize these Things, and see them *as they are,* they would sooner rush upon a drawn Sword, or leap into a burning Furnace, than farther incense the eternal Majesty against their Souls, and venture upon everlasting Damnation. But their Misery is, that they have no feeling Apprehension of these Things. They consider them but as the Rumbling of remote Thunder; and as Affairs of no special Consequence to them: and thus they will consider them, unless the Spirit of God sets home the important Concern upon their Mind; and gives them a lively Sense of what they are doing, and whither they are going. But if once the blessed Spirit undertakes the Work, he will make the long neglected and slighted Means of Grace effectual to open their Eyes, that they may see their State as it is. Tho' they could before sit under the most powerful Ministry from Year to Year, without Care, Fear, or sensible Apprehension of their Danger: Yet now an ordinary Sermon, or a particular Passage in a Sermon, which perhaps they had heard hundreds of Times before without Concern, shall awaken their sleepy Consciences, and make them with *Trembling* and *Astonishment* cry out, *What shall I do to be saved?* Why, what's the Matter now? Whence is this wonderful Change? Why can't the poor Sinner do now as he was wont to do? Why can't he go on in his Mirth and Jollity, in his worldly Pursuits and sensual Gratifications? What means this Darkness and Distress, this melancholly Countenance and solemn Concern? Is this the Man, that lately laugh'd at Preciseness; that banter'd serious Godliness, and ridicul'd vital Piety, as *Enthusiasm,* or a heated Imagination? Whence is he now as much an Enthusiast, as any of those whom he lately derided and scoff'd at? Whence is *he* now so afraid of Hell and Damnation, that could lately *mock at Fear; and laugh at the shaking of God's Spear?* This wonderful Alteration is wholly wrought by the almighty Spirit's impressing a *lively View* of what the secure Sinner could have no feeling Sense of before. Now he sees his *Sins,* in their Number, Nature and Aggravations. Now he sees his *Danger;* and thence feels that *it's a fearful Thing to fall into the Hands of the living God.* He sees it in such a View, that he can be no longer quiet and easy, in such a State of Guilt and Misery. But this (tho' open to every one's Observation, and plainly visible from the Word of God, and the Nature of Things) is what he never would have seen to Purpose, unless the Comforter had be'n sent to *convince him of Sin.* And the Reason is assigned, 2. *Cor.* iv. 4. *The God of this World hath blinded the Minds of them which believe not.* And Isai. 1. 3. *Israel doth not know; my People doth not consider.*

2. If we consider the Case with Respect to a Sinner's *Humiliation,* the Spirit of God works this also in the Soul, by *shewing him his State as it is;* and by giving him a realizing Sight of his *Unworthiness* of Divine Mercy, of his spiritual *Impotency,* and utter Inability to help himself. These are indeed Truths plainly revealed in Scripture, as well as necessary Deductions from the Light of Nature. By both these it is clearly manifest, that we are guilty Creatures, and thereby obnoxious to the Wrath [of] God; that we are imperfect Creatures, and therefore cannot fulfil the Demands of the Law of Nature; much less can we make Satisfaction for our past Offences. But, though these Things are in themselves evident as the Light, they have no Impression upon the Minds of the Generality of Mankind. Though deserving Nothing but Destruction and Death, they are as easy and secure, as though they had a Title to God's Favour, and a Claim to eternal Happiness. Though utterly uncapable to change their own Hearts, or to deserve that God should do it for them, they are yet attempting their Salvation *in their own Strength,* if they attempt it at all; and *being ignorant of God's Righteousness, they go about to establish their own Righteousness, not submitting themselves to the Righteousness of God.* Even those who are convinced of their Guilt and Danger, are usually struggling after Deliverance in their own Strength; and betaking themselves to some Self-righteous Refuge or other. And thus in their highest Attainments, will they continue to *compass themselves about with Sparks of their own Kindling,* till the Spirit of Grace by his powerful Influences humble them at God's Foot; and shew 'em that they are *poor, and miserable, and wretched, and blind, and naked.* And how is this done, but by giving them a *Sight of their Case as it is?* They had a *doctrinal* Knowledge before, that they were sinful, guilty, helpless, and hopeless in themselves: But this had no special Influence upon their Affections, or their Conduct. But when they have a *feeling* Sense of this, it must bring them low. They now see their Sin and Guilt, that there is no resting in their present Condition. They see the Defects of their Duties, that these cannot recommend 'em to God's Favour. They see their own Impotency, that they cannot take away the

Heart of Stone out of their Flesh; and give themselves a Heart of Flesh. They see the strict Demands of God's Law, that it's impossible to come up to 'em. They see the Purity and Holiness of God's Nature, that He cannot look upon Sin and Sinners with Approbation. They see that they have no Capacity to help themselves, though they are utterly undone in their present Condition. And what is the necessary Result of a realizing Sight of such a lost, helpless, perishing Condition, but that (*Psalm* cxxx. 3.) *If thou, Lord, shouldst mark Iniquity, O Lord, who should stand?* Or that (*Neh.* ix. 15.) *Behold, we are before thee in our Trespasses; for we cannot stand before thee, because of this!* What should be the Result of this Prospect, but that they lie at God's Footstool, as condemned Malefactors, having nothing to plead, save unmerited and forfeited Mercy, why Sentence should not be executed upon them, to their eternal Confusion!

3. In the same Manner, is a convinced Sinner brought to a *sollicitous Inquiry after an Interest in Christ.* This also is wrought in him, by a lively *View* of his Case *as it is.* We are all indeed from our earliest Age, indoctrinated in this essential Article of the Christian Faith, That *there is not Salvation in any other but Christ,* and that *there is no other Name under Heaven and among Men, whereby we must be saved.* And yet the most of the World are *whole, and need not the Physician.* They are more concern'd about any Thing else, than about an Interest in Christ. It is beyond human Art and Means, to make them at all sollicitous about this great Salvation, though they know that their eternal Welfare depends upon it. And what can be the Reason, that this *Madness is in the Hearts of Men?* Can condemned perishing Sinners be unconcern'd, about the

only Method of Escape from eternal Damnation? Can they set more Value by their Lusts and Pleasures by the World and it's Vanities, and even by the meerest Trifles imaginable, than by Christ and his saving Benefits? Can they rather choose to perish eternally, and to lose all the Glories of the heavenly World, than to *come to Christ, that they might have Life?* How astonishing soever this Conduct appears, it is visibly the Case of the World of Mankind in general. And what Reason can possibly be imagin'd of such unparallel'd Stupidity, but this, that they have not (they cannot have, while under the Power of a blind and carnal Mind) any realizing View of this great Concern? Could they but see their Case *as it is,* a condemned Malefactor could as easily set Light by a Pardon, or a drowning Man by Deliverance, as these perishing Sinners by an offered Saviour. We accordingly find, that when the Spirit of God comes upon them with his Illuminations, and opens their Eyes to see their Misery and Impotency, they can be no longer careless about an Interest in Christ. They can no longer make Excuses; and *go their Way, one to his Farm; and another to his Merchandize.* They can no longer amuse themselves with divers Lusts and Pleasures; and forget their necessity of Christ and his Salvation. No! they have now Nothing so much at Heart, as the securing an Interest in this blessed Saviour. Now this Thought lies down and rises with them, *What must I do to be saved?* How shall I obtain an Interest in Christ? Now their distressed Souls are groaning out these pathetick Desires, *O for an Interest in Christ! Let me have Christ, whatever I want!* The World now with all it's Blandishments, all its Riches and Glory, dwindles to Nothing in the Eyes of such a humbled Sinner, when compared with this excellent and needed Saviour. I may appeal to every one that have been truly converted to

God, at an Age of Observation, whether they han't experienced these Things in their own Hearts. And indeed these Operations of the Mind are so rational that it would be in the Nature of Things impossible we should neglect a most active Concern about an Interest in Christ, if the Eyes of our Understanding were enlighten'd. But alas! *The Light shines in Darkness; and the Darkness comprehendeth it not.* We see by Experience, that Men never do (never will) shew themselves thorowly in earnest about this everlasting Concern, till the Spirit of God *open their Eyes, and turn them from Darkness to Light;* and that when they are thus illuminated, they can't do otherwise. This wonderful Change in Men's Desires and Pursuits, is a necessary Consequence of Divine Illumination and of a just and reasonable View of Things. Without this, they cannot attain it: With this, they cannot fail of it. To this therefore the Apostle ascribes it. 2 *Cor.* iv. 6. *For God who commanded the Light to shine out of Darkness, hath shined in our Hearts, to give the Light of the Knowledge of the Glory of God, in the Face of Jesus Christ.*

4. In the same Manner also is the *actual Conversion* of a Sinner accomplish'd. In Order to this, the Spirit of God gives him a realizing Sight of the Fulness and Sufficiency that there is in Christ; and of his Willingness and Readiness to save him. The Attainments before described, do not necessarily imply a saving Conversion to God. Tho' these are the Influences of the blessed Spirit, they are not his special and saving Operations. The Sinner is not brought into a State of Favour with God, till he accepts a tendred Saviour upon his own Terms. Tis by *receiving him, that we have Power to become the Sons of God.* The first Act of saving *Faith* is that Conversion, by which the Sinner affectually turns from Sin *to God,* passes *from Death to Life,* and becomes interested in Christ and all his saving Benefits. Now, which Way is the Sinner bro't to this, but by an impressed lively *Discovery* of Things *as they are?* By a lively Sight of his *Sin* and *Danger,* powerfully applied to his Mind and Conscience, and appearing *as it is,* he is awaken'd to an earnest Inquiry after the Way of Salvation. By a clear Discovery of his *Unworthiness* and *Impotence,* he is bro't to the Footstool of God's Sovereignty, and to an earnest Desire of an Interest in Christ; as I observ'd before. But here the Soul is often plunged into greatest Darkness and Distress: His *Guilt* stares him in the Face; He sees he has no Claim to Mercy, Nothing that can intitle him to it; He has been struggling in vain, to mortify his Corruptions, to enliven his Affections, and to do something to recommend himself to God's Favour; and is now perhaps ready to give up the Case as helpless and hopeless; He can't see how God can have Mercy upon such a guilty, polluted, hard-hearted, hellish Sinner, as he is. Propose to him the only *Remedy* for such lost Sinners; and how many *Objections* will be in the Way! How many Arguments will he bring against believing in Christ; from his own Unworthiness and want of Qualifications to come to him; from the Decrees of God; from his having sinned away the Day of Grace, and the like; even till he runs into Despair, unless the Spirit of God disperse the dark Cloud, and give him a *right view* of redeeming Mercy! But when once such a distressed Soul sees this as it is, when once he has an impressed Sense of Gospel-Grace and is brought to see indeed, that he is invited to come to Christ, notwithstanding all his Guilt and Unworthiness; and that this precious Saviour is able and willing to bestow all that Salvation upon him, which

he stands in Need of, then his Objections are silenced; and he cannot refrain from heartily complying with the Offer. Then he can commit his Soul to him; for he sees that there is utmost Safety in doing it. Then he can depend upon him as the *Author of his eternal Salvation;* for he sees that he has no *whither else to go,* and that Christ *has the Words of eternal Life.*

It is remarkable, that the Scriptures every where annex Salvation to *Faith,* and to the *Belief of the Truth;* and we are told, I *Joh.* v. I. *Whosoever believeth that Jesus is the Christ, is born of God.* But what are we to understand by this Belief? Will a cold and unactive Assent to this Truth interest us in Christ and his Salvation? No! *Faith is the Substance of Things hoped for, and the Evidence of Things not seen.* Heb. xi. 1. In which is more than a bare Assent imply'd. It implies such a realizing View as makes all the Offers of Salvation by Christ certain, and his purchased Benefits present to the Believer. And when a weary and heavy-laden Soul hath such a Sight of the Fulness and Sufficiency, of the Kindness and Compassion of Christ; and of his willingness to save him upon his coming to him, as makes this comfortable Truth as it were personally present to his Mind; when he has such a View that this Saviour is offered freely to him, *without Money and without Price;* it is impossible for him to do otherwise than consent to such reasonable Terms of Salvation. How can he refuse his Consent to these Terms, when his Distress of Soul had before prepar'd him for a Compliance with any Terms of obtaining God's Favour? It's impossible for him to do otherwise than set the highest Value by such a Saviour, when he has this Sight, that Grace here, and Glory hereafter is imply'd in his Interest in Christ. It's impossible for him to do otherwise than have his Dependance upon Christ only,

when he has this Sight, that *in him all Fulness dwells,* and that there is no Safety any where else. But I hope (if God will) more particularly to describe a true saving Faith. I'm now only endeavouring to shew, that the Spirit of God works this Grace in us by illuminating our Minds; and giving us a right Exercise of our Understandings.

5. The Spirit of God does likewise carry on the Work of Grace in a Believer's *Sanctification,* by continued *Views* of spiritual Things *as they are.* By Faith, the Soul is united to the Lord *Jesus Christ;* and becomes *one Spirit* with him. By Faith, Believers have an Interest in all the Benefits of Christ's Redemption. They have thereby a Claim to all the Promises of the Covenant of Grace, and may safely and confidently depend upon the Faithfulness of God, that *he will give them Grace and Glory;* that *they shall be kept by his Power, through Faith, unto Salvation;* that *he who hath begun a good Work in them, will perform it* unto the Day of Jesus Christ; *that he who spared not his own Son, but delivered him up for them all, will with him also freely give them all things;* and that upon their *believing in Christ, out of their Bellies shall flow Rivers of living Water.* And what Way is this glorious Work of Grace carried on in the Soul, but by the continued Assistances of the blessed Spirit to act *reasonably;* and to maintain a lively Apprehension and Impression of invisible Realities? How comes the Believer to *hate every false Way;* but by a lively View of the Vileness and Unreasonableness of sinning against God? What excites him to live in the Love of God; but a realizing Impression of the Excellency of his Nature, the infinite Value of his Favour, and the endearing Attractives of his Goodness, Kindness and Compassion? What makes him in Love with Holiness; but a sensi-

ble Discovery of it's internal Beauty and agreeableness to a reasonable Being? How comes he wean'd from the World; but by a true Sight of it's Vanity, and utter Insufficiency to satisfy the Desires of an immortal Nature? How come his Affections placed upon the Things above; but from a like Discovery of the Value and Importance of Things unseen and eternal? What is Communion with God; but a just Impression of what pertains to God and Godliness? And what [are] the Evidences of God's Favour; but a realizing Sight of the Actings of Grace in our Souls, and of the Truth of the Invitations and Promises of the Gospel? The extraordinary Influences of the Spirit in his immediate Communications of Light and Joy to the Believer, are but still a brighter Discovery of Things *as they are*. In a Word, in whatever Aspect this Case is consider'd, what I am pleading for will (I think) appear to be Truth. The whole Work of Sanctification is carried on by Illumination, and by the Soul's being brought, through the Influences of God's Spirit, to the Exercise of Knowledge and Understanding; and to this the Apostle ascribes it. Eph. i. 17, 18. *That the God of our Lord Jesus Christ, the Father of Mercy, may give unto you the Spirit of Wisdom and Revelation, in the Knowlege of him: The Eyes of your Understanding being enlightened, that you may know what is the Hope of his Calling; and what the Riches of the Glory of his Inheritance in the Saints.*

Upon the whole, I can't see that the Spirit of God does in any other manner work this wonderful Change in the Hearts of Sinners, than by giving them a just *View* of Things *as they are*, by bringing them to act *reasonably*, worthy the Dignity of their rational Nature, and the intellectual Powers they are endued with. By this he conquers the Enmity to God there is in their Hearts; and brings them from the Power of their Lusts, of Satan, and the World, into the Fear and Favour of God. By *opening their Eyes, he turns them from Darkness to Light, and from the Pow[er] of Satan unto God, that they may have an Inheritance among those that are sanctified.*

If it be *objected*, That the *Will* must be changed and renewed, as well as the Understanding enlightened, in the Conversion of a Sinner; *That the Spirit of God works in us both to will and to do of his good Pleasure;* and Christ's *People must be made willing in the Day of his Power:* This is readily granted. But the Question is, In what *Manner* is the Will changed; and how doth the Lord Jesus Christ bring the stubborn obdurate Will of the Sinner into Subjection to himself? To this I answer as before; By giving them a *realizing affecting Sight* of Things as they are. It's impossible for a reasonable Being to do otherwise than *will* what appears to be, in all Circumstances, *best* for him and most agreable and desirable to him. Did therefore carnally secure Sinners see Things *as they are;* did they realize to themselves the Folly and Danger of their Lusts, the Misery of an unconverted State, their Need of a Saviour, the Excellency of Christ, the Advantage of an Interest in him, the Benefits of a Life of Religion with Respect both to this World and that to come; I say, did they *see* these Things in a just and powerful Light, their *Wills* would necessarily be changed. They would no longer choose the Way of Destruction and Death, before the Path of Life and Peace. They would no longer venture eternal Damnation, rather than accept of Happiness here and for ever. We are not therefore to suppose, that the Spirit of God properly puts any *Force* upon Men's Inclinations, when he changes their Wills. The Will admits no Violence. He does but give them a true Discovery, a realizing View and powerful Impression of what is best for them; and that necessarily determines their Choice. Let Sinners, if they can, be willing to rush upon the Pikes of God's Displeasure, when the Spirit by strong Convictions and Illuminations gives them a full and clear Sight of their Sins, and of the flaming Vengeance, that hangs over their guilty Heads. Let them, if they can, refuse a tendred Saviour, when they are brought to see their extreme Necessity of him, with his Fulness, Sufficiency, and Readiness to save them. Or let them, if they can, choose the Service of Sin and Satan before the Service of God, when they have a feeling Sense of the Danger and Misery of the one; and the Excellency, Desirableness, and Safety of the other. In a Word, Tho' Men may have the greatest Degree of *doctrinal* Knowledge, in the Things now treated of, understand them well, discourse of 'em rationally and distinctly; and receive 'em for Truth, without any Change of their Wills and Affections: yet if through the Spirit they had any *lively* and *affecting Apprehensions* of these unseen and eternal Concerns, they must of Necessity have an Influence upon their Hearts and Lives, proportionable to the *Kind* and Degree of the Light impressed on their Minds. Tho' a notional Knowledge of these Things will serve no other Purpose, but to leave the Sinner the more inexcusable: yet when the Spirit of God sets them home with Power upon the Soul, in their own proper Light and Evidence, this Prospect cannot fail of a blessed Effect.

CHAPTER FOUR

TROUBLE IN THE CHURCHES

WELL before the Awakening, Gilbert Tennent and the other Log College graduates were discontented with the dominant faction in the Synod of Philadelphia. Looking to Scotland or Ulster for their models, most of these conservatives valued rigid orthodoxy and a traditional education over piety and spirited preaching. They disparaged the training William Tennent gave his students and resented their intensity and aggressiveness. In a move to exclude Log College men, the synod in 1738 required that all candidates for a preaching license present a degree from Harvard, Yale, or a European university. To prevent Tennent's men from capturing vacant congregations or from evangelizing people without a church, the synod also forbade preaching before such groups without unanimous approval from the presbytery. Angered by the implicit rebukes, Gilbert Tennent and his friends contested both rules, but without success.

As the Middle Colonies awakened following Whitefield's visit in 1740, however, Tennent took the offensive. In 1740 he delivered a sermon at Nottingham in Pennsylvania, a vacant congregation, on the dangers of an unconverted ministry (No. 23) . Mercilessly lashing the conservatives, he made them out as enemies of Christ, not merely ineffectual, but as obstacles to conversion. Unfortunate souls sitting under unregenerate ministers were admonished to separate themselves and seek out preachers who dispensed the words of life. The sermon, published in both Philadelphia and Boston, at once became notorious.

Tennent's doctrine offended moderate New Lights as well as the Old Lights who were his intended targets. The approval of separations, it was feared, threatened to destroy the churches. Malcontents as well as conscientious objectors might abandon a minister as they pleased.

No pastor's authority was secure. Tennent himself had misgivings about his rash statements after he saw how Davenport's wholesale censures of the clergy discredited the revival, and after people began in fact to separate in large numbers. More moderate New Lights like Solomon Williams (1700–1776), a Connecticut pastor and cousin of Jonathan Edwards's, berated the extremists for undermining the churches. In one of the two letters which he and Eleazar Wheelock, his colleague in Lebanon, wrote to Davenport, Williams argued for the legitimacy of church government as established by Christ (No. 24). A minister's authority depended on a proper ordination according to scriptural rules rather than piety or effectual preaching. People were not to break up the churches to get a pastor to their liking.

By the time Williams wrote, the revival ferment had already begun to split the churches. The most dramatic division occurred in the Presbyterian synod in 1741 when the tension between the Log College men and the European-oriented conservatives came to a head. The previous year Gilbert Tennent and Samuel Blair had charged their opponents with departures from Calvinist orthodoxy and unconscionable opposition to the revival. When the synod met again, Robert Cross, one of the long time enemies of the Log College men, read a *Protestation* which culminated with the demand that the revivalists be excluded from the synod (No. 25). After a confused and heated clash, the signers of the protest were found to be in the majority, and the Log College men withdrew. For four years they existed simply as the "Conjunct Presbyteries of New Brunswick and Londonderry," the areas in New Jersey and southern Pennsylvania where most of the Log College men labored, and were popularly called New Side Presbyterians in contrast to the Old Side conservatives. In 1745 the Conjunct Presbyteries joined the New York Presbytery, which had long been restive in the Synod of Philadelphia, to form the Synod of New York. So long as revival animosities still rankled, New Side and Old Side were irreconcilable, but as the disadvantages of a divided church became more obvious, proposals for reunification were made. Finally in 1758 the two synods made their peace. By then the dominance of the Awakening party within the Presbyterian Church was assured, and Gilbert Tennent moderated the first combined meeting.

In New England where there was no central ecclesiastical power to fight over, separations occurred in individual congregations. Small groups, or even an individual like Nathan Cole, broke away to find more moving preaching or to sit under less constraining ecclesiastical rule. Some shortly returned to the old church. Others, like the group in Norwich, Connecticut, formed their own church and ordained a minister, usually a layman like themselves (No. 26). The established church attempted to discipline these schismatics to no effect. The Separates believed the pastor and their former brethren to be without authority and scoffed at censures and excommunication. The established church was no more successful in collecting ecclesiastical taxes. The Separates refused to pay on grounds of conscience, contending that forced payment was an unwarranted invasion of their right to worship as they pleased. They went to prison rather than compromise. Relief came only gradually as individual town meetings found the tax laws impossible to enforce and as many Separates became Baptists, a denomination officially tolerated and therefore exempt.

Wherever the separating brethren ended up, a common yearning for a pure and holy church motivated their quest. Ebenezer Frothingham (1719–1798), one of the laymen who entered the ministry in the Separatist movement, expressed the common desire for a society devoid of scoffers and hypocrites where the spirit of God reigned supreme (No. 27). Well into the 1750s, a great many people were to pursue that vision in one fashion or another, regardless of the cost to the established ecclesiastical order.

A Qualified Ministry

23. Gilbert Tennent, *The Danger of an Unconverted Ministry*, 1740

[Gilbert Tennent, *The Danger of an Unconverted Ministry, Considered in a Sermon on Mark VI. 34* . . . (Boston, 1742), 2–8, 10–12]

MARK VI. 34.

And Jesus, when he came out, saw much People and was moved with Compassion towards them, and because they were as Sheep not having a Shepherd.

As a faithful Ministry is a great Ornament, Blessing and Comfort, to the Church of GOD; even the Feet of such Messengers are beautiful: So on the contrary, an ungodly Ministry is a great Curse and Judgment: These Caterpillars labour to devour every green Thing.

There is nothing that may more justly call forth our saddest Sorrows,

and make all our Powers and Passions mourn, in the most doleful Accents, the most incessant, insatiable, and deploring Agonies; than the melancholly Case of such, who have no faithful Ministry! This Truth is set before our Minds in a strong Light, in the Words that I have chosen now to insist upon! in which we have an Account of our LORD's Grief with the Causes of it.

We are informed, That our dear Redeemer was moved with Compassion towards them. The Original Word signifies the strongest and most vehement Pity, issuing from the innermost Bowels.

But what was the Cause of this great

and compassionate Commotion in the Heart of Christ? It was because he saw much People as Sheep, having no Shepherd. Why, had the People then no Teachers? O yes! they had Heaps of Pharisee-Teachers, that came out, no doubt after they had been at the Feet of *Gamaliel* the usual Time, and according to the Acts, Cannons, and Traditions of the Jewish Church. But notwithstanding of the great Crowds of these Orthodox, Letter-learned and regular Pharisees, our Lord laments the unhappy Case of that great Number of People, who, in the Days of his Flesh, had no better Guides: Because that those were as good as none (in many Respects) in our Saviour's Judgment. For all them, the People were as Sheep without a Shepherd.

From the Words of our Text, the following Proposition offers itself to our Consideration, *viz.*

That the Case of such is much to be pitied, who have no other but Pharisee-Shepherds, or unconverted Teachers.

In discoursing upon this Subject, I would

I. *Enquire into the Characters of the Old Pharisee-Teachers.*

II. *Shew, why the Case of such People, who have no better, should be pitied. And*

III. *Shew how Pity should be expressed upon this mournful Occasion!* And

First I am to enquire into the *Characters of the Old Pharisee-Teachers.* Now, I think the most notorious Branches of their Character, were these, viz. *Pride, Policy, Malice, Ignorance, Covetousness,* and *Bigotry to human Inventions in religious Matters.*

The old Pharisees were very proud and conceity; they loved the uppermost Seats in the Synagogues, and to be called Rabbi, Rabbi; they were masterly and positive in their Assertions, as if forsooth Knowledge must die with them; they look'd upon others that dif-

fered from them, and the common People with an Air of Disdain; and especially any who had a Respect for JESUS and his Doctrine, and dislik'd them; they judged such accursed.

The old Pharisee-Shepherds were as crafty as Foxes; they tried by all Means to ensnare our Lord by their captious Questions, and to expose him to the Displeasure of the State; while in the mean Time, by sly and sneaking Methods, they tried to secure for themselves the Favour of the Grandees, and the People's Applause; and this they obtained to their Satisfaction. *John* 7. 48.

But while they exerted the Craft of Foxes, they did not forget to breathe forth the Cruelty of Wolves, in a malicious Aspersing the Person of Christ, and in a violent Opposing of the Truths, People and Power of his Religion. Yea, the most stern and strict of them were the Ring-leaders of the Party: Witness *Saul's* Journey to *Damascus,* with Letters from the Chief-Priest, to bring bound to *Jerusalem* all that he could find of that Way. It's true the Pharisees did not proceed to violent Measures with our Saviour and his Disciples just at first; but that was not owing to their good Nature, but their Policy; for they feared the People. They must keep the People in their Interests: Ay, that was the main Chance, the Compass that directed all their Proceedings; and therefore such sly cautious Methods must be pursued as might consist herewith. They wanted to root vital Religion out of the World; but they found it beyond their Thumb.

Although some of the old Pharisee-Shepherds had a very fair and strict Out-side; yet were they ignorant of the New-Birth: Witness Rabbi *Nicodemus,* who talk'd like a Fool about it. Hear how our LORD cursed those plaister'd Hypocrites, Mat. 23. 27, 28. *Wo unto you, Scribes and Pharisees, Hypocrites;*

for ye are like whited Sepulchres, which indeed appear beautiful outward, but are within full of dead Bones, and of all Uncleanness. Even so ye also appear righteous unto Men, but within ye are full of Hypocrisy and Iniquity. Ay, if they had but a little of the Learning then in Fashion, and a fair Out-side, they were presently put into the Priests' Office, though they had no Experience of the New-Birth. O sad!

The old Pharisees, for all their long Prayers and other pious Pretences, had their Eyes, with *Judas,* fixed upon the Bag. Why, they came into the Priest's Office for a Piece of Bread; they took it up as a Trade, and therefore endeavoured to make the best Market of it they could. O Shame!

. . . .

The Second General Head of Discourse, is to shew, *Why such People, who have no better than the Old Pharisee-Teachers, are to be pitied?* And

1. Natural Men have no Call of GOD to the Ministerial Work under the Gospel-Dispensation.

Isn't it a principal Part of the ordinary Call of GOD to the Ministerial Work, to aim at the Glory of GOD, and, in Subordination thereto, the Good of Souls, as their chief Marks in their Undertaking that Work? And can any natural Man on Earth do this? No! no! Every Skin of them has an evil Eye; for no Cause can produce Effects above its own Power. Are not wicked Men forbid to meddle in Things sacred? Ps. 50. 16. *But unto the Wicked, GOD faith, What hast thou to do to declare my Statutes, or that thou shouldst take my Covenant in thy Mouth?* Now, are not all unconverted Men wicked Men? Does not the Lord JESUS inform us, *John* 10. 1. That *he who entreth not by the Door into the Sheep-fold, but climbeth up some other Way, the same is a Thief and a Robber?* In the *9th V.* Christ tells us, That *He is the Door;* and that *if any*

Man enter in by him, he shall be saved, by him, i. e. By Faith in him, (says *Henry.*) Hence we read of a *Door of Faith,* being opened to the Gentiles. *Acts* 14. 22. It confirms this Gloss, that Salvation is annexed to the Entrance before-mentioned. Remarkable is that Saying of our Saviour, *Matth.* 4. 19. *Follow me, and I will make you Fishers of Men.* See, our LORD will not make Men Ministers, 'till they follow him. Men that do not follow Christ, may fish faithfully for a good Name, and for worldly Pelf; but not for the Conversion of Sinners to God. Is it reasonable to suppose, that they will be earnestly concerned for others Salvation, when they slight their own? Our LORD reproved *Nicodemus* for taking upon him the Office of instructing others, while he himself was a Stranger to the New Birth, *John* 3. 10. *Art thou a Master of Israel, and knowest not these Things?* The Apostle *Paul* (in 1 *Tim.* 1. 12.) thanks GOD for counting him faithful, and putting him into the Ministry; which plainly supposes, That GOD Almighty does not send Pharisees and natural Men into the Ministry: For how can these Men be faithful, that have no Faith? It's true Men may put them into the Ministry, thro' Unfaithfulness, or Mistake; or Credit and Money may draw them, and the Devil may drive them into it, knowing by long Experience, of what special Service they may be to his Kingdom in that Office: But God sends not such hypocritical Varlets. Hence *Timothy* was directed by the Apostle *Paul,* to commit the ministerial Work to faithful Men. 2 *Tim.* 2. 2. And do not these Qualifications, necessary for Church-Officers, specified 1 *Tim.* 3. 7, 3, 9, 11. and *Tit.* 1. 7, 8. plainly suppose converting Grace? How else can they avoid being greedy of filthy Lucre? How else can they hold the Mystery of Faith in a pure Conscience, and be faithful in all Things? How else can they be Lovers of Good, sober, just, holy, temperate?

2. The Ministry of natural Men is uncomfortable to gracious Souls.

The Enmity that is put between the Seed of the Woman and the Seed of the Serpent, will now and then be creating Jarrs: And no wonder; for as it was of old, so it is now, *He that was born after the Flesh, persecuted him that was born after the Spirit.* This Enmity is not one Grain less, in unconverted Ministers, than in others; tho' possibly it may be better polished with Wit and Rhetorick, and gilded with the specious Names of Zeal, Fidelity, Peace, good Order, and Unity.

Natural Men, not having true Love to Christ and the Souls of their Fellow-Creatures, hence their Discourses are cold and sapless, and as it were freeze between their Lips. And not being sent of GOD, they want that divine Authority, with which the faithful Ambassadors of CHRIST are clothed, who herein resemble their blessed Master, of whom it is said, That *He taught as one having Authority, and not as the Scribes.* Matth. 7. 29.

And Pharisee-Teachers, having no Experience of a special Work of the Holy Ghost, upon their own Souls, are therefore neither inclined to, nor fitted for, Discoursing, frequently, clearly, and pathetically, upon such important Subjects. The Application of their Discourses, is either short, or indistinct and general. They difference not the Precious from the Vile, and divide not to every Man his Portion, according to the Apostolical Direction to *Timothy.* No! they carelesly offer a common Mess to their People, and leave it to them, to divide it among themselves, as they see fit. This is indeed their general Practice, which is bad enough: But sometimes they do worse, by misapplying the Word, through Ignorance, or Anger. They often strengthen the Hands of the Wicked, by promising him Life. They

comfort People, before they convince them; sow before they plow; and are busy in raising a Fabrick, before they lay a Foundation. These fooling Builders do but strengthen Men's carnal Security, by their soft, selfish, cowardly Discourses. They have not the Courage, or Honesty, to thrust the Nail of Terror into sleeping Souls; nay, sometimes they strive with all their Might, to fasten Terror into the Hearts of the Righteous, and so to make those sad, whom GOD would not have made sad! And this happens, when pious People begin to suspect their Hypocrisy, for which they have good Reason. I may add, That inasmuch as Pharisee-Teachers seek after Righteousness as it were by the Works of the Law themselves, they therefore do not distinguish, as they ought, between *Law* and *Gospel* in their Discourses to others. They keep Driving, Driving, to Duty, Duty, under this Notion, That it will recommend natural Men to the Favour of GOD, or entitle them to the Promises of Grace and Salvation: And thus those blind Guides fix a deluded World upon the false Foundation of their own Righteousness; and so exclude them from the dear Redeemer. All the Doings of unconverted Men, not proceeding from the Principles of Faith, Love, and a new Nature, nor being directed to the divine Glory as their highest End, but flowing from, and tending to Self, as their Principle and End; are doubtless damnably Wicked in their Manner of Performance, and do deserve the Wrath and Curse of a Sin-avenging GOD; neither can any other Encouragement be justly given them, but this, That in the Way of Duty, there is a Peradventure or Probability of obtaining Mercy.

And natural Men, wanting the Experience of those spiritual Difficulties, which pious Souls are exposed to, in this Vale of Tears; they know not how to speak a Word to the Weary in Season. Their Prayers are also cold; little child-like Love to God or Pity to poor perishing Souls, runs thro' their Veins. Their Conversation hath nothing of the Savour of Christ, neither is it perfum'd with the Spices of Heaven. They seem to make as little Distinction in their Practice as Preaching. They love those Unbelievers that are kind to them, better than many Christians, and chuse them for Companions; contrary to *Ps.* 15. 4. *Ps.* 119. 115. & *Gal.* 6. 10. Poor Christians are stunted and starv'd, who are put to feed on such bare Pastures, and such dry Nurses; as the Rev. Mr. *Hildersham* justly calls them. It's only when the wise Virgins sleep, that they can bear with those dead Dogs, that can't bark; but when the LORD revives his People, they can't but abhor them. O! it is ready to break their very Hearts with Grief, to see how lukewarm those Pharisee-Teachers are in their publick Discourses, while Sinners are sinking into Damnation, in Multitudes! But

3. The Ministry of natural Men, is for the most part unprofitable; which is confirmed by a three-fold Evidence, *viz.* of Scripture, Reason, and Experience. Such as the Lord sends not, he himself assures us, shall not profit the People at all. *Jer.* 23. 32. Mr. *Pool* justly glosseth upon this Passage of sacred Scripture, thus, viz. *'That none can expect GOD's Blessing upon their Ministry, that are not called and sent of GOD into the Ministry.'* And right Reason will inform us, how unfit Instruments they are to negotiate that Work they pretend to. Is a blind Man fit to be a Guide in a very dangerous Way? Is a dead Man fit to bring others to Life? a mad Man fit to give Counsel in a Matter of Life and Death? Is a possessed Man fit to cast out Devils? a Rebel, an Enemy to GOD, fit to be sent on an Embassy of Peace, to bring Rebels into a State of Friendship with GOD? a Captive bound in the Massy Chains of Darkness and Guilt, a

proper Person to set others at Liberty? a Leper, or one that has Plague-sores upon him, fit to be a good Physician? Is an ignorant Rustick, that has never been at Sea in his Life, fit to be a Pilot, to keep Vessels from being dashed to Pieces upon Rocks and Sand-banks? *'Is'nt an unconverted Minister like a Man who would learn others to swim, before he has learn'd it himself, and so is drowned in the Act, and dies like a Fool?'* I may add, That sad Experience verifies what has been now observed, concerning the Unprofitableness of the Ministry of unconverted Men. Look into the Congregations of unconverted Ministers, and see what a sad Security reigns there; not a Soul convinced that can be heard of, for many Years together; and yet the Ministers are easy; for they say they do their Duty! Ay, a small Matter will satisfy us in the Want of that, which we have no great Desire after. But when Persons have their Eyes opened, and their Hearts set upon the Work of God; they are not so soon satisfied with their Doings, and with Want of Success for a Time. O! they mourn with *Micah,* that they are as those that gather the Summer-Fruits, as the Grape-gleaning of the Vintage. Mr. *Baxter* justly observes, *'That those who speak about their Doings in the aforesaid Manner, are like to do little Good to the Church of God.'* *'But many Ministers* (as Mr. Bracel *observes) thinks the Gospel flourishes among them when the People are in Peace, and many come to hear the Word, and to the Sacrament.'* If with the other they get the Salaries well paid; O then it is fine Times indeed! in their Opinion. O sad! And they are full of Hopes, that they do good, tho they know nothing about it. But what Comfort can a consciencious Man, who travails in Birth, that Christ may be form'd in his Hearers Hearts, take from what he knows not? Will a hungry Stomach be satisfied with Dreams about Meat? I believe not; tho' I confess a full one may.

.   .   .   .

Third general Head was to shew, *How Pity should be expressed upon this mournful Occasion?*

My Brethren, We should mourn over those, that are destitute of faithful Ministers, and sympathize with them. Our Bowels should be moved with the most compassionate Tenderness, over those dear fainting Souls, that are *as Sheep having no Shepherd;* and that after the Example of our blessed LORD.

Dear Sirs! we should also most *earnestly pray* for them, that the compassionate Saviour may preserve them, by his *mighty* Power, thro' Faith unto Salvation; support their sinking Spirits, under the *melancholy Uneasinesses of a dead Ministry;* sanctify and sweeten to them the *dry* Morsels they get under such blind Men, when they have none better to repair to.

And more especially, *my Brethren,* we should pray to the LORD of the Harvest, to send forth faithful Labourers into his Harvest; seeing that the Harvest truly is plenteous, but the Labourers are few. And O Sirs! how humble, believing, and importunate should we be in this Petition! O! let us follow the LORD, Day and Night, with Cries, Tears, Pleadings and Groanings upon this Account! For GOD knows there is great *Necessity* of it. *O! thou Fountain of Mercy, and Father of Pity, pour forth upon thy poor Children a Spirit of Prayer, for the Obtaining this important Mercy! Help, help, O Eternal GOD and Father, for Christ's sake!*

And indeed, *my Brethren,* we should join our Endeavours to our *Prayers.* The most likely Method to stock the Church with a faithful *Ministry,* in the present Situation of Things, the publick Academies being so much corrupted and abused generally, is, To encourage private Schools, or Seminaries of Learning, which are under the Care of skilful and experienced Christians; in which those only should be admitted, who upon strict Examination, have in the Judgment of a reasonable *Charity,* the plain Evidences of experimental Religion. Pious and experienced Youths, who have a good natural Capacity, and great Desires after the Ministerial Work, from good Motives, might be sought for, and found up and down in the *Country,* and put to Private Schools of the Prophets; especially in such Places, where the Publick ones are not. This Method, in my Opinion, has a *noble Tendency,* to build up the Church of God. And those who have any Love to Christ, or Desire after the Coming of his Kingdom, should be *ready,* according to their Ability, to give somewhat, from time to time, for the Support of such poor Youths, who have nothing of their own. And truly, Brethren, this *Charity* to the Souls of Men, is the most noble kind of *Charity*—O! if the Love of God be in you, it will constrain you to do something, to promote so noble and necessary a Work. It looks Hypocrite-like to go no further, when other Things are required, than *cheap Prayer.* Don't think it much, if the Pharisees should be offended at such a Proposal; these subtle selfish Hypocrites are wont to be scar'd about their Credit, and their Kingdom; and truly they are both little worth, for all the Bustle they make about them. If they could help it, they wo'dn't let one faithful Man come into the Ministry; and therefore their Opposition is an encouraging Sign. Let all the Followers of the Lamb stand up and act for GOD against all Opposers: Who is upon GOD's Side? who?

THE IMPROVEMENT of this Subject remains. And

1. If it be so, That the Case of those, who have no other, or no better than Pharisee-Teachers, is to be pitied: Then

what a Scrole and Scene of Mourning, and Lamentation, and Wo, is opened! because of the Swarms of Locusts, the Crowds of Pharisees, that have as *covetously* as *cruelly,* crept into the Ministry, in this adulterous Generation! who as nearly resemble the Character given of the old Pharisees, in the Doctrinal Part of this Discourse, as one Crow's Egg does another. It is true some of the modern Pharisees have learned to prate a little more *orthodoxly* about the New Birth, than their Predecessor *Nicodemus,* who are, in the mean Time, as great Strangers to the feeling Experience of it, as he. They are blind who see not this to be the Case of the Body of the Clergy, of this Generation. And O! that our Heads were Waters, and our Eyes a Fountain of Tears, that we could *Day* and *Night* lament, with the utmost Bitterness, the doleful Case of the poor Church of God, upon this account.

2. From what has been said, we may learn, That such who are contented under a *dead Ministry,* have not in them the Temper of that Saviour they profess. It's an awful Sign, that they are as blind as Moles, and as dead as Stones, without any spiritual Taste and Relish. And alas! isn't this the Case of Multitudes? If they can get one, that has the Name of a Minister, with a Band, and a black Coat or Gown to carry on a *Sabbath-days* among them, although never so coldly, and *insuccessfully;* if he is free from gross Crimes in Practice, and takes good Care to keep at a due Distance from their Consciences, and is never troubled about his Insuccessfulness; O!

think the poor Fools, that is a fine Man indeed; our Minister is a prudent charitable Man, he is not always harping upon Terror, and sounding Damnation in our Ears, like some rash-headed Preachers, who by their uncharitable Methods, are ready to put poor People out of their Wits, or to run them into Despair; O! how terrible a Thing is that Dispair! Ay, our Minister, honest Man, gives us good Caution against it. Poor silly Souls! consider *seriously* these Passages, of the Prophet, *Jeremiah* 5. 30,31.

3. We may learn, the Mercy and Duty of those that enjoy a *faithful Ministry.* Let such *glorify* GOD, for so distinguishing a Privilege, and labour to walk worthy of it, to all Well-pleasing; lest for their Abuse thereof, they be exposed to a greater Damnation.

4. If the Ministry of natural Men be as it has been represented; Then it is both lawful and expedient to go from them to hear Godly Persons; yea, it's so far from being sinful to do this, that one who lives under a pious Minister of lesser Gifts, after having honestly endeavour'd to get Benefit by his Ministry, and yet gets little or none, but doth find real Benefit and more Benefit elsewhere; I say, he may *lawfully* go, and that *frequently,* where he gets most Good to his precious Soul, after regular Application to the Pastor where he lives, for his Consent, and proposing the Reasons thereof; when this is done in the Spirit of Love and Meekness, without Contempt of any, as also without rash *Anger* or vain *Curiosity.*

24. A Plea for Moderation: Solomon Williams, A Letter, 1744

[Solomon Williams and Eleazar Wheelock, *Two Letters From the Reverend Mr. Williams and Wheelock of Lebanon, to The Rev. Mr. Davenport, Which were The principal Means of his late Conviction and Retraction* . . . (Boston, 1744), 3–7, 11–14, 19–20]

Dear Sir,

YOU desire my Thoughts respecting that Part of your Conduct which relates to your publick censuring of Ministers as unconverted, and promoting Separations from their Ministry under that Fear or Apprehension of them, and I think you gave me to understand the Principles you acted from were especially these, *viz.*

1. That it is unlawful for an unconverted Man to undertake the Work of the Ministry: Whence it must follow, that if a Man be found in an unconverted State in the Work of the Ministry, it must be unlawful for him to go on, and unlawful for his People to attend his Ministry; and therefore they ought to be warned of their Danger in it, and he ought to be born Witness against.

2. That at that Time you had a very great and extraordinary Concern upon your Heart about the Danger of an unconverted Ministry, and for the Welfare of precious and immortal Souls, and from thence was ready to conclude, that God had prepared and fitted you for this Work; and while you was doing this, you was confirmed in it by some extraordinary Appearance of Success.

As to the first Principle of your Acting, I am in the same Sentiments with you, that it is unlawful, and a very dangerous Thing for a Person knowing himself to be, or having a prevailing Perswasion that he is unconverted, to undertake the Work of the Gospel Ministry. But the Consequences you draw from it, I cannot see will at all follow: That if a Man be found in the Judg-

ment of other Ministers, or of private Christians, to be unconverted, that therefore he is no Minister, or that it is unlawful for him to go on in the Work of the Ministry, or that it is lawful for that Reason for his People to separate from him; and much less is it lawful for a particular Minister from such a Fear or Judgment to advise them to do so, and openly treat him as no Minister.

It appears to me that all ordinary Ministers of the Gospel are made and constituted according to the known and standing Laws of Christ's visible Kingdom found in his Word, and can be made no otherwise. Now it is certain that these Laws impower, and give Right to a visible Church to call a Person whom in the best Judgment they can make, they esteem qualified according to the Gospel Rule to be their Minister. When the Apostles had by special Designation of the Holy Ghost appointed two Persons to be offered to the Church for their Choice or Determination of one, even to the Apostleship, they did by Lot choose *Matthias*, Act. i. 15,21,27. and in *Act*.xiv.22.23. it is said, *When they had ordained them Elders by Suffrage in every Church, and had prayed with Fasting, they commended them to the Lord.* It is also certain, that the Laws of Christ direct and impower the Presbytery, upon the best Judgment they can make of the Regularity of such a Call, and the Qualifications of such a Person, to seperate him by solemn Ordination to the Work and Office of the Ministry; that this Power is confer'd by the laying on of the Hands of the Presbytery is proved from, 1 *Tim*.iv.14. and that this is to be done on a Trial and Judgment as before intimated, is evident from 1 Tim.v.22. where Ministers are directed to *lay Hands suddenly on no Man*, which must necessarily imply, that when the best Trial has been made, they are able according to Gospel Directions to make, and the best Judgment they can form, has been formed, they are to do it.

When therefore the Church and Ministers have so far as can be known by them from the Word of God attended the Rules of that Word, in chusing, or calling, and ordaining a Minister; that Man is a lawful Minister of the Gospel, and has lawful Right and Authority from Christ to perform all Parts of the ministerial Work. 'Tis true, his Call and Ordination or Institution, give him no Right (if after all he be an unconverted Man) to preach another Gospel, or to administer other Seals of the Covenant than those of Christ, nor to administer the Seals which Christ has appointed in any other Manner than he has appointed. Nor does the Office of the Ministry, and Institution in it, give any more Power to a godly Man than to an ungodly Man to do so: But every Man who is so instituted in, and introduced into the Work of the Ministry, has received Power and Authority from Christ to preach that Gospel which is his, and to administer those Sacraments and Ordinances which are his, according to the Rules of his Word: If after all the Care abovesaid, Mens Judgments are mistaken as to that great Qualification (the regenerating Grace of God in the Man's Heart) and he be really an unconverted Man, he is a lawful Minister not withstanding: tho' he is not like to be a good Minister, or faithful, yet this does not vacate his Commission, nor make it that he had no Commission; much less does the Judgment, Fear, or Suspicion of another Minister, or of private Chris-

tians, that he is unconverted. This may never be set against both the private and publick Judgment which has been made before, according to the Laws of Christ's visible Kingdom in his Word, so far as they could be known by those who by these Laws were call'd to make such a Judgment: This I say cannot vacate his Commission, or be an Evidence that he had no Commission, nor warrant a Separation from his Ministry. Because

1. Tho' Conversion be a necessary Qualification to his own Approbation before God, and without it he will not, he cannot discharge this Office so, as thro' Grace to obtain a Crown of Glory hereafter, nor be faithful in it; yet it is not necessary to his having a lawful Right to execute the Office of the Ministry: if it was, it would be absolutely necessary that those who by God's Word have Right and Power to call and ordain him, should be able to make an infallible Judgment of his State, or else that God should make it known by immediate Revelation: Neither of which is true or Fact, and the Supposition of either is a denial of the Sufficiency of the Word of God as a Rule for the Government of the visible Kingdom of Christ.

. . . .

4. If a lawful Right to the Ministry depends on the inward State of the Man's Mind, or on the Judgment which another Man makes about him, then the Ordinances of Christ as to their Validity and Efficacy, must depend on the Man himself who administers them, or on the Work of God in the Man, or on another Man's Judgment concerning that Work, and not on the Institution of Christ, and his Blessing conveyed through his own Institution, which 'tis certain it does entirely depend upon; Exod.20. 24. *In all Places where I record my Name I will come unto thee, and I will bless thee.* And to look either

to Man, or to the Work of God in another Man, or to the Judgment of one Man concerning another, for the Efficacy of Ordinances, is to transfer the Honour of Christ to a Creature, or to his Work in a Creature, or to a Judgment made by Man about that Work.

5. When a particular visible Church of Christ and a Presbytery have, so far as can be discerned from the Word of God, acted according to the visible Laws of Christ's Kingdom, in introducing a Man into the Work of the Ministry, no particular Minister or private Christian have Right to act publickly towards that Man, as if he was no Minister. He may not openly oppose an open solemn Declaration, visibly made and profess'd to be made according to the Laws of Christ's visible Kingdom, unless he certainly knows that that Declaration was not really made; and this no Man can be certain of but by the standing Laws of the Bible, or by special Revelation of the Holy Ghost. To suppose he can know it in the first of these Ways is a Contradiction in Terms, and whoever pretends to know it in the other Way, must be an extraordinary Minister of Christ, and able to shew his Commission by Miracles, else no Man may believe him, which Christ himself declares with respect to himself, Joh. 15. 24. *If I had not done among them the Works which none other Man did, they had not had Sin.* Therefore no Man may openly oppose his own private Judgment or Fear to such an open and solemn Declaration, nor publickly act as if that was false, 'till it openly appears to be so by the evident Light of God's Word.

For tho' our private Actions may be grounded on our private Knowledge, and sometimes on private Grounds of Fear and Suspicion, yet our publick Actions must be ever grounded on Things publick, and publickly known, and evident, and never on our private Suspicions, Doubts or Fears. And yet Fears, and Doubts, Hopes, and strong Perswasion of the Mind are as far as any Christian dare ordinarily go with respect to Conversion or Non-Conversion in another Man—'Tis easy to see how disagreable such Treatment is to the Apostle's Injunction, 1 Tim. 5. 19. *Against an Elder receive not an Accusation but before two or three Witnesses.*

Again, For a particular Minister or private Christian without publick Reason, or Evidence publickly known, to treat a Minister publickly as unconverted, and on that Account to advise to a Seperation, or to seperate from his Ministry, is a great Venture, even on the Principle you acted. For after all, it may be he is a godly Man; and if so, he who treats him in the Manner beforementioned is certainly guilty of beating his Fellow Servant, and hindering his Usefulness, and forbidding him to do what Christ has set him about; and I think no Man need inquire what Thanks he may expect from his Master for this Service. But if the Man be really what you suspect or fear, yet your Opinion, or the Declaration of that Opinion, carries no Light, and if any Body acts upon it he puts you in the Place of God, and therefore he acts formally, and essentially wrong, altho' the Action were materially right.

. . . .

An unconverted Ministry is without Controversy one of the greatest Calamities that can befall a Church: But if we have the strongest Reason to fear this is the sad Case of any particular Place, yet particular Ministers or private Persons have no Warrant to oppose or pull it down, but according to the Methods prescribed by Christ, and the known Rules of proceeding given us in his Word. We should fervently and unceasingly pray, that the Lord would convert all his Ministers, and thrust forth faithful Labourers into his Harvest; but we must remember that he who purchased the Church with his own Blood, loves it infinitely better than we do; and he always governs it by a secret mysterious Providence, and a most wise and faithful Care. But he does not trust us to govern it (who he knows are utterly unfit for the mighty Work) nor to have any Hand in doing it, any otherwise than according to the standing, known, plain, open Laws of his visible Kingdom, all found in his Word.

Thus my dear Brother, instead of many Things which might have been said, I have given you in haste, a few of my Thoughts on the Subject you desired. I have done it in hearty Love to you, and I think also to our *good and divine Master the blessed Jesus,* and to his *poor but dear Church.* If I am mistaken in my Thoughts, pray God would make me see Truth. If I am right, and you receive the least Advantage by it, bless God alone, but still pray for your poor Brother,

SOLOMON WILLIAMS

Separations

25. The Synod of Philadelphia Divides: *Records of the Presbyterian Church,* 1741

[William Morrison Engles, ed., *Records of the Presbyterian Church in the United States of America* (Philadelphia, 1841), 157–160]

A Protestation presented to the Synod, June 1, 1741.

Reverend Fathers and Brethren,

We, the ministers of Jesus Christ, and members of the Synod of Philadelphia, being wounded and grieved at our very hearts, at the dreadful divisions, distractions, and convulsions, which all of a sudden have seized this infant church to such a degree, that unless He, who is King in Zion, do graciously and seasonably interpose for our relief, she is in no small danger of expiring outright, and that quickly, as to the form, order, and constitution, of an organized church, which hath subsisted for above these thirty years past, in a very great degree of comely order and sweet harmony, until of late—we say, we being deeply afflicted with these things which lie heavy on our spirits, and being sensible that it is our indispensable duty to do what lies in our power, in a lawful way, according to the light and direction of the inspired oracles, to preserve this swooning church from a total expiration: and after the deliberate and unprejudiced inquiry into the causes of these confusions which rage so among us, both ministers and people, we evidently seeing, and being fully persuaded in our judgments, that besides our misimprovement of, and unfruitfulness under, gospel light, liberty, and privileges, that great decay of practical godliness in the life and power of it, and many abounding immoralities: we say, besides these, our sins, which we judge to be the meritorious cause of our present doleful distractions, the awful judgment we at present groan under, we evidently see that our protesting brethren and their adherents, were the direct and proper cause thereof, by their unwearied, unscriptural, antipresbyterial, uncharitable, divisive practices, which they have been pursuing, with all the industry they were capable of, with any probability of success, for above these twelve months past especially, besides too much of the like practices for some years before, though not with such barefaced arrogance and boldness:

. . . .

Reverend and dear Brethren, we beseech you to hear us with patience, while we lay before you as briefly as we can, some of the reasons that move us thus to protest, and more particularly, why we protest against our protesting brethren's being allowed to sit as members of this Synod.

1. Their heterodox and anarchical principles expressed in their Apology, pages twenty-eight and thirty-nine, where they expressly deny that Presbyteries have authority to oblige their dissenting members, and that Synods should go any further, in judging of appeals or references, etc. than to give their best advice, which is plainly to divest the officers and judicatories of Christ's kingdom of all authority, (and plainly contradicts the thirty-first article of our Confession of Faith, section three, which these brethren pretend to adopt,) agreeable to which is the whole superstructure of arguments which they advance and maintain against not only our synodical acts, but also all authority to make any acts or orders that shall bind their dissenting members, throughout their whole Apology.

2. Their protesting against the Synod's act in relation to the examination of candidates, together with their proceeding to license and ordain men to the ministry of the gospel, in opposition to, and in contempt of said act of Synod.

3. Their making irregular irruptions upon the congregations to which they have no immediate relation, without order, concurrence, or allowance of the Presbyteries or ministers to which congregations belong, thereby sowing the seeds of division among people, and doing what they can to alienate and fill their minds with unjust prejudices against their lawfully called pastors.

4. Their principles and practice of rash judging and condemning all who do not fall in with their measures, both ministers and people, as carnal, graceless, and enemies to the work of God, and what not, as appears in Mr. Gilbert Tennent's sermon against unconverted ministers, and his and Mr. Blair's papers of May last, which were read in open Synod; which rash judging has been the constant practice of our protesting brethren, and their irregular probationers, for above these twelve months past, in their disorderly itinerations and preaching through our congregations, by which, (alas! for it,) most of our congregations, through weakness and credulity, are so shattered and divided, and shaken in their principles, that few or none of us can say we enjoy the comfort, or have the success among our people, which otherwise we might, and which we enjoyed heretofore.

5. Their industriously persuading people to believe that the call of God whereby he calls men to the ministry, does not consist in their being regularly ordained and set apart to that work, according to the institution and rules of the word; but in some invisible motions and workings of the Spirit, which none can be conscious or sensible of but the person himself, and with respect to which he is liable to be deceived, or play the hypocrite; that the gospel preached in truth by unconverted ministers, can be of no saving benefit to souls; and their pointing out such ministers, whom they condemn as graceless by their rash judging spirit, they effectually carry the point with the poor credulous people, who, in imitation of their example, and under their patrociny, judge their ministers to be grace-

less, and forsake their ministry as hurtful rather than profitable.

6. Their preaching the terrors of the law in such a manner and dialect as has no precedent in the word of God, but rather appears to be borrowed from a worse dialect; and so industriously working on the passions and affections of weak minds, as to cause them to cry out in a hideous manner, and fall down in convulsion-like fits, to the marring of the profiting both of themselves and others, who are so taken up in seeing and hearing these odd symptoms, that they cannot attend to or hear what the preacher says; and then, after all, boasting of these things as the work of God, which we are persuadad do proceed from an inferior or worse cause.

7. Their, or some of them, preaching and maintaining that all true converts are as certain of their gracious state as a person can be of what he knows by his outward senses; and are able to give a narrative of the time and manner of their conversion, or else they conclude them to be in a natural or graceless state, and that a gracious person can judge of another's gracious state otherwise than by his profession and life. That people are under no sacred tie or relation to their own pastors lawfully called, but may leave them when they please, and ought to go where they think they get most good.

For these and many other reasons, we protest, before the Eternal God, his holy angels, and you, Reverend Brethren, and before all here present, that these brethren have no right to be acknowledged as members of this judicatory of Christ, whose principles and practices are so diametrically opposite to our doctrine, and principles of government and order, which the great King of the Church hath laid down in his word.

How absurd and monstrous must that union be, where one part of the members own themselves obliged, in conscience, to the judicial determinations of the whole, founded on the word of God, or else relinquish membership; and another part declare, they are not obliged and will not submit, unless the determination be according to their minds, and consequently will submit to no rule, in making of which they are in the negative.

Again, how monstrously absurd is it, that they should so much as desire to join with us, or we with them, as a judicatory, made up of authoritative officers of Jesus Christ, while they openly condemn us wholesale; and, when they please, apply their condemnatory sentences to particular brethren by name, without judicial process, or proving them guilty of heresy or immorality, and at the same time will not hold Christian communion with them.

Again, how absurd is the union, while some of the members of the same body, which meet once a year, and join as a judicatory of Christ, do all the rest of the year what they can, openly and above board, to persuade the people and flocks of their brethren and fellow members, to separate from their own pastors, as graceless hypocrites, and yet they do not separate from them themselves, but join with them once every year, as members of the same judicatory of Christ, and oftener, when Presbyteries are mixed. Is it not most unreasonable, stupid indolence in us, to join with such as are avowedly tearing us in pieces like beasts of prey?

Again, is not the continuance of union with our protesting brethren very absurd, when it is so notorious that both their doctrine and practice are so directly contrary to the adopting act, whereby both they and we have adopted the Confession of Faith, Catechisms and Directory, composed by the Westminster Assembly?

Finally, is not continuance of union

absurd with those who would arrogate to themselves a right and power to palm and obtrude members on our Synod, contrary to the minds and judgment of the body?

In fine, a continued union, in our judgment, is most absurd and inconsistent, when it is so notorious, that our doctrine and principles of church government, in many points, are not only diverse, but directly opposite. For how can two walk together, except they be agreed?

Reverend Fathers and Brethren, these are a part, and but a part, of our reasons why we protest as above, and which we have only hinted at, but have forborne to enlarge on them, as we might, the matter and substance of them are so well known to you all, and the whole world about us, that we judged this hint sufficient at present, to declare our serious and deliberate judgment in the matter; and as we profess ourselves to be resolvedly against principles and practice of both anarchy and schism, so we hope that God, whom we desire to serve and obey, the Lord Jesus Christ, whose ministers we are, will both direct and enable us to conduct ourselves, in these trying times, so as our consciences shall not reproach us as long as we live. Let God arise, and let his enemies be scattered, and let them that hate him fly before him, but let the righteous be glad, yea, let them exceedingly rejoice. And may the spirit of life and comfort revive and comfort this poor swooning and fainting church, quicken her to spiritual life, and restore her to the exercise of true charity, peace, and order.

Although we can freely, and from the bottom of our hearts, justify the Divine proceedings against us, in suffering us to fall into these confusions for our sins, and particularly for the great decay of the life and power of godliness among all ranks, both ministers and people, yet we think it to be our present duty to bear testimony against these prevailing disorders, judging that to give way to the breaking down the hedge of discipline and government from about Christ's vineyard, is far from being the proper method of causing his tender plants to grow in grace and fruitfulness.

As it is our duty in our station, without delay, to set about a reformation of the evils whereby we have provoked God against ourselves, so we judge the strict observation of his laws of government and order, and not the breaking of them, to be one necessary mean and method of this necessary and much to be desired reformation. And we doubt not, but when our God sees us duly humbled and penitent for our sins, he will yet return to us in mercy, and cause us to flourish in spiritual life, love, unity, and order, though perhaps we may not live to see it, yet this testimony that we now bear, may be of some good use to our children yet unborn, when God shall arise and have mercy on Zion.

Ministers: Robert Cross, John Thomson, Francis Alison, Robert Cathcart, Richard Zanchy, John Elder, John Craig, Samuel Caven, Samuel Thomson, Adam Boyd, James Martin, Robert Jamison.

Elders: Robert Porter, Robert McKnight, William McCulloch, John McEuen, Robert Rowland, Robert Craig, James Kerr, Alexander McKnight.

26. The Separates in Norwich, Connecticut, 1745–1752

A. Joseph Griswold Interrupts a Sermon, 1745

[Daniel C. Gilman, ed., Papers Relating to the First Church in Norwich during the Ministry of Rev. Benjamin Lord, D.D. Chiefly in his Handwriting. Arranged 1859, Bound MS, 5-A, Connecticut State Library, Hartford, Conn.]

Whereas Joseph Griswould did on the 10th of Feb. last. 1744/5 Speak out In Sermon Time, Unto the Minister by way of Enquiring Into something relating to A passage in his Sermon, And this to the interruption of his fellow Worshippers—Having been Since Made Sensible of *his Mistake* Concerning that passage In the Sermon which was not as he Recieved it, and of his Error In *Speaking* as he did, he is Now Sorry for it, and asks forgiveness of God and his people: Read publickly and openly Consented to by Jos: Griswould

Test: Benj. Lord

B. The Separates Called to Account, 1745

[Daniel C. Gilman, ed., Papers Relating to the First Church in Norwich during the Ministry of Rev. Benjamin Lord, D.D. Chiefly in his Handwriting. Arranged 1859, Bound MS, 8-A, Connecticut State Library, Hartford, Conn.]

To Hugh Calkins, Jedidia Hide, Wm. Lothrop, Samll Leffingwell, Joseph Griswould, John Smith, James Backus, Isaac Backus, John Leffingwell, and Daniel Chapman, and also Phebe, the Wife of Hugh Calkins, the Wido Eliz Backus, and Lydia the Wife of Joseph Kelley, Members of the first Church of Christ in Norwich—

Whereas You have Each one, Actually separated YourSelves from the publick Worship of God, and Communion of the Church and the ordinances of Christ therein, and have held and do hold a Separate Meeting on the holy Sabbath; which appears to be a disorderly Walking, Contrary to the Gospel Rule in Heb. 10.25. Ephes. 4.2,3. etc. and So appears to be a Causing of divisions and offenses Contrary to the Gospel, and to Your Solemn Convenanting with God and his people, as also Contrary to the Platform of discipline Which this Church have professed Special regard to—

And Whereas the Church have by their Committee (Chosen for that purpose) Laboured Your Conviction and Recovery, (i.e.) of Such of You, as they had opportunity then, to discourse with, and other More private Methed, have been taken, and all without the desired Effect.

Therefore, A Meeting of this Church is Warned to be on the 31st Day of this Instant July. in the Meeting house, att one of the Clock in the afternoon then and there to have this Matter of Your Seperation, laid before them for them to Consider of the Same, in order to take Such Farther Steps in the Case, As the Gospel Directs—Accordingly

You are Each and Every of You, hereby Notified of Said Meeting of the Church, and the occasion thereof, and Cited or warned to attend on the Same, att Time and place above mentioned, to make answer to what Shall be observed to the Church, and objected against that Conduct touching Your Seperation etc. As Abovesaid—

Norwich, July. 23d. 1745.
> BENJA. LORD: Pastor
> of the first Church of Christ
> In Norwich

Deacon Ebenezer Huntington is desired to Read this abovewritten, to the Persons within Named, and if they Desire it to Leave a Copy with Some one of Them—

C. EXPLANATIONS FOR WITHDRAWAL, 1745

[Frederic Denison, *Notes of the Baptists, and Their Principles, in Norwich, Conn., From the Settlement of the Town to 1850* (Norwich, 1857), 21–22, 24–26]

THE REASONS WHICH THE SEPARATES GAVE IN BEFORE THE CHURCH OF THEIR SEPARATION.

JEDIDIA HIDE'S REASONS:

1. Errors in the Church; i.e. *first,* The Church not making conversion a term of Communion, or, [as he explained it] not making Regeneration the only term of Communion. *Secondly,* The body's being imperfect till it has all its members, but this Church has not all, because it hath not Ruling Elders.
2. The Body of the Church denying the power of godliness, and especially the Minister's denying it in his [said Hide's] soul in this late glorious time.
3. Edification elsewhere.
4. The Gospel not preached here.

WILLIAM LOTHROP'S REASONS:

1. The Minister's denying the power of godliness, though not in word, yet in practice.
2. Insisting on Imprudencies and not speaking up for that which is good.
3. Not praying for their meetings, and not giving thanks for the late glorious work.
4. Not a friend to Lowly Preaching

and Preachers, particularly not letting Mr. Jewett preach once, and once forbidding Mr. Croswell.
5. Not having the Sacrament for Six Months in the most glorious part of the late Times; and often enough since the Church is in Difficulty: and oftener now than ever.

SAMUEL LEFFINGWELL'S REASONS:

1. Mr. Lord's going off from the Platform and Settlement.
2. Other Reasons, and the same as Mr. Hide's.

JOSEPH GRISWOLD'S REASONS:

1. Better edification.
2. The Gospel better preached, and that Scripture mentioned as what weighed with him, 'Where the carcasses are, there the Eagles are gathered together.'

ISRAEL BACKUS' REASONS:

The same as the others, as he said.

JOHN LEFFINGWELL'S REASONS:

The same with others, but moreover,
1. The minister's not apt to teach.
2. A point of Doctrine objected against, as he took it to be delivered,

(viz.:) If Christians Lived as they should, the World would Love them.

3. The Minister's not Spiritual in Conversation with him.

HUGH CALKINS' wife desired to be excused from saying any thing.

The Widow ELIZABETH BACKUS said little, but in general said her reasons were the same with others.

LYDIA KELLY'S REASONS:

1. I came to this place as long as I could be edified, and rather longer too —explained thus: I was not edified here and went where I was more edified.

2. Sometimes he (Mr. Lord,) would preach precious truths, and then pull them down again, as it appeared to me.

3. I have not, as it apppeared to me, departed from one child of God.

4. I thought the Church was as much Separate as I, and had gone off from the Settlement.

JAMES BACKUS' REASONS:

1. Mr. Lord's making the motion to the Church to go to the Association, and the Church's giving way thereto, which, as he (Mr. B.) alledged, discovered the unfaithfulness of the Church.

2. Reasons contained and given in the words of Mr. Wise's Book, page 101.

3. As to Mr. Lord's Doctrine, he objected that he (Mr. Lord) said, If Christians Lived as they should do, the world would Love them.

4. The general course of Mr. Lord's preaching has appeared to me not to be the Gospel of Christ, not with a tendency to awaken (and) convert Sinners, and build up Christians, but said he

should mention none, though owned that he sometimes preached well.

5. His (Mr. Lord's) unfaithfulness in the general course of his conversation, and not being particular in his preaching.

6. Mr. Lord has often declared in public such things as that was not agreeable, especially with respect to flying stories; particularly what he said respecting the non-necessity of Conviction before Conversion, as in danger of spreading or beginning to spread.

7. It appeared to me he (Mr. Lord) hath not the Qualifications of a Bishop, or Teacher, which are mentioned in Timothy and Titus.

8. Corruption in the Church; they profess well but are corrupt in practice, in admission of members, opening the Door too wide, Letting in even all sorts of persons, without giving any evidence at all of their faith in Christ and repentance towards God.

9. Another Reason. The method of admitting adult persons to Baptism, and of Baptized persons owning the Covenant, and of children to Baptism.

MARY LATHROP'S REASONS:

1. As to Communion in the Church at the Sacrament, I did not commune because I was in the dark, and thought I was not fit.

2. Another Reason, because I was not edified.

3. Because the power of godliness, it seems to me, is denied here, and is (exists) elsewhere.

4. By Covenant I am not held here any longer than I am edified.

D. Suspension from Communion, 1745

[Daniel C. Gilman, ed., Papers Relating to the First Church in Norwich during the Ministry of Rev. Benjamin Lord, D.D. Chiefly in his Handwriting. Arranged 1859, Bound MS, 10-A, Connecticut State Library, Hartford, Conn.]

Att a Meeting of the first Church in Norwich, on October 17th: 1745, by Adjournment.

The following Act of Suspension agreed on, and Voted In these Words — (viz.)

Whereas this Church hath att their last Meeting, allowed the Persons, hereafter Named, Time to Consider of the Warning then given of their Seperation; which hath been Judged by the Church, to be unwarrantable, and a disorderly Walking; and in this Time, not having any Intimations, of their Desire to Retract the Same and Return —This church in pursuance to their own Judgment and agreable to the Nature and Reason of the thing, and Express Scripture to withdraw from Every Brother that walketh Disorderly, and Especially after due Warning given of the Evil thereof;

Do now declare it is not fit that they. (viz.) Jededia Hide, Wm. Lothrop, Samll Leffingwell, Joseph Griswould, Isaac Backus, John Leffingwell, Junr, Phebe, the Wife of Hugh Calkins, and the Wido Eliz: Backus, Junr, should have Communion with this Church, while they thus manifestly withdraw from, and refuse to have Communion therewith: And Accordingly in faithfulness to Christ and their Souls doe hereby *Suspend* them From The Communion thereof in Special ordinances; till they Shall receive better Light and Manifest their desire to Return to the Communion thereof with proper Reflections on their past Conduct in Seperating therefrom.

This was published by Publick Reading it on Novemb, the 10th. 1745.

A True Copy. Test:
BENJA LORD Pastor,

Norwich. March. 11. 1745/6

The Pastor Desires that Deacon Ebenezer Huntington do read the Above written to all the Persons included therein—

E. Refusal to Pay Taxes, 1748

[Connecticut Archives, Ecclesiastical Affairs, XI, 35a, Connecticut State Library, Hartford, Conn.]

To the Honorable General Assembly of his Majesty's english Colony of Connecticut in New England in America, to be holden at Hartford in Said Colony on the Second Thursday of May Instant

The Memorial of the first Society in Norwich in the County of New London in Said Colony, by their Agent Ebenezer Backus of Said Society Esqr., humbly shews that there are of the Inhabitants of Said Society to the Number of thirty Persons, most of them Heads of Families (Viz) John Smith, John Reed Jur., Theophilus Rogers, Samuel Leffingwell, Joseph Griswold, Nathanael Post, Samuel [———], Daniel Chapman, James Backus, Peres Tracy, Gamaliel Reynolds, Jedediah Hide, Samuel Leffingwell Jur., Benjamin Wentworth, Josiah Backus, Moses Chapman, Samuel Leffingwell the 3d, Charles Hill, Elizabeth Backus Jur., Isaac Backus, Elijah Backus, William Lothrop, Hugh Calkins, Samuel

Backus, John Leffingwell Jur., Elisha Munsell, Ebenezr. Grover, Ebenezer Grover Jur. Ebenezer Thomas and John Burchard Who have Separated themselves from the Established Worship and Discipline of the Church in Said Society, under the Pastoral Care and Charge of the Revd. Mr. Benjn. Lord (who is, and hath for a long Time been, their Lawful Minister), who also refuse to pay any Thing towards his, the Said Mr. Lord's Support or towards Building or Maintaining a Meetinghouse or otherwise Supporting the Gospel in Said Society, in any other Way or Form than that which they themselves have Set up (having Ordained Said Jedediah Hide their Minister and Attending his Administrations as Such pleading Conscience in all) and many of our Said Society are of Opinion that it Can't be right to force Men to that, (in Matters of Religion) which they declare to be against their Consciences, and we being well assured that no Rates can be recovered of the Said Separates (for the Purposes above Said) without using the Severities of the Law, which will have a Tendency not only to impoverish many of their Poor Families, but greatly to Disturb and disquiet our said Society, And we would further Inform your Honors that Said Separates appear in all our Society Meetings and they together with those who are tender

of them Negative Granting any Salary for the Support of our Minister the said Mr. Lord So that we were Oblig'd in the Month of Dec. last to have Sundry Society Meetings before we Could Grant any Rate for our Minister and we have not, neither Can we have any Collector Who will receive any Rate Bill wherein the Body of Said Separates are Rated, to Collect any Such Rate from them as they are not willing to pay: And we are now, with your Honors Leave about to Build a new Meeting: house in and for Said Society: wherefore we Pray your Honors to Enact that Said Separates Shall be Excused from Paying anything towards the Support of our Minister, and also towards the Building Said Meeting: house in Said Society And that they (for the Future) shall have no Right to vote in any of our Society Meetings in any Thing Relating thereto; or Enact that we, by our Major Vote in Society Meeting may excuse them therefrom, on Condition that they refrain from Voting in our Society Meetings respecting the aforesaid Matters, or in Some other Way Grant Relief; and we (as Duty Bound) Shall ever Pray.

Dated in Said Society the 9th Day of May, 1748—

EBENEZER BACKUS

Agent for Said Society

F. TWO SEPARATES IN PRISON, 1752

[Frederic Denison, *Notes of the Baptists, and Their Principles, in Norwich, Conn., From the Settlement of the Town to 1850* (Norwich, 1857), 28–30]

NORWICH, NOV. 4, 1752.

DEAR SON: *

I have heard something of the trials among you of late, and I was grieved

* Elizabeth Backus was the mother of Isaac Backus, leader of the Baptists in New England in the latter part of the century. [Ed.]

till I had strength to give up the case to God, and leave my burthen there. And now I would tell you something of our trials. Your brother Samuel lay in prison twenty days. October 15 the collector came to our house and took me away to prison about nine o'clock, in a dark rainy night. Brothers Hill and Sabin were brought there next night. We lay in prison thirteen days, and then were set at liberty, by what means, I know not. Whilst I was there a great many people came to see me; and some said one thing, and some another. O, the innumerable snares and temptations that beset me; more than I ever thought of before! But, O, the condescension of Heaven! Though I was bound when I was cast into the furnace, yet was I loosed, and found Jesus in the midst of the furnace with me. O, then I could give up my name, estate, family, life and breath, freely to God. Now the prison looked like a palace to me. I could bless God for all the laughs and scoffs made at me. O, the love that flowed out to all mankind! Then I could forgive, as I would desire to be forgiven, and love my neighbor as myself. Deacon Griswold was put in prison the 8th of October, and yesterday old brother Grover; and (officers) are in pursuit of others; all which calls for humiliation. This Church hath appointed the 13th of November to be spent in prayer and fasting on that account. I do remember my love to you and your wife, and the dear children of God with you, begging your prayers for us in such a day of trial. These from your loving mother,

ELIZABETH BACKUS.

Norwich Goale, November the I Day, 1752.
Mr. Lord, Sir, I take this opertunity to present you with these fu lines which I should have thout you would have Pervented By visiting us. pray Sir consider wheather or no you Do not neglect to minister to Christ, for inasmuch as they did it not to them, etc. and further If you come not to see us theire is oather prisoners heare, and as you sustain the caracter of a minister see to it you neglect them not, and I should be glad of opertunity to see you. But being informed you Refuse to come I shall take Liberty to tell you that I judge it moast unscriptral and unreasonable that I am imprisoned thus by you. Ye lay heavy Burdens and Refuse to touch them with one of your fingers. You say it is the Athority; Simeon and Levi are brethren; instruments of cruelty are in their habitations. Genesis, xlix. 5–7.

Pray Sir Read the 3 Chapter of Mikes Provesy and may the Lord mack the aplycatyon. Consider also that our Lord Jesus hath toald us that his Kingdom is not of this world, also that he that taketh the sword shall perish by the sword. I could wish you a Deliverance from Mistacal Babelon and from her merchandize. my soul looks to and longs to see hir Receive the cup of the Lord's vengens and that all his Plages may come upon hir In one Day and that God's children may come out of hir and that the Kingdom may be given to the saints of the moast high. these lines with oure cause I Leave with God who will I trust Defend it, and so subscribe myself a Prisoner of hope.

CHARLES HILL.

27. The Failings of the Churches: Ebenezer Frothingham,
    The Articles of Faith and Practice, 1750

[Ebenezer Frothingham, *The Articles of Faith
and Practice, with the Covenant, That is confessed by the Separate Churches of Christ in
general in this Land* . . . (Newport, 1750),
340–343]

The Churches that we have separated from generally hold, that external Morality is the Door into the Church, and that the Lord's Supper is a converting Ordinance; or that all have a Right to join with the Church, that will make an outward public Profession of Christianity, altho' they be unconverted. Now therefore consider if Christ be the Foundation or Rock that his Church is built upon, then it certainly followeth, that external Morality, or a bare Profession of Christianity, is not that Faith by which, and in which Christ's Church is built, namely, A real, true, divine Belief, that Jesus Christ is the Son of the Living God, and the only Rock to build upon, both in Faith and Practice, *Matt.* 16 chap. 16, 17, 18. is as wide asunder from external Morality, or a bare Profession only, as Grace is from Nature, or Heaven from Hell; for the one is upon the Rock Christ, and the other is upon the Sands, chap. 7 24 to 27 ver. We therefore ask the Reader, wherein we have transgressed for leaving the sandy Foundation, to build upon the Rock Christ? for such a Church and People as we have left, the Word of God requires us to separate from. For Instance; the Churches that we have left, professedly hold, that Believers and Unbelievers, should covenant together in Church standing, and partake of the Ordinances together; and such a People or Church we are commanded to separate from, 2 *Cor.* 6 chap. 14, 17, 18 ver. *Be ye not unequally yoked together with Unbelievers; for what Fellowship hath Righteousness with Un-righteousness? and what Communion hath Light with Darkness? Wherefore come out from among them, and be ye separate, saith the Lord, and touch not the unclean Thing; and I will receive you, and I will be a Father unto you, and ye shall be my Sons and Daughters, saith the Lord Almighty.*

Again. In the Churches that we have left, there are many that are hardened, and believe not, but speak evil of the Ways, Work, and Power of God, and are awful Mockers at the Spirit of God, and the Saints that are under the Influence of the same Spirit; and these Persons are indulged in the Churches: Therefore we have a just Right and Warrant in the Word of God, to separate from them, *Acts* 19 chap. 9. *But when divers were hardened, and believed not, but spake evil of that Way before the Multitude, he departed from them, and separated the Disciples, disputing daily in the School of one* Tyrannus. 1 *Cor.* 5 chap. 11. *If any Man that is called a Brother, be a Fornicator, or covetous, or an Idolator, or a Railer, or a Drunkard, or an Extortioner, with such an one, no not to eat.*

Again. The Churches that we have left, have dwindled away into a dead, dry, lifeles Form of Godliness, and have denied the Power and Life of Godliness, and from such we are to turn away, see 2 *Tim.* 3 chap. 5. *Having a Form of Godliness, but denying the Power thereof, from such turn away.*

Again. The Churches that we have left, are stuffed full of hypocrites or Dissemblers; for they professedly take in the unconverted; and when they are in the Church, they profess themselves Saints, and are counted and treated as such, which is manifest Hypocrisy in the sight of God, and his Saints, *Psa. 26. 4, 5. I have not sat with vain Persons, neither will I go in with Dissemblers. I have hated the Congregation of evil Doers; and will not set with the Wicked. Isa.* 29 chap. 13, 14. Now as to our leaving the House of God: Multitudes are deceived by a traditional Practice in this Matter, and so take that to be God's House, which is not. We have Reason to think, that there are Multitudes, that can give no other Reason why that is the House of God where they meet only this; That the Society, or their Fathers, have always met there to pray, and hear preaching, and attend upon the Ordinances, and it is the Place appointed; therefore it is God's House, etc. Now the same Argument the Papist can bring, to prove, that where they meet is the House of God; for they pray, preach, and attend Ordinances also; therefore those that can give no other Reason than this, speak what they do not know, when they say, that we have left the House of God; For the Truth is, that we have left the House of dead Formality, and spiritual Idolatry, and meet where the sovereign Lord of Heaven and Earth grants his gracious Spirit, in its divine, quick'ning, and sanctifying Influences; so that thereby we are enabled to worship him in Spirit and in Truth. It is not any Meeting Place, or House, that is appointed by Man only, that makes God's House; No! for what makes a Place to be God's House, is his special, spiritual Presence; and where his Children meet, under the Divine Influence of his blessed Spirit, for social and Spiritual Worship, whether it be a public Meeting-House, or a private House, or the open Wilderness.

CHAPTER FIVE

ASSESSMENTS

M OST of the Calvinist ministry welcomed Whitefield and the revival in 1740. The Awakening was a fulfillment of their hopes
for many years past. Especially in New England few dared speak against
him for some months. The Anglicans were the first to object. They
knew Whitefield's reputation among the English clergy and they dis-
liked his cavalier disregard for Church conventions. He slighted the
ecclesiastical differences between Anglicans and dissenters, which
Churchmen stressed in their competition with Presbyterians and Congregationalists, and instead concentrated entirely on the new birth.
Joining the Anglican clergy in this hostility were Gilbert Tennent's
enemies among the Old Side Presbyterians. Whitefield's blessing on
the Log College men strengthened their influence with the general
public, and his censures of dead preaching confirmed Tennent's rebuke
in the Nottingham sermon. The Old Side Presbyterians at once recognized Whitefield as an enemy. New England conservatives mobilized
more slowly, but first Tennent and then Davenport aroused their fears.
From 1742 on, vocal opposition grew in intensity. In 1744 and 1745
Harvard and Yale both came out against Whitefield and thus implicitly
registered their official disapproval of the Awakening.

Samuel Finley (1715–1766), one of the Log College men and
pastor at Nottingham in Pennsylvania, understood the opposition as
the natural hatred of ungodly men for the work of God (No. 28). He
stood shoulder to shoulder with Gilbert Tennent in the battle with the
Presbyterian conservatives and wrote his letter in the same spirit that
moved *The Danger of an Unconverted Ministry*. Finley was not, however, merely a firebrand. He opened a school in the parsonage at
Nottingham that later trained a number of men who went on to
eminence, among them Benjamin Rush, the famous physician and

publicist of Revolutionary years. In 1761 Finley became one of the long line of distinguished evangelists who succeeded to the presidency of the College of New Jersey at Princeton.

As more and more disturbances occurred, the Old Lights steadily added to their brief against the Awakening. Charles Chauncy (1705–1787), pastor of the First Church in Boston, assiduously collected adverse stories from all over New England, as well as extensive passages from the Puritan fathers, for publication in his lengthy indictment of the Awakening, *Seasonable Thoughts on the State of Religion in New England* (1743). That work established him as champion of the antirevival forces; the *Letter . . . to Mr. George Wishart* of the previous year pungently summarized his feelings as he began the larger book (No. 29). Above all Chauncy feared the loss of control. Whitefield's extravagant preaching invited people to release their passions when the purpose of religion and morality was to restrain them. Small wonder that antinomianism, the belief that a person with grace was above the law, followed in the wake of the revival. The disintegration of ecclesiastical order was the natural outgrowth of the loss of personal control. Lay preaching, censure of ministers, irresponsible itineracy, and separation all accorded with the chaotic spirit of the Awakening.

Jonathan Edwards (1703–1758) was Chauncy's counterpart on the New Light side. A much more astute antagonist than Finley, Edwards delighted in the Awakening, but was not blinded by its unwonted excesses. He condemned the errors as vigorously as Chauncy. After 1741 he expended considerable effort to distinguish true religion from the false zeal and assurance of enthusiasts. But despite his recognition of the unfortunate side effects of the revival, Edwards never denied that God's Spirit worked in the Awakening. All of the excesses were in fact perfectly understandable. The cataclysmic transformation at conversion necessarily aroused the affections and resulted in some untoward behavior (No. 30). While he tried to dampen every kind of ecclesiastical irregularity, he sympathized with the common yearning to reform the churches. (His own efforts to exclude the unconverted from the church at Northampton led to his dismissal.) Edwards cautioned his colleagues not to oppose the revival on account of its faults lest they be found to fight against God.

As the controversy raged, both parties sought to demonstrate that the preponderance of clerical opinion was on their side. At the annual convention of Massachusetts ministers in May of 1743, a group of Old Lights pushed through a statement enumerating the errors of the revival which they published as *The Testimony of the Pastors of the Churches* (No. 31). The title implied that the Massachusetts clergy as a body had censured the Awakening disorders. Only a brief paragraph at the end credited the revival with any good effects. A number of ministers, led by Joshua Gee of Boston, objected to the implication of the title. The convention, they argued, was only an informal gathering which represented but a small portion of the clergy. Of that group only a small majority (thirty-eight out of about seventy) were content with the unduly modest praise of the revival. Gee called on the ministers of the province to meet again in July following the Harvard commencement and speak their mind more truly. *The Testimony and Advice of an Assembly* was the outcome of this meeting (No. 32). Ultimately 111 ministers, 90 from Massachusetts alone, subscribed to this more favorable appraisal, although 15 of them wished that the testimony had more forcefully denounced the errors.

In juxtaposition, the two statements demonstrate that virtually all the ministry saw both good and evil in the Awakening; they only differed on how to divide the praise and blame. But this measure of disagreement was sufficient to disturb the clergy for years to come.

28. The Priests Are Blind: Samuel Finley, *Letter,* 1741

[Samuel Finley, *A Letter to a Friend* ([Boston], 1741)]

My dear FRIEND,

IT is a lamentable Truth, that when ever the Gospel is preach'd with such Power and Purity as to shake the strong Holds of Satan, and rouse a World lying securely in Wickedness then those who ought, and seem'd to be Pillars of God's House, and Religion's only Friends, do always make the most violent Opposition against it. The Church of God has always had its Ebbings and Flowings; sometimes flourishing, and again declining; and whoever will look into the History of it, with any Care and Attention, will be oblig'd to grant the Truth of the following Observations among many others. *First,* that, in whatever State it was, there was always such People, such Priests. If the Church was in a declining State (and sometimes there was hardly Faith to be found on the Earth) in such Times the Priests were all of a Piece with the

People, alike Secure and Blind; neither could it ordinarily be otherwise, because the Priests too must be taken out of the same Lump, the same way leavened. And *Secondly,* we may observe, that whenever God would reform his Church and revive his People, he always did something extraordinary; he rais'd up some eminent Men to Alarm the World of their Danger; and to these gave Qualifications suited to the Circumstances the Church was in. *Thirdly,* we may observe, that these were always opposed and rejected, by that Set of Priests who were then established when a Reformation began: It was the Builders, who always set at nought the Chief Corner Stone. No wonder then, that a rushing mighty Wind should make their House reel and totter and fall to the Ground. Thus the false Prophets persecuted the true Ones; and the Scribes and Pharisees who sat in *Moses* his Seat, persecuted our Saviour and his Apostles; and from the very Beginning of the World, to this Day, the Observations will hold good. *Fourthly*, we may observe that Pride and Interest always hinder'd the Generality of these Ecclesiasticks from Embracing CHRIST; they would not humble themselves so far as to own their Ignorance or Prejudice; and their Interests made them always strive to stir up the People against Christ and his Gospel, that so they might keep them on their own Side; and thus, by insensible Degrees, they have stop'd their Ears and Shut their Eyes, and would neither see nor hear; and have still, alas! turn'd away much People from the Lord, being neither willing to enter into the Kingdom of Heaven themselves, nor yet to suffer those who were entering to go in. Hence, have they been judicially harden'd of God, and become his bitterest Enemies. But *Fifthly*, we may observe, that the very Methods they have us'd to suppress the People of God, those very Methods has God, in his Wisdom, made use of to raise his People higher, and to confound those who devis'd them. The very Ashes of the Martyrs have become the Seed of the Church. But *Sixthly*, we may also observe, that the Prophets, and Christ, and his Apostles, and all other eminent Reformers, in Order to promote the Gospel, have always dash'd the Credit of a carnal Set of Teachers, that so the People might be free from one great Prejudice which they labour'd under, that is the bold Contradictions of their own Teachers, in whose Favour they are apt to be blindly prepossess'd. And *Lastly*, we may observe, that the common People do generally hear Christ gladly, to the great Dissatisfaction of the Scribes and Pharisees: *Have any of the Rulers or Pharisees believ'd on him? No, but this People who know not the Law are accursed.*

Now in order to run a Parallel, between past and present Times, I will take it for granted, that the World has long been very secure; there has been little Stir among Professors about the State of their Souls; few groaning under a sense of their Sins; few broken Reeds or smoaking Flax few seeking after Jesus, but only seeking after Ordinances in a lifeless formal Manner: Now God is pleased to send the Comforter into the World, to convince it of Sin, of Righteousness, and of Judgment, And now a stiff-necked and rebellious People do always resist the Holy Ghost, as their Predecessors, the Scribes and Pharisees, and their Adherents did formerly, so they do now. The Scribes and Pharisees, who were Office Bearers in Christ's Church, gave him the worst Treatment, stirr'd up the People against him, call'd him a Deceiver, said he had a Devil, and was beside himself; and would account for all his Miracles from Spells and Charms; went about to ensnare him in his Words; had they come with a sincere Desire of Information, this had been well, but they came to trap him, with captious, ensnaring Questions, that they might have wherewith to accuse him; they said he spoke Blasphemy and would not let the People hear him; that he was for making himself a temporal Kingdom; would not submit to their Church Government, nor walk according to the Traditions of the Fathers. How did they bespatter his Character! No doubt their Pulpits were fill'd with Invectives against him. And what was the Reason of this Bitter Outcry against Christ? Why, he called the Scribe and Pharisees a Pack of Hypocrites, to their Faces; told the People to beware of them and their Doctrines: He kept aloof from them, and damned them, for their rotten Performances, Prayers, Fastings and Alms. This, this was what provok'd their Spleen, and did whet their Malice; because of this, they said he spoke against the Law of God, which commanded the Performance of them. O the babling ignorant Priests, that would seem so great Friends to Holiness; and under a Disguise of Religion deceive the People, who do not understand the Gospel! Thus the Scribes and Pharisees and their Allies, have always, either ignorantly or wilfully mistaken Christ, and stumbled at that stumbling Stone, that Rock of Offence, and have been broken as many as have fallen upon it; but that is not all, for while they lie unrecovered, the same Stone will fall on them, and grind them to Powder. Alas! how many of their Successors do pray for the Day of the Lord, and yet know it not now when it is come: Wo to them, for the Day of the Lord is to them Darkness, and not Light, full of Stumbling Blocks and Offences, and not at all according to their liking. How do they cavil at this and that; for the natural Man, receiveth not the Things of the Spirit of God, for they are Foolishness to him, and he cannot possibly know them, because they are spiritually descerned: The meanest Believer knows more of these Things than the most learned faithless Rabbi: For why, the one has felt and experienced them, and the other has only heard of them. And when the roused World begins to stand aghast, being Powerfully convinced by God's Spirit of their miserable State and are made to cry out under their Burden, then carnal Souls, who have never felt these Things, do imagine that Priest and People are beside themselves; and will tell you, this is all the Power of Fancy, the Passions and Affections a little mov'd; which might be done to at good Purposes by an old *Quaker* Wife, or an Actor of Tragedies; and some are so bold as to call it a Work of the Devil. And as for Mr. *Whitefield* and the *Tennents,* they are disorderly Brethren, do not walk according to the Traditions of the Elders,

(*i.e.* when they preceive them to have a Tendency to hinder the Progress of Christ's Gospel) they go about to get the Applause of the World, and make themselves a Party; their Doctrines are unsound, because they damn their formal Prayers, and speak against carnal Ministers, and warn the People to take Care of them; they talk of Assurance of God's Love, and Joy in the Holy Ghost, as the Priviledge of all Believers: They talk of the Necessity of deep Convictions, and amuse the People with some new Notions and Modes; and a great deal of Stuff to this Purpose, which I need not wait now to confute; Nay more, to compleat an ugly Character, they are called by some, wandering Stars, blazing Comets, that will appear for a while in Brightness, and then Vanish into Smoke: Are not these the Devil's Advocates and Pleaders of his Cause! whose Spirit comes from them?

Now I would gladly learn from these diabolical Reasoners, (be they Ministers or People) whether it be the Devil's Custom to set the World in an Uproar about the State of their Souls; I used to think and say, that when *the strong Man armed keeps the House, all his Goods are at Peace;* but, if what they say be true, I must change my Opinion of Satan, and think he is grown a Penitent Reformer. And if the Power of Fancy is so great, as to convince the World powerfully of Sin, to make them feel its Burden as they never did before, to make them cry fervently and importunately Night and Day to God for Mercy; to fill their Hearts with strong Desires after Jesus, and make him precious to their Souls, altogether lovely and desireable, the chiefest among ten Thousand; to make them restless and unsatisfied until they find Jesus, their Souls best beloved; and nothing will quiet or please them but some Token of his Special Love and pardoning Grace to their own Souls; if it makes them leave their Waters Pots, and worldly Concerns, their former Pursuits, and all their Darling Pleasures and Profits, and flock to hear the true Doctrines of the Gospel preach'd and press'd warmly and powerfully, and solemnly apply'd; to hear Doctrines so directly contrary to their natural Desires of Peace and Ease and Security: to hear themselves condemned; their dreadful Doom display'd; their former peaceful Hopes destroy'd and cut down; to hear Sermons that search them to the quick; that scorch their Conscience, and distress them to the utmost Degree; that makes them cry out in the Bitterness of their Souls, *What shall we do to be saved?* Now, I say if this be not the Work of God, but only a fanciful Delusion, then farewell Reason and common Sense! then, my Soul, thou are no longer able to distinguish between Light and Darkness! Virtue and Vice, Holiness and Wickedness are empty Names and lie wholly confus'd an undistinguished Mixture, and insepperable Heap! Then farewel all our Knowledge! farewel Scripture Promises and sacred History! all are Deceit, Delusions, enthusiastick Notions; Then it might be the Power of a warm Imagination, that caus'd three Thousand convicted Souls to cry out, *Men and Brethren, what shall we do?* Then I will confess that an old *Quaker* Wife, or an expert Tragedian, may, by their Craft, work up the Passions and Affections of their Hearers so far as to make them go Weeping and Mourning as they go, enquiring the Way to Zion, with their Faces thitherward; and may convince the World of Sin, of Righteousness, and Judgment so powerfully, that we cannot distinguish between them, and the Workings of God's Spirit. I do not in the least doubt, but those who commanded the Apostles not to preach in the name of Jesus, did strive to persuade the People that those three

Thousand who cryed out, were got into a whimsical, fanciful, enthusiastick Fit, and would come to themselves again; that this was sudden Commotion of the Passions and Affections; and possibly some reverend Scribe might tell the Members of the Synagogue, that he had seen or heard of an Assembly of *Pagans* as much melted as that, by hearing an eloquent and warm Speech from *Cicero* the *Roman* Orator; and concluded firmly that this was not to be taken any Notice of. Oh Ministers of Satan! Enemies of all Righteousness! who thus, like *Elimas,* do seek to turn the People away from the Faith. Are there yet Masters in *Israel* who have no Knowledge of a wounded Spirit! Why do they talk so ignorantly, so maliciously of the Work of God on his People's Hearts! When they talk of Convictions, they seem to mean nothing but an ineffectual dry Conviction; a Conviction of the Understanding that never affects the Heart. They cannot hear of People crying out under them; no, this is Nonsense: Let them search the Records of *Scotland's* Reformation, and they will find, that some have fallen dead, and fainted, and cried out under God's powerful Workings. What will they understand, by the Commandment coming and slaying a Person, by breaking up the fallow Ground, renting the Heart, wounding the Spirit, by being weary, labouring and heavy laden? Is all this without feeling? They can talk of the Duties of Holiness, and will Propose Rewards, and tell the Happiness of Heaven: They can declaim against gross Out Breakings, and damn the persisting Doers to devouring Flames; but the Devil cares not how much they Preach thus, if they never reach the Heart, if a Match with Christ be not attained. Do they discover the hidden Corners of the Heart, and confound the self deceiving Hypocrite, and unmask the carnal Professor? Do they lay his

Heart open to his own View, that he goes away self condemned: If this were closely done, we should have had more News of wounded Spirits. If I had time I would set these Things in a clearer Light; but I must hasten to a Conclusion.

I have heard Mr. *Whitefield's* Character is falsly and maliciously bespatter'd; that he is represented as a vain Fellow, a Self-seeker, Proud, a Deceiver of the People; that he is getting Money to purchase an Estate to himself, and the like; or something that will bear the same Sense: I will only observe, that Mr. *Whitefield* is very sure of God's eternal Love, and is not afraid that ever he shall be asham'd of his Hope. Let those then, who thus revile him, first consider, whether they can confute his Evidences of God's Favour, or whether they have as good themselves? If none of these can be done, let them be disregarded as Persons that do no harm to the Lord's Prophets, and touch his Anointed. His Behaviour may be set in an ugly ridiculous Light; but the World knows the Gravity, Humility, Undisguisedness, Heavenliness, Meekness, Self-Denial, Temperance and Modesty, that appear plainly in all his Conduct. He is bold as a Lyon in his Master's Cause, and bids Defiance to Earth and Hell, to Devils and wicked Men. He is zealous, lively and diligent, which cannot be denied; and his Doctrine sound, which cannot be condemned, unless by those who would cavil at Words, not attending to the Strain of his Sermons: (I will not condemn any one that would come in the Spirit of Meekness in a fit Season, to be inform'd of what they doubt of.)

But what nettles some of them most, and makes them catch at any Pretence to quarrel with Mr. *Whitefield*, is his Preaching against carnal Ministers, and confounding their Manner of Teaching and Doctrines, and telling the People to beware of them, as his Master did; forasmuch as they are but only Wolves, tho' they may have Sheep Cloathing. I know not what blind fatality it is, that makes any of them show a dislike to this Doctrine: Are they afraid that they shall be found to be the carnal Teachers? Does their Conscience apply it to them? If so, they might make a better Improvement of it, than to quarrel with it. If not, why are they offended at it? why do they not join in it? why do some of them preach, that it's no matter whether a Minister of the Gospel be graceless or gracious? Now, Sir, I leave you to judge, whether the Parallel will not run much better between those who oppose the Work of God, and the ancient Scribes and Pharisees, and their Adherents, than between Mr. *Whitefield* and an old *Quaker* Wife, or a dissembling Tragedian.

—I do not aim by what I have said, against any but those Ministers and People, who oppose the Work of God, and speak contemptuously of it; who Mock and Deride poor convinced Souls, that are not able to bear the Load of a deeply wounded Spirit, but are forced to cry out in the Bitterness of the Souls, whenever God opens their Eyes, to see their miserable, their damnable Condition, in order to make them fly to Jesus, the Redeemer of a perishing World. He it is, that will bind up their broken, wounded Hearts, that will heal their Souls, and forgive their Sins, and save them from 'em. He it is, that will put a New Song in their Mouths, even Praises to the God of their Salvation, and Hosannas to the Son of *David*. They shall eternally rejoice, when the prophane, laughing, mocking World shall eternally mourn. Let Despisers come and behold, and wonder and perish: They may, indeed, occasion much Tribulation to the Saints here on Earth, but can never climb to Heaven to disturb them there.

Sir, you may make what Use you please of these Lines, I profess them to be the fixed Sentiments of my Soul, and am ready to defend them, oppose them who will: Forasmuch as I firmly believe, that neither my Station, or Youth, or any other Thing can possibly excuse me, if I should refuse to appear to Day for God's Cause; to stand up for the Lord against the Mighty, of whatever Rank, Age, or Station they be. But if I have written any thing that is unjustifiable, when I am conceived of it, I will not be asham'd to acknowledge to the World that I was in an Error. If any Man will be offended, and drawn away from Christ, I cannot help it; I pray that God may open his Eyes.

I am, Sir, Yours, etc.
SAMUEL FINLY.

29. Overheated Passions: Charles Chauncy, *A Letter . . . to Mr. George Wishart*, 1742

[(Charles Chauncy), *A Letter from a Gentleman in Boston, to Mr. George Wishart, One of the Ministers of Edinburgh, Concerning the State of Religion In New-England* (Edinburgh, 1742), 5–15, 17–24]

Reverend Sir,

I Perceive by a printed Letter from a Friend in *Edinburgh,* containing *Excerpts of Letters concerning the Success of the Gospel in these Parts,* that marvellous Accounts have been sent Abroad of a most glorious Work of Grace going on in *America,* as begun by Mr. *Whitefield,* and helpt forward by those in his way of preaching and acting. I should be glad there had been more Truth in those Accounts. Some of the Things related are known Falsehoods, others strangely enlarged upon; and the Representations, in general, such, as exhibit a wrong Idea of the *religious* State of Affairs among us. I had Thoughts of sending you the needful Corrections of that *Pamphlet;* but my Circumstances being such, at present, as not to allow of this, must content myself with giving you the following *summary* Narration of things as they have appeared among us.

The Minds of People in this Part of the World, had been greatly prepossest in Favour of Mr. *Whitefield,* from the Accounts transmitted of him, from time to time, as a *Wonder of Piety, a Man of God,* so as *no one was like him:* Accordingly, when he came to *Town,* about two Years since, he was received as though he had been an *Angel of God;* yea, *a God come down in the Likeness of Man.* He was strangely flocked after by all Sorts of Persons, and much admired by the *Vulgar,* both *great* and *small.* The *Ministers* had him in Veneration, at least in Appearance, as much as the People; encouraged his Preaching, attended it themselves every Day in the Week, and mostly *twice* a Day. The grand Subject of Conversation was Mr. *Whitefield,* and the whole Business of the Town to run, from Place to Place, to hear him preach: And, as he preach'd under such uncommon Advantages, being high in the Opinion of the People, and having the Body of the Ministers hanging on his Lips, he soon insinuated himself still further into the Affections of Multitudes, in so much that it became dangerous to mention his Name, without saying something in commendation of him.

His Reception, as he past through *this* and the neighbouring Governments of *Connecticut* and *New-York,* till he came to *Philadelphia,* was after much the same Manner; save only, that he met with no Admirers among the *Clergy,* unless here and there one, any where but in *Boston:* And, whether the Ministers here in general, really thought better of him than they did elsewhere, I will not be too positive to affirm. 'Tis possible, they might act as tho' they had a great Veneration for him, and so as to lead People into such an Apprehension, from *Cowardice, Affectation of Popularity,* or a *rigid Attachment to some Sentiments in Divinity,* they might imagine there was now an Advantage to establish and propagate: And I would not undertake to prove, that they might none of them be under an undue Influence from some or other of these Motives.

Much began to be now said of a *glorious Work of God* going on in the Land. *Evening-lectures* were set up in one Place and another; no less than six in this Town, *four* weekly, and *two* monthly ones, tho' the Town does not consist of above 5000 Families at the largest Computation. At some of these Lectures, it was common to mention Mr. *Whitefield* by Name, both in the *Prayers* and *Sermons;* giving God Thanks for sending such an *extraordinary* Man among us, and making him the Instrument of *such extraordinary Good* to so many Souls. He was indeed spoken of, as *the Angel flying through Heaven with the everlasting Gospel,* and such Honours sacrificed to him as were due to no meer Man: Nay, to such a Height did this Spirit rise, that all who did not express a very high Thought of Mr. *Whitefield,* were lookt upon with an evil Eye; and as to those who declared their Dislike of what they judged amiss of the Times, they were stigmatised as *Enemies of God* and *true Religion;* yea, they were openly represented, both from the *Pulpit* and the *Press,* as in danger of committing *the*

Sin against the Holy Ghost, if not actually guilty even of this *unpardonable* Sin.

And here you will doubtless be disposed to enquire, what was the *great Good* this *Gentleman* was the Instrument of?

In answer whereto, I freely acknowledge, wherever he went he generally moved the *Passions,* especially of the *younger* People, and the *Females* among them; the Effect whereof was, a great Talk about Religion, together with a Disposition to be perpetually hearing Sermons, to neglect of all other Business; especially, as preach'd by those who were Sticklers for the *new Way,* as it was called. And in these things *chiefly* consisted the Goodness so much spoken of. I deny not, but there might be here and there a Person stopp'd from going on in a Course of Sin; and some might be made really better: But so far as I could judge upon the nicest Observation, the Town, in general, was not much mended in those things wherein a Reformation was greatly needed. I could not discern myself, nor many others whom I have talked with, and challenged on this Head, but that there was the same Pride and Vanity, the same Luxury and Intemperance, the same lying and tricking and cheating, as before this Gentleman came among us. There was certainly no *remarkable* Difference as to these things: And 'tis vain in any to pretend there was. This, I am sure of, there was raised such a Spirit of bitter, censorious, uncharitable judging, as was not know before; and is, wherever it reigns, a Scandal to all who call themselves Christians: Nor was it ever evident to me, but that the greatest Friends to Mr. *Whitefield* were as much puffed up with Conceit and Pride as any of their Neighbours; and as to some of them, and the more eminent too, I verily believe they possess a *worse Spirit* than before they heard of his Name, and it had been as well for them if they had never seen his Face.

But I have only entred as yet upon that Scene of Things, which has made so much Noise in the Country. A Number of Ministers, in one Place and another, were by this Time formed into Mr. *Whitefield's* Temper, and began to appear and go about preaching, with a Zeal more flaming, if possible, than his. One of the most famous among these was Mr. *Gilbert Tennent,* a Man of no great Parts or Learning; his preaching was in the *extemporaneous* Way, with much Noise and little Connection. If he had taken suitable Care to prepare his Sermons, and followed Nature in the Delivery of them, he might have acquitted himself as a *middling* Preacher; but as he preached, he was an *awkward Imitator* of Mr. *Whitefield,* and too often turned off his Hearers with *mere Stuff,* which he uttered with a Spirit more bitter and uncharitable than you can easily imagine; all were *Pharisees, Hypocrites, carnal unregenerate Wretches,* both Ministers and People, who did not think just as he did, particularly as to the Doctrines of *Calvinism;* and those who opposed him, and the Work of God he was sure he was carrying on, would have opposed *Christ Jesus himself* and *his Apostles,* had they lived in their Day. This Gentleman came from *New-Brunswick* in the *Jersies* to *Boston,* in the Middle of Winter, (a Journey of more than 300 Miles) to *water the good Seed sown by Mr.* Whitefield in this Place. It was indeed at Mr. *Whitefield's* Desire, and in consequence of a Day of *Fasting and Prayer,* kept on purpose to know the Mind of God as to this Matter, that he came among us; the *Ministers in the Town,* though *fourteen* in Number, being thought insufficient to carry on the *good Work* he had begun here in the Hearts of People. And though the

Design this Gentleman professedly came upon, was a bare-faced Affront to the *Body of the Ministers,* yet not only the People, (which is not to be wondred at) but some of the Ministers themselves admired and followed him, as much as they had done Mr. *Whitefield* before him; and here he was, by their Encouragement, a great Part of the Winter, preaching every Day in the Week, to the taking People off from their Callings, and the introducing a Neglect of all Business but that of hearing him preach. He went from *Boston* to the *eastward,* to visit the Places where Mr. *Whitefield* had been; and on his Return home passed through the Country, preaching every where as he went along, in the same Manner, and with the same Spirit he did here in *Boston.*

And now it was, that Mr. *Whitefield's* Doctrine of *inward Feelings* began to discover itself in Multitudes, whose *sensible Perceptions* arose to such a Height, as that they *cried out, fell down, swooned away,* and, to all Appearance, were like Persons in *Fits;* and this, when the Preaching (if it may be so called) had in it as little well digested and connected good Sense, as you can well suppose. Scores in a Congregation would be in such Circumstances at a Time; nay some hundreds in some Places, to the filling the Houses of Worship with Confusion not to be expressed in Words, nor indeed conceived of by the most lively Imagination, unless where Persons have been Eye and Ear-witnesses to these Things. Though I may add here, that to a Person in possession of himself, and capable of Observation, this surprising Scene of Things may be accounted for: The *Speaker* delivers himself, with the *greatest Vehemence* both of *Voice* and *Gesture,* and in the most *frightful Language* his Genius will allow of. If this has its intended Effect upon *one* or *two weak Women,* the Shrieks catch from one to another, till a great Part of the Congregation is affected; and some are in the Thought, that it may be too common for those *zealous in the new Way* to *cry out themselves,* on purpose to move others, and bring forward a *general Scream. Visions* now became common, and *Trances* also, the Subjects of which were in their own Conceit transported from Earth to Heaven, where they saw and heard most glorious Things; conversed with *Christ* and *holy Angels;* had opened to them the *Book of Life,* and were permitted to read the Names of Persons there, and the like. And what is a singular Instance (so far as I remember) of the working of Enthusiasm, *laughing, loud hearty laughing,* was one of the Ways in which our *new Converts,* almost every where, were wont to join together in expressing their Joy at the Conversion of others.

'Tis scarce imaginable what Excesses and Extravagancies People were running into, and even encouraged in; being told such Things were Arguments of the *extraordinary Presence of the Holy Ghost* with them. The same Houses of Worship were scarce emptied Night nor Day for a Week together, and unheard of Instances of supposed Religion were carried on in them. In the same House, and at the same time, some would be *praying,* some *exhorting,* some *singing,* some *clapping their Hands,* some *laughing,* some *crying,* some *shrieking and roaring out;* and so invincibly set were they in these Ways, especially when encouraged by any Ministers, (as was too often the Case) that it was a vain Thing to argue with them, to shew them the Indecency of such Behaviour; and whoever indeed made an Attempt this Way, might be sure aforehand of being called an *Opposer* of the *Spirit,* and a *Child of the Devil.*

At these Times there were among the People what we call here Exhorters; these are such as are esteemed to be *Converts* in the *new Way.* Sometimes they are *Children, Boys* and *Girls,* sometimes *Women;* but most commonly *raw, illiterate, weak* and *conceited young Men,* or *Lads.* They pray with the People, call upon them to come to Christ, tell them they are dropping into Hell, and take upon them what they imagine is the Business of preaching. They are generally much better thought of than any Ministers, except those in the *new Way,* I mean by the Friends to the *Extraordinaries* prevalent in the Land; and they are the greatest Promoters of them. 'Tis indeed at the *Exhortations* of these poor ignorant Creatures, that there is ordinarily the most Noise and Confusion: And what may be worth a particular Remark, 'tis *seldom* there are any great Effects wrought, till the Gloominess of the Night comes on. It is in the *Evening,* or more late in the *Night,* with only a *few Candles* in a *Meeting-house,* that there is the *screaming* and *shrieking* to the greatest Degree; and the Persons thus affected are generally *Children, young People,* and *Women.* Other Instances there may have been, but they are more rare; these bear the chief Part.

.   .   .   .

You may be ready perhaps to think I have here given you a romantick Representation of Things; but it is the real Truth of the Case without a Figure; yea, this has been the Appearance in all Parts of the Land more or less, and so known to have been so, that there is no room for Debate upon the Matter: Nay, those who are Friends to the *new Way* were *once* so far from being ashamed of these Things, that they boasted of them, and entertained an ill Opinion of all who did not speak of them as *Evidences* of the *wonderful Power of the Spirit of God:* I say, they *at first* boasted of these Things, and some of them do so still; though the Generality have begun, for some time, to speak publickly of the *Subtilty of Satan,* to tell People he may appear as *an Angel of Light,* and to warn them against being carried away by his Devices. Nay Mr. *Tennent* himself, one of the main Instruments of all our Disorders, has, in a couple of Letters to some of his Friends, published in the *Prints,* expressed his Fears lest the Churches should be undone with a *Spirit of Enthusiasm,* and *these Exhorters* which have risen up every where in the Land. He seems indeed to have quite turned about: The Reason whereof may be this; the *Moravians* who came to *Philadelphia* with Count *Zinzendorf,* have been among his People, and managed with them as he did elsewhere, and brought the like Confusion among them; and now he cries out of Danger, and expresses himself much as those did, whom before he had sent to the Devil by wholesale.

Various are the Sentiments of Persons about this *unusual Appearance* among us. Some think it to be a *most wonderful Work of God's Grace;* others a *most wonderful Spirit of Enthusiasm;* some think there is a *great deal* of *Religion,* with some *small Mixture* of Extravagance; others, a *great deal of Extravagance* with some *small Mixture* of that which may be called *good;* some think the *Country* was never in such a *happy* State on a *religious* account, others that it was never in a *worse.*

For my self, I am among those who are clearly in the Opinion, that there never was such a *Spirit* of *Superstition* and *Enthusiasm* reigning in the Land before; never such *gross Disorders* and *barefaced Affronts* to *common Decency;* never such *scandalous Reproaches* on the *Blessed Spirit,* making him the Author of the greatest *Irregularities* and *Confusions:* Yet, I am of Opinion also, that the Appearaces among us (so

much out of the ordinary Way, and so unaccountable to Persons not acquainted with the History of the World) have been the Means of awakening the Attention of many; and a good Number, I hope, have settled into a truly *Christian* Temper: Tho' I must add, at the same time, that I am far from thinking, that the Appearance, in *general,* is any other than the Effect of *enthusiastick Heat.* The Goodness that has been so much talked of, 'tis plain to me, is nothing more, in general, than a *Commotion in the Passions.* I can't see that Men have been made *better,* if hereby be meant, their being formed to a nearer Resemblance to the *Divine Being* in *moral Holiness.* 'Tis not evident to me, that Persons, generally, have a better Understanding of Religion, a better Government of their Passions, a more Christian Love to their Neighbour, or that they are more decent and regular in their Devotions towards God. I am clearly of the Mind, they are worse in all these Regards. They place their Religion so much in the *Heat* and *Fervour* of their *Passions,* that they too much neglect their *Reason* and *Judgment:* And instead of being more kind and gentle, more full of Mercy and good Fruits, they are more bitter, fierce and implacable. And what is a *grand discriminating Mark of this Work,* wherever it takes Place, is, that it makes Men *spiritually proud* and *conceited* beyond Measure, infinitely *censorious* and *uncharitable,* to *Neighbours,* to *Relations,* even the nearest and dearest; to *Ministers* in an especial Manner; yea, to all Mankind, who are not as they are, and don't think and act as they do: And there are few Places where *this Work* has been in any *remarkable* manner, but they have been filled with Faction and Contention; yea, in some, they have divided into Parties, and openly and scandalously separated from one another.

Truly the Accounts sent Abroad,

were sent too soon; too soon, I am satisfied, to reflect Honour upon the Persons who wrote them: And they bewray such a want of Judgment, as I was really sorry to see them falling into. There are few Persons now, perhaps none but such as are evidently overheated, but begin to see that Things have been carried too far, and that the Hazard is great, unless God mercifully interpose, lest we should be over-run with *Enthusiasm.* And to speak the plain Truth, my Fear is, lest the End of these things should be *Quakerism* and *Infidelity:* These we have now chiefly to guard against.

A particular Account of one Mr. *James Davenport,* with his *strange Conduct* in this *Town* and *elsewhere,* I doubt not would have been agreeable:

But I have exceeded already. He is the *wildest Enthusiast* I ever saw, and acts in the wildest manner; and yet, he is vindicated by some in all his Extravagancies.

I now beg Pardon, Sir, for thus trespassing upon your Patience. As Mr. *Whitefield* has been in *Scotland,* and *human Nature* is the *same every where;* this Narration of the Effects he has been the Instrument of producing here, may excite your Zeal to guard the People in time against any such Extravagancies, if there should be Danger of them where you may be concerned. I am,

Reverend Sir,

With all due Regard, etc.

Boston, August 4.

1742.

30. A Work of God: Jonathan Edwards, *The Distinguishing Marks*, 1741

[Jonathan Edwards, *The Distinguishing Marks Of a Work of the Spirit of God* . . . (Boston, 1741), 62–64, 66–79]

As to this Work that has lately been carried on in the Land, there are many Things concerning it that are notorious, and known by every Body, (unless it be some that have been very much out of the Way of observing and hearing indeed) that unless the Apostle *John* was out in his Rules, are sufficient to determine it to be in general, the Work of God. 'Tis notorious that the Spirit that is at work, takes off Persons Minds from the Vanities of the World, and engages them in a deep Concern about a future and eternal Happiness in another World, and puts them upon earnestly seeking their Salvation, and convinces them of the Dreadfulness of Sin, and of their own guilty and miserable State as they are by Nature. It is notorious that it awakens Mens Consciences, and makes 'em sensible of the

Dreadfulness of God's Anger, and causes in them a great Desire, and earnest Care and Endeavour to obtain his Favour. It is notorious, that it puts them upon a more diligent Improvement of the Means of Grace which God has appointed. It is also notorious, that in general, it works in Persons a greater Regard to the Word of God, and desire of hearing and reading of it, and to be more conversant with the holy Scriptures than they used to be. And it is notoriously manifest that the Spirit that is at work, in general, operates as a Spirit of Truth, making Persons more sensible of what is really true, in those Things that concern their eternal Salvation: As that they must die, and that Life is very short and uncertain; that there is a Great, Sin-hating God, that they are accountable to, and will fix them in an eternal State in another World, and that they stand in great Need of a Saviour. It is furthermore notorious, that the Spirit that is at work makes Persons more sensible of the Value of that Jesus that was crucified, and their Need of him; and that it puts them upon earnestly seeking an Interest in him. It can't be but that these Things should be apparent to People in general through the Land; for these Things ben't done in a Corner; the Work that has been wrought has not been confined to a few Towns, in some remoter Parts of the Land, but has been carried on in many Places in all Parts of the Land, and in most of the principal, and most populous, and publick Places in it, (Christ in this Respect has wrought amongst us, in the same Manner that he wrought his Miracles in *Judea*) and has now been continued for a considerable Time; so that there has been a great deal of Opportunity to observe the Manner of the Work. And all such as have been much in the Way of observing the Work, and have been very conversant with those that have been the Subjects of it, do see a great deal more that, by the Rules of the Apostle, does clearly and certainly shew it to be the Work of God.

. . . .

And as I am One that, by the Providence of God, have for some Months past, been much amongst those that have been the Subjects of that Work, that has of late been carried on in the Land; and particularly, have been abundantly in the Way of seeing and observing those extraordinary Things that many Persons have been much stumbled at; such as Persons crying out aloud, shrieking, being put into great Agonies of Body, and deprived of their bodily Strength, and the like; and that in many different Towns; and have been very particularly conversant with great Numbers of such, both in the Time of their being the Subjects of such extraordinary Influences, and afterwards, from Time to Time, and have seen the Manner and Issue of such Operations, and the Fruits of them, for several Months together; many of them being Persons that I have long known, and have been intimately acquainted with them in Soul Concerns, before and since: So I look upon my self called on this Occasion to give my Testimony, that so far as the Nature and Tendency of such a Work is capable of falling under the Observation of a By-stander, to whom those that have been the Subjects of it have endeavour'd to open their *Hearts,* or can be come at by diligent and particular Inquiry, this Work has all those Marks that have been spoken of; in very many Instances, in every Article; and particularly in many of those that have been the Subjects of such extraordinary Operations, all those Marks have appeared in a very great Degree.

Those in whom have been these uncommon Appearances, have been of two Sorts; either those that have been in great Distress, in an Apprehension of their Sin and Misery; or those that have been overcome with a sweet Sense of the Greatness, Wonderfulness and Excellency of divine Things. Of the Multitude of those of the former Sort, that I have had Opportunity to observe, and have been acquainted with, there have been very few, but that by all that could be observed in them, in the Time of it, or afterwards, their Distress has arisen from real, proper Conviction, and a being in a Degree sensible of that which was the Truth. And tho' I don't suppose, when such Things were observed to be common, that Persons have laid themselves under those violent Restraints, to avoid outward Manifestations of their Distress, that perhaps they otherwise would have done; yet there have been very few in whom there has been any Appearance of feigning or affecting such Manifestations, and very many for whom it would have been undoubtedly utterly impossible for 'em to avoid them. Generally those that have been in these Agonies have appeared to be in the perfect Exercise of their Reason; and those of them that have been able to speak, have been well able to give an Account of the Circumstances of their Minds, and the Cause of their Distress, in the Time of it, and well able to remember, and give an Account afterwards. I have known a very few Instances of those, that in their great Extremity, have for a short Space been deprived, in some Measure of the Use of Reason; but among the many Hundreds, and it may be Thousands, that have lately been brought to such Agonies, I never yet knew one, lastingly deprived of their Reason. In some that I have known, Melancholly has evidently been mixt; and when it is so, the Difference is very apparent; their Distresses are of another Kind, and operate quite after another Manner, than when their Distress is from meer Conviction: 'Tis not Truth only that distresses them, but many vain Shadows and Notions, that won't give Places either to Scripture or Reason. Some in their great Distress, have not been well able to give an Account of themselves, or to declare the Sense they have of Things, or to explain the Manner and Cause of their Trouble to others, that yet I have had no Reason to think were not under proper Convictions, and in whom there has been manifested a good Issue. But this won't be at all wonder'd at, by those who have had much to do with Souls under spiritual Difficulties. Some Things that they are sensible of are altogether new to them, their Ideas and inward Sensations are new, and what they therefore knew not how to accommodate Language to, or to find Words to express. And some

who in first Inquiry, say they know not what was the Matter with them, on being particularly Examined and Interrogated, have been able to represent their Case, tho' of themselves they could not find Expressions, and Forms of Speech to do it.

Some say they think that the Terrors that such Persons are in, that have such Effects on their Bodies, is only a *Fright*. But certainly there ought to be a Distinction made between a very great Fear, and extream Distress, arising from an Apprehension of some dreadful Truth, that is a Cause that is fully proportionable to such an Effect, and a needless causless Fright: which is of two Kinds; either when Persons are terrified with that which is not the Truth; (of this I have seen very few Instances unless in Case of Melancholy;) Or secondly, when Persons are under a childish Fright, only from some terrible outward Appearance and Noise, and a general Notion thence arising, that there is something or other Terrible, they know not what; without having in their Minds the Apprehension of any particular terrible Truth whatsoever; of such a Kind of Fright I have seen very little Appearance, either among Old or Young.

Those that are in such Extremity, commonly express a great Sense of their exceeding Wickedness, the Multitude and Aggravations of their actual Sins, and the dreadful Pollution, Enmity and Perverseness of their Hearts, and a dreadful Obstinacy and hardness of Heart; a Sense of their great Guilt in the Sight of God; and the Dreadfulness of the Punishment that Sin exposes to: Very often they have a lively Idea of the horrible Pit of eternal Misery; and at the same Time it appears to them, that a Great God that has them in his Hands, is exceeding Angry with them; his Wrath appears amazingly terrible to them; God appearing to them so much provoked, and his great Wrath so incensed, they are apprehensive of great Danger, that we will not bear with them any longer; but will now, forthwith, cut 'em off, and send them down to the dreadful Pit they have in View; at the same Time seeing no Refuge: They see more of the Vanity of every Thing they used to trust to, and flatter themselves in; 'till they are brought wholly to despair in all, and to see that they are at the Disposal of the meer Will of the God that is so angry with them. Very many, in the midst of their Extremity, have been brought to an extraordinary Sense of their fully deserving that Wrath and Destruction, which is then before their Eyes; and at the same Time, that they have feared every Moment, that it would be executed upon them, they have been greatly convinced that it would be altogether just that it should, and that God is indeed absolutely Sovereign: and very often, some Text of Scripture expressing God's Sovereignty, has been set home upon their Minds, whereby their Minds have been calm'd, and they have been brought as it were to lie at God's Foot; and after great Agonies, a little before Light has arisen, they have been composed and quiet, in a Kind of Submission to a Just and Sovereign God; but their bodily Strength much spent; and sometimes their Lives, to Appearance almost gone; and then Light has appeared, and a glorious Redeemer, with his wonderful, all-sufficient Grace, has been represented to them, often, in some sweet Invitation of Scripture. Sometimes the Light comes in suddenly, sometimes more gradually, filling their Souls with Love, Admiration, Joy and Self-Abasement; drawing forth their Hearts in Longing after the excellent lovely Redeemer, and Longings to lie in the Dust before him; and Longings that others might behold him, and embrace him, and be delivered by him;

and Longings to live to his Glory: but sensible that they can do nothing of themselves; appearing Vile in their own Eyes, and having much of a Jealousy over their own Hearts. And all the Appearances of a real Change of Heart have followed; and Grace has acted, from Time to Time, after the same Manner that it used to act in those that were converted formerly, with the like Difficulties, Temptations, Buffetings, and like Comforts; excepting that in many, Light and Comfort has been in higher Degree than ordinary. Many very young Children have been thus wro't upon. There have been some Instances very much like those Demoniacks that we read of, *Mar.* I. 26. and *Chap.* 9. 26. of whom we read, that *when the Devil had cried with a loud Voice, and rent them fore, he came out of them.* And probably those Instances were designed for a Type of such Things as these. Some have several Turns of great Agonies, before they are delivered: and some have been in such Distresses, and it has passed off, and no Deliverance at all has followed.

Some object against it, as great Confusion, when there is a Number together, in such Circumstances, making a Noise; and say, God can't be the Author of it, because he is the God of Order, not of Confusion. But let it be considered, what is the proper Notion of Confusion, but the breaking that Order of Things whereby they are properly disposed, and duly directed to their End, so that the Order and due Connection of Means being broken, they fail of their End; but Conviction and Conversion of Sinners is the obtaining the End of religious Means. Not but that I think that Persons that are thus extraordinarily moved shou'd endeavour to refrain from such outward Manifestations, what they well can, and should refrain to their utmost, in the Time of the solemn Worship. But if

God is pleased to convince the Consciences of Persons, so that they can't avoid great outward Manifestations, even to the interrupting, and breaking off those publick Means they were attending, I don't think this is Confusion, or an unhappy Interruption, any more than if a Company should meet on the Field to pray for Rain, and should be broken off from their Exercise by a plentiful Shower. Would to God that all the publick Assemblies in the Land were broken off from their publick Exercises with such Confusion as this the next Sabbath Day! We need not be sorry for the breaking the Order of the Means, by obtaining the End to which that Order is directed: He that is going a Journey to fetch a Treasure, need not be sorry that he is stopped by meeting the Treasure in the midst of his Journey.

Besides those that are overcome with Conviction and Distress, I have seen many of late, that have had their bodily Strength taken away with a Sense of the glorious Excellency of the Redeemer, and the Wonders of his dying Love; with a very uncommon Sense of their own Littleness, and exceeding Vileness attending it, with all Expressions and Appearances of the greatest Abasement and Abhorrence of themselves: And not only new Converts, but many that were, as we hope, formerly converted, whose Love and Joy has been attended with a Flood of Tears, and a great Appearance of Contrition and Humiliation, especially for their having lived no more to God's Glory since their Conversion; with a far greater Sight of their Vileness, and the Evil of their Hearts than ever they had; with an exceeding Earnestness of Desire to live better for the Time to come, but attended with greater Self-Diffidence than ever: And many have been even overcome with Pity to the Souls of others and longing for their Salvation.

And many other Things I might mention in this extraordinary Work, answering to every one of those Marks that have been insisted on. So that if the Apostle *John* knew how to give Signs of a Work of the true Spirit, this is such a Work.

Providence has cast my lot in a Place where the Work of God has formerly been carried on: I had the Happiness to be settled in that Place two Years with the venerable STODDARD: and was then acquainted with a Number that, during that Season, were wro't upon, under his Ministry, and have been intimately acquainted with the Experiences of many others, that were wro't upon before under his Ministry, in a Manner agreeable to his Doctrine, and the Doctrine of all orthodox Divines; and of late that Work has been carried on Their, with very much of these uncommon Opperations: but 'tis apparent to all to be the same Work, not only that was wro't there six or seven years ago, but elder Christians there know it to be the same Work that was carried on there, in their former Pastors's Days, tho' there be some new Circumstances. And certainly we must throw by all the Talk of Conversion and Christian Experience; and not only so, but we must throw by our Bibles, and give up revealed Religion, if this be not in general the Work of God, Not that I suppose that the Degree of the Influence of the Spirit of God, is to be determined by the Degree of Effect of Men's Bodies, or that those are always the best Experiences, that have the greatest Influence on the Body.

And as to the Imprudences and Irregularities and Mixture of Delusion that have been; it is not at all to be wondered at that a Reformation, after a long continued, and almost universal Deadness, should at first when the Revival is new, be attended with such Things. In the first Creation God did not make a compleat World at once; but there was a great deal of Imperfection, Darkness, and Mixture of *Chaos and Confusion,* after God first said, *Let there be Light,* before the whole stood forth in perfect Form. When God at first began his great Work for the Deliverance of his People, after their long continued Bondage in *Egypt,* there were false Wonders mix'd with true, for a while; which harden'd the unbelieving *Egyptians,* and made 'em doubt of the Divinity of the whole Work. When the Children of *Israel* first went about bringing up the Ark of God, after it had long been neglected, and had been long absent, they *sought not the Lord after the due Order,* I Chron. 15. 13. At the Time when the Sons of God came to present themselves before the Lord, *Satan came also among them.* And *Solomon's* Ships when they *brought Gold and Silver and Pearls,* also brought *apes and Peacocks.* When Day Light first appears, after a Night of Darkness, we must expect to have Darkness mixt with Light, for a while, and not to have perfect Day, and the Sun risen at once. The Fruits of the Earth are first green, before they are ripe, and come to their proper Perfection gradually; and so Christ tells us, *is the Kingdom of God.* Mark 4. 26, 27, 28. *So is the Kingdom of God; as if a Man should cast Seed into the Ground, and should Sleep, and rise Night and Day; and the Seed should spring and grow up, he knoweth not how: for the Earth bringeth forth Fruit of her self; first the Blade; then the Ear; then the full Corn in the Ear.*

The Imprudences and Errors that have attended this Work, are the less to be wonder'd at, if it be considered, that it is chiefly young Persons that have been the Subjects of it, who have less steadiness and Experiences, and are in the Heat of Youth, and much more ready to run to Extreams. Satan will keep Men secure as long as he can; but when he can do that no longer, he often endeavours to drive them to Extreams, and so to dishonour God, and wound Religion that Way. And doubtless it has been one Occasion of much of the Misconduct there has been, that in many Places, People that are the Subjects of this Work of God's Spirit, see plainly that their Ministers have an ill Opinion of the Work; and therefore with just Reason, durst not apply themselves to 'em as their Guides in this Work; and so are without Guides: and no Wonder that when a People are as Sheep without a Shepherd, they wander out of the Way. A People, in such Circumstances especially, stand in great and continual Need of Guides, and their Guides stand in continual Need of much more Wisdom than they have of their own. And if a People have Ministers that favour the Work, and rejoyce in it, yet 'tis not to be expected that, either People or Ministers should know so well how to conduct themselves in such an extraordinary State of Things, while it is new, and what they never had any Experience of before, as they may, after they have had Experience, and Time to see the Tendency, Consequences, and Issue of Things. The happy Influence of Experience is very manifest at this Day, in the People among whom God has settled my Abode. The Work of God that has been carried on there this Year, has been much purer than that which was wrought there six Years before; It has seem'd to be more purely spiritual; freer from natural and corrupt Mixtures, and any Thing favouring of enthusiastick Wildness and Extravagance: It has wrought more by deep Humiliation and Abasement before God and Men; and they have been much freer from Imprudences and Irregularities. And particularly there has been a remarkable Difference in this Respect, That whereas many before, in their Comforts and Rejoycings, did too much forget their Distance from God, and were ready in their Conversation to-gether of the Things of God, and of their own Experiences, to talk with too much of an Air of Lightness, and something of Laughter; now they seem to have no Disposition to it, but rejoyce with a more solemn, reverential, humble Joy; as God directs the Princes of the Earth, *Psal.* 2. 11. 'Tis not because the Joy is not as great, and in many of them much greater: There are many among us, that were wro't upon in that former Season, that have now had much greater Communications from Heaven than they had then; but their Rejoycing operates in another Manner: it only abases and solemnizes them; breaks their Hearts, and brings them into the Dust: Now when they speak of their Joys, it is not with Laughter, but a Flood of Tears. Thus those that laughed before, weep now; and yet, by their united Testimony, their Joy is vastly purer and sweeter than that which before did more raise their animal Spirits.

31. Errors and Disorders: *The Testimony of the Pastors of the Churches*, 1743

[*The Testimony of the Pastors of the Churches in the Province of the Massachusetts-Bay in New-England, at their Annual Convention in Boston, May 25. 1743. Against several Errors in Doctrine, and Disorders in Practice* . . . (Boston, 1743), 5–13]

We, the *Pastors* of the *Churches* of CHRIST in the PROVINCE of the MASSA-CHUSETTS-BAY in NEW-ENGLAND, at our *annual* Convention, *May* 25th. 1743, taking into Consideration several *Errors in Doctrine,* and *Disorders in Practice,* that have of late obtained in *various Parts of the Land,* look upon our selves bound, in *Duty* to our great LORD and MASTER, JESUS CHRIST, and in *Concern* for the *Purity* and *Welfare* of these Churches, in the most public Manner, to bear our *Testimony* against them.

I. As to *Errors in Doctrine;* we observe, that some in our Land look upon what are called *secret Impulses* upon their Minds, without due Regard to the *written Word,* the *Rule* of their Conduct; that none are *converted* but such as *know* they are converted, and the *Time when;* that *Assurance* is of the *Essence* of *saving Faith;* that *Sanctification* is no *Evidence* of *Justification,* with other ANTINOMIAN and FAMILISTI-CAL Errors, which flow from these: All which, as we judge, are contrary to the pure Doctrines of the Gospel, and testified against and confuted, by Arguments fetched from *Scripture* and *Reason,* by our venerable *Fathers,* in the Acts of the Synod of August 1637; as printed in a Book entitled, *The Rise, and Reign, and Ruin, of* ANTINOMIANISM etc. in NEW-ENGLAND.

II. As to *Disorders in Practice,* we judge,

1. The *Itinerancy,* as it is called, by which either *ordained Ministers,* or *young Candidates,* go from Place to Place, and without the Knowledge, or contrary to the Leave of the *stated* Pastors in such Places, assemble their People to hear *themselves* preach, arising, we fear, from too great an Opinion of *themselves,* and an uncharitable Opinion of *those Pastors,* and a Want of Faith in the great *Head* of the Churches, is a Breach of *Order,* and contrary to the *Scriptures.*

. . . .

2. *Private* Persons of *no Education,* and but *low Attainments* in Knowl-

edge, in the great Doctrines of the Gospel, without any *regular Call,* under a
Pretence of *exhorting,* taking upon
themselves to be *Preachers* of the Word
of GOD, we judge to be an heinous
Invasion of the *ministerial Office,* offensive to GOD, and destructive of these
Churches, contrary to *Scripture* . . .

. . . .

III. The *ordaining* and *separating* of
any Persons to the Work of the *evangelical Ministry,* at *large,* and without any
special Relation to a *particular Charge,*
which some of late have unhappily
gone into, we look upon as contrary to
the *Scriptures,* and directly opposite to
our *Platform,* . . .

. . . .

IV. The Spirit and Practice of *Separation* from the *particular Flocks* to
which Persons belong, to join themselves with and support, *lay Exhorters,*
or *Itinerants* is very subversive to the
Churches of CHRIST, opposite to the
Rule of the Gospel . . .

. . . .

V. Persons assuming to themselves
the Prerogative of GOD, to *look* into
and *judge* the *Hearts* of their Neighbours, *censure* and *condemn* their
Brethren, especially their *Ministers,* as
Pharisees, Arminians, blind, and *unconverted,* etc., where their Doctrines are
agreable to the Gospel, and their Lives
to their Christian Profession, is, we
think, most contrary to the Spirit and
Precepts of the Gospel, and the Example of CHRIST, and highly unbecoming
the Character of those who call themselves the Disciples of the meek and
lowly JESUS . . .

. . . .

VI. Though we deny not, that the
human Mind, under the Operation of
the Divine SPIRIT, may be overborn
with *Terrors* or *Joys;* yet, the many
Confusions that have appeared in some
Places, from the Vanity of Mind, and

ungoverned Passions of People, either
in the Excess of *Sorrow* or *Joy,* with the
disorderly Tumults and *indecent Be-
haviours* of Persons, we judge to be so
far from an Indication of the *special
Presence of* GOD with those Preachers
that have industriously excited and
countenanced them, or in the Assemblies where they prevail, that they are a
plain Evidence of the Weakness of
human Nature; as the History of the
Enthusiasms that have appear'd in the
World, in several Ages, manifests. . . .
At the same Time, we bear our Testimony against the *impious Spirit* of
those, that, from hence, take Occasion
to reproach the *Work of the Divine*
SPIRIT, in the Hearts of the Children of
GOD.

Upon the whole, we earnestly recommend the *Churches* of this *Country* to
the gracious Care and Conduct of the
great *Shepherd of the Sheep,* with our
thankful Acknowledgement for his merciful Regard to them, in supplying
them with faithful Pastors, and protect-
ing them from the Designs of their Enemies, and advancing his spiritual Kingdom in the Souls of so many from the
Foundations of this Country to this
Day; and where there is any special
Revival of pure Religion in any Parts
of our Land, at this Time, we would
give unto GOD all the Glory. And earnestly advise all our Brethren in the
Ministry, carefully to endeavour to
preserve their Churches pure in their
Doctrine, Discipline, and Manners, and
guard them against the Intrusions of
Itinerants and *Exhorters,* and to uphold the Spirit of Love towards one
another, and all Men; which, together
with their fervent Prayers, will be the
most likely Means, under GOD, to promote the true Religion of the *Holy*
JESUS, and hand it uncorrupt to succeeding Generations.

NATHANAEL EELLS, Moderator.

32. An Effusion of the Holy Spirit: *The Testimony and Advice* of an Assembly, 1743

[*The Testimony and Advice of an Assembly of Pastors of Churches in New-England, At a Meeting in Boston July 7. 1743. Occasion'd By the late happy Revival of Religion in many Parts of the Land . . .* (Boston, 1743), 5–12, 15]

If it is the Duty of every one, capable of Observation and Reflection, to take a constant religious Notice of what occurs in the daily Course of common Providence; how much more is it expected that those Events in the divine Economy, wherein there is a signal Display of the Power, Grace and Mercy of God in behalf of the Church, should be observ'd with sacred Wonder, Pleasure and Gratitude? Nor should the People of GOD content themselves with a *silent* Notice, but *publish with the Voice of Thanksgiving, and tell of all his wondrous Works.*

More particularly, When CHRIST is pleas'd to come into his Church in a plentiful Effusion of his Holy Spirit, by whose powerful Influences the Ministration of the Word is attended with uncommon Success, Salvation-Work carried on in an eminent Manner, and his Kingdom, which is *within Men,* and consists *in Righteousness and Peace and Joy in the Holy Ghost,* is notably advanced, THIS is an Event which above all other invites the Notice, and bespeaks the Praises of the Lord's People, and should be declar'd abroad for a *Memorial* of the divine Grace; as it tends to confirm the Divinity of a despised Gospel, and manifests the Work of the Holy Spirit in the Application of Redemption, which too many are ready to reproach; as it may have a happy Effect, by the divine Blessing, for the Revival of Religion in other Places, and the Enlargement of the Kingdom of CHRIST in the World; and as it tends to enliven the Prayers, strengthen the

Faith, and raise the Hopes, of such as are *waiting for the Kingdom of God,* and the coming on of the Glory of the latter Days.

But if it is justly expected of all who profess themselves the Disciples of CHRIST, that they should openly acknowledge and rejoice in a Work of this Nature, wherein the Honour of their divine Master is so much concerned; How much more is it to be look'd for from those who are employ'd in the *Ministry of the LORD JESUS,* and so stand in a special Relation to Him, as Servants of his Houshold, and Officers in his Kingdom? *These* stand as *Watchmen* upon the Walls of *Jerusalem;* and it is their Business not only to give the Alarm of War when the Enemy is approaching, but to sound the Trumpet of Praise when *the King of Zion cometh,* in a *meek* Triumph, *having Salvation.*

For these and other Reasons, We, whose Names are hereunto annexed, Pastors of Churches in *New-England,* met together in *Boston,* July 7th 1743, think it *our* indispensable Duty, (without judging or censuring such of our Brethren as cannot at present see Things in the same Light with us) in this open and conjunct Manner to declare, to the Glory of sovereign Grace, our full Perswasion, either from what we have seen our selves, or received upon credible Testimony, That there has been a *happy* and *remarkable Revival of Religion in many Parts of this Land, thro' an uncommon divine Influence;* after a long Time of great Decay and Deadness, and a sensible and very awful Withdraw of the Holy Spirit from his Sanctuary among us.

Tho' the Work of Grace wro't on the Hearts of Men by the Word and Spirit of GOD, and which has been more or less carried on in the Church from the Beginning, is always the same for Substance, and agrees, at one Time and another, in one Place or Person and another, as to the main Strokes and Lineaments of it, yet the *present Work* appears to be remarkable and extraordinary,

On Account of the *Numbers wrought upon*—We never before saw so many brought under Soul-Concern, and with Distress making the Inquiry, *What must we do to be saved?* And these Persons of all Characters and Ages. With Regard to the *Suddenness* and *quick Progress* of it—Many Persons and Places were surprized with the gracious Visit together, or near about the same Time; and the heavenly Influence diffus'd it self far and wide like the Light of the Morning. Also in Respect of the *Degree of Operation,* both in a Way of *Terror* and in a Way of *Consolation;* attended in many with unusual *bodily Effects.*

Not that all who are accounted the Subjects of the present Work, have had these extraordinary Degrees of previous Distress and subsequent Joy. But many, and we suppose the greater Number, have been wrought on in a more gentle and silent Way, and without any other Appearances than are common and usual at other Times, when Persons have been awakened to a solemn Concern about Salvation, and have been thought to have pass'd out of a State of Nature into a State of Grace.

As to those whose *inward Concern* has occasioned extraordinary *outward Distresses,* the most of them when we came to converse with them, were able to give, what appear'd to us, a rational

Account of what so affected their Minds; *viz.* A quick Sense of their *Guilt, Misery* and *Danger;* and they would often mention the Passages in the Sermons they heard, or particular Texts of Scripture, which were set home upon them with such a powerful Impression. And as to such whose *Joys* have carried them into *Transports* and *Extasies,* they in like Manner have accounted for *them,* from a lively Sense of the Danger they hop'd they were freed from, and the Happiness they were now possess'd of; such clear Views of divine and heavenly Things, and particularly of the Excellencies and Loveliness of JESUS CHRIST, and such sweet Tastes of redeeming Love as they never had before. The Instances were very few in which we had Reason to think these Affections were produced by *visionary* or sensible Representations, or by any other Images than such as the Scripture it self presents unto us.

And here we think it not amiss to declare, that in dealing with these Persons we have been careful to inform them, That the Nature of Conversion does not consist in these passionate Feelings; and to warn them not to look upon their State safe, because they have pass'd out of deep Distress into high Joys, unless they experience a Renovation of Nature, follow'd with a Change of Life, and a Course of vital Holiness. Nor have we gone into such an Opinion of the *bodily Effects* with which this Work has been attended in some of its Subjects, as to judge them any Signs that Persons who have been so affected, were *then* under a *saving Work* of the Spirit of God. No; we never so much as call'd these bodily Seizures, *Convictions;* or spake of them as the *immediate* Work of the Holy Spirit. Yet we do not think them inconsistent with a Work of GOD upon the Soul at that very Time; but judge that those inward Impressions which come from the Spirit of GOD, those Terrors and Consolations of which He is the Author, may, according to the natural Frame and Constitution which some Persons are of, occasion such bodily Effects. And therefore that these extraordinary outward Symptoms, are not an Argument that the Work is delusive, or from the Influence and Agency of the evil Spirit.

With Respect to Numbers of those who have been under the Impressions of the present Day, we must declare there is good Ground to conclude they are become *real Christians;* the Account they give of their Conviction and Consolation agreeing with the Standard of the Holy Scriptures, corresponding with the Experiences of the Saints, and evidenc'd by the external Fruits of Holiness in their Lives: So that they appear to those who have the nearest Access to them, as so many *Epistles of Christ,* written not with Ink, but by the Spirit of the living God, attesting to the *Genuineness* of the present Operation, and representing the *Excellency* of it.

Indeed many who appear'd to be under Convictions, and were much alter'd in their external Behaviour, when this Work began, and while it was most flourishing, have lost their Impressions, and are relaps'd into their former Manner of Life: Yet of those who were judg'd hopefully converted, and made a publick Profession of Religion, there have been *fewer Instances* of *Scandal* and *Apostacy* than might be expected. So that, as far as we are able to form a Judgment, the Face of Religion is lately chang'd much for the better in many of our Towns and Congregations; and together with a *Reformation* observable in diverse Instances, there appears to be more *experimental Godliness,* and *lively Christianity,* than the most of us can remember we have ever seen before.

Thus we have freely declar'd our Tho'ts as to the Work of GOD so re-

markably reviv'd in many Parts of this Land. And now, We desire to *bow the Knee in Thanksgiving to the God and Father of our Lord Jesus Christ,* that our *Eyes have seen,* and our *Ears heard* such Things. And while these are our Sentiments, we must necessarily be grieved at any Accounts sent abroad, representing this Work as all *Enthusiasm, Delusion* and *Disorder.*

Indeed it is not to be denied that in some Places many Irregularities and Extravagancies have been permitted to accompany it, which we would deeply lament and bewail before GOD, and look upon our selves oblig'd, for the Honour of the HOLY SPIRIT, and of his blessed Operations on the Souls of Men, to bear a publick and faithful Testimony against; tho' at the same Time it is to be acknowledg'd with much Thankfulness, that in *other Places,* where the Work has greatly flourish'd, there have been few if any of these Disorders and Excesses. But who can wonder, if at such a Time as this Satan should intermingle himself, to hinder and blemish a Work so directly contrary to the Interests of his own Kingdom? Or, if while so much good Seed is sowing, *the Enemy should be busy to sow Tares?* We would therefore, in the *Bowels of Jesus,* beseech such as have been Partakers of this Work, or are zealous to promote it, that they *be not ignorant of* Satan's *Devices;* that they *watch* and *pray* against Errors and Misconduct of every Kind, lest they blemish and hinder that which they desire to honour and advance. Particularly,

That they do not make *secret Impulses* on their Minds, without a due Regard to the *written Word,* the Rule of their Duty: A very dangerous Mistake which we apprehend some in these Times have gone into—That to avoid *Arminianism* they do not verge to the opposite Side of *Antinomianism;* while we would have others take good Heed to themselves, lest they be by some led into, or fix'd in, *Arminian Tenets,* under the Pretence of opposing *Antinomian Errors.* That *Laymen* do not invade the Ministerial Office, and under a Pretence of *Exhorting* set up *Preaching;* which is very contrary to Gospel Order, and tends to introduce Errors and Confusion into the Church. That *Ministers* do not invade the Province of others, and in *ordinary Cases* preach in another's Parish without his Knowledge, and against his Consent: Nor encourage *raw* and *indiscreet* young *Candidates,* in rushing into particular Places, and preaching publickly or privately, as some have done to the no small Disrepute and Damage of the Work in Places where it once promis'd to flourish. Tho' at the same Time we would have Ministers shew their Regard to the spiritual Welfare of their People, by suffering them to partake of the Gifts and Graces of *able, sound* and *zealous Preachers of the Word,* as GOD in his Providence may give Opportunity therefor: Being perswaded GOD has in this Day remarkably bless'd the Labours of *some* of his Servants who have *travelled* in preaching the Gospel of CHRIST. That People beware of entertaining Prejudices against their *own Pastors,* and don't run into *unscriptural* Separations. That they don't indulge a *disputatious Spirit,* which has been attended with mischievous Effects; nor discover a Spirit of *Censoriousness, Uncharitableness,* and rash *judging* the State of others; than which scarce any Thing has more blemish'd the Work of GOD amongst us. And while we would meekly *exhort* both Ministers and Christians, so far as is consistent with *Truth* and *Holiness,* to *follow the Things that make for Peace;* we would most earnestly *warn* all Sorts of Persons

not to *despise* these Out-pourings of the Spirit, lest a holy GOD be provok'd to withhold them, and instead thereof to pour out upon this People the Vials of his Wrath, in temporal Judgments and spiritual Plagues; and would *call* upon every one to improve this remarkable Season of Grace, and put in for a Share of the heavenly Blessings so liberally dispensed.

Finally,

We exhort the Children of GOD to *continue instant in Prayer,* that He, with whom is *the Residue of the Spirit,* would grant us fresh, more plentiful and extensive Effusions, that so this Wilderness, in all the Parts of it, may become a fruitful Field: That the present Appearances may be an *Earnest* of the glorious Things promis'd to the Church in the latter Days; when she shall *shine with the Glory of the LORD arisen upon her,* so as to dazzle the Eyes of Beholders, confound and put to Shame all her Enemies, rejoice the Hearts of her solicitous and now sadned Friends, and have a strong Influence and Resplendency throughout the Earth. *AMEN! Even so come LORD JESUS; Come quickly!*

After solemn repeated Prayer, free Inquiry and Debate, and serious Deliberation, the above Testimony and Advice signed by, [fifty-three names follow].

. . . .

We whose Names are under-written concur with the Testimony for the Substance of it, excepting against that Article of Itinerancy, or Ministers, and others, intruding into other Ministers Parishes without their Consent, which great Disorder we apprehend not sufficiently testify'd against, therein.

[Fifteen names follow].*

. . . .

* Ultimately 111 ministers subscribed to the testimony in one way or another. [Ed.]

CHAPTER SIX

NEW DIRECTIONS

A FEW ministers had grown dissatisfied with traditional Calvinism well before the Awakening stirred up controversy about the way to salvation. In the 1730s Robert Breck, a young man suspected of Arminian leanings, offered himself as a candidate for a pulpit in Springfield, Massachusetts. Jonathan Edwards and other Connecticut Valley clergymen did all in their power to block his ordination, but a number of prominent ministers, unabashed by Breck's dilution of Calvinism, supported him and thus implicitly sustained his beliefs. In these same years Jonathan Parsons of Lyme frankly confessed to being an Arminian. More commonly, ministers who had never openly repudiated the old doctrines simply omitted grace from their sermons in favor of teaching good works. Not until after the Awakening polarized opinion did these proto-Arminians frankly express their misgivings about the injustice of an arbitrary election of grace without regard to personal merit.

Experience Mayhew (1673–1758) was one of the first publicly to raise objections to salvation by grace alone. According to his introduction, Mayhew had long brooded over the problem before he published his book, *Grace Defended,* in 1744 (No. 33). The question he could not extinguish was why God appeared to offer salvation to all while granting it only to the elect. Was it fair to save some and damn others for no apparent reason? At last Mayhew concluded that all who truly sought God were rewarded with grace. Not that men saved themselves by good works; Mayhew wished to defend grace, not to eliminate it. But saving grace came in response to an earnest effort.

Though not an important figure in theological history, Mayhew raised a question that was to occupy ministers for years to come, and his answer, in one variation or another, was commonly accepted. Ultimately this line of thought led to Unitarianism, which as a movement, though not a denomination, emerged about this time, with Jonathan Mayhew, Experience's still more liberal son, as a leader. More ortho- dox theologians also struggled to enlarge the realm of human volition, albeit without diminishing the sovereignty and glory of God, and by the early nineteenth century many of them, such as Charles G. Fin- ney and Nathaniel W. Taylor, ended up as Arminians as well.

Before the ascendance of Arminianism, however, pristine Calvin- ism enjoyed a resurgence. During the Awakening and after, Edwards, Tennent, and Dickinson all expounded the impotency of man and his utter dependence on grace. The main thrust of their writings was to glorify God and bring man into subjection to Him. The apparent injustice in Calvinism which Mayhew complained of resulted from this yearning to grant God absolute sovereignty in the dispensation of salvation as in all else. Joseph Bellamy (1719–1790), a Connecticut New Light, was most concerned in his treatise on true religion (No. 34) to prevent the self from raising itself up as a rival to God. God's infinite glory and beauty demanded in return infinite love and obedi- ence without regard to self. Arminian aspirations to earn grace, Bel- lamy believed, were egotistical, motivated by self-love, not the love of God. The righteousness of unregenerate men was wholly inadequate to their salvation, and reliance on their own good works a pitiful and detestable evidence of pride. Arminians' claims on God were wisps of straw in the fiery furnace. Christ's atonement and redeeming grace were the only hope. Not until men gave up their pretensions to merit of any kind, were they humble enough to rely solely on Christ who alone was mighty enough to save.

Bellamy studied in Edwards's parsonage after graduation from Yale and became a leading figure in the development of the New England theology which emerged from the Awakening. Behind the movement was a vision of selfless love which Edwards himself best described in his work on *The Nature of True Virtue* (No. 35). Ed- wards saw all the perceiving intelligences in the universe interlaced with God in a perfect harmony of pure being. Neither hope for ad- vancement nor delight in God's beauty initially drew men to Him. The benevolence binding mind to mind was entirely disinterested, a perfect union of different beings like the notes of a chord. That was the absorbing love for which Bellamy yearned and which the presumptu- ous self disturbed.

Edwards and Bellamy expressed in theological language a desire for harmony that characterized eighteenth-century thought on many levels. In the same spirit, the forcing of will, the dominion of one over another, repelled this generation and compelled them to seek forms of order in which union was wholly voluntary. Nowadays we usually think of the Old Lights as the proponents of coercion in the creation of ecclesiastical order. They passed the laws in Connecticut restricting itineracy and they excluded the Log College men from the Synod of Philadelphia. But to the Old Light way of thinking, the New Lights were the coercive ones. John Caldwell, one of the most vitriolic opponents of the Awakening among the Boston ministry, complained that the New Lights delivered their judgments as if they spoke from Sinai (No. 36). Differing opinions were castigated as demonic, thus frightening people into compliance. Caldwell urged each man to judge for himself and not to put his conscience at the mercy of fanatics. He was in effect pleading for an order grounded in toleration of differences.

Actually the New Lights would not have entirely disagreed with Caldwell's principle. The ideal union of redeemed spirits could only be achieved within the church, not in society at large. There some form of tolerance was necessary. The Separates in Connecticut asked for tolerance just as Caldwell did (No. 37). And Samuel Davies (1723–1761) demanded liberty of conscience for his Presbyterian congregations in Anglican Virginia (No. 38). A second-generation New Light, as it were, Davies studied with Samuel Blair at Fagg's Manor before his assignment to Virginia in 1747, where small gatherings of converts had formed near the latter end of the revival. The Act of Toleration had guaranteed religious liberty to Presbyterians, but Virginia churchmen thought the dissenters to whom Davies ministered were malcontents rather than true converts. Davies wished to persuade the Bishop of London, who supervised the colonial church, that their commitment was made in good faith. Eventually Davies won the toleration he had worked for and rose to prominence among New Side Presbyterians in the middle colonies. From 1759 until his death in 1761 he presided over the College of New Jersey.

The pluralistic society which tolerance implied, and for which Davies and the Separates worked, fell far below the New Lights' ultimate expectations. Beyond the unity of mere tolerated differences, they desired the unity of love and holiness. In the early years of the Awakening, Edwards believed that America was moving rapidly toward this joyous state. In 1742 he gathered together his Northampton congregation and pledged them to forego their contention and selfishness and knit their hearts together as one (No. 39). As conversions slacked off and controversy increased in the later years of the Awakening, he saw the day of ultimate peace postponed, but he never abandoned his belief that God was preparing the world for the millenial reign through the outpouring of His Spirit. The predicted cataclysms and the violent destruction of evil were not a necessary prelude either. Edwards located these prophesied events at the end of the millenium (making him a postmillenialist). The ordinary workings of grace such as the colonies had experienced during the Awakening were sufficient to bring in the reign of Christ. That belief put the millenium within reach.

Aaron Burr, Edwards's son-in-law who presided over the College of New Jersey just before it moved to Princeton, differed with his father-in-law on the millenial calendar. Burr thought the calamities would precede the time of peace (making him a premillenialist). But the two men shared the prevailing hope for an age when the earth would be filled with the knowledge of the Lord as the waters cover the sea (No. 40). While the Awakening started innumerable ecclesiastical contentions and protracted theological debates, its intended goal, as the millenial expectations disclosed, was a society of joy, love, and union. Toward that goal the heirs of the Awakening, well into the nineteenth century, zealously directed their best efforts.

Moralism and Piety

33. The Injustice of Primitive Calvinism: Experience Mayhew, *Grace Defended*, 1744

[Experience Mayhew, *Grace Defended, in a Modest Plea for an Important Truth; Namely, That the Offer of Salvation made to Sinners in the Gospel, comprises in it an Offer of the Grace given in Regeneration* . . . (Boston, 1744), iii–v, 146–147, 172–175, 194–199]

I have been from my Youth naturally inclined to endeavour to understand what I believe; and why I believe this or that Proposition to be true: And yet I very readily acknowledge, That when any Proposition is evidently delivered in the Scriptures of Truth, I ought for that Reason to believe it to be true, tho' I cannot fully comprehend the same, and am not able to answer all Objections that can be made against it: But then I must be sure that it is indeed delivered in the divine Oracles —in which Case *every Tho't should be*

captivated to the Obedience of CHRIST.

In the little Reading for which I have had Leisure and Opportunity, I have been chiefly conversant in the Writings of *Calvinists;* yet I confess I have endeavoured not to be wholly ignorant of the Principles of those who embrace or incline to the *Arminian Hypothesis;* and have always preferred the Former as much as best of the Two: So that I cannot justly be looked upon as endeavoring to overthrow the First, and establish the Other. This is what I do not at all intend; but what I endeavour is, to remove some Things out of the Way, commonly asserted by *Calvinists,* which I think may be dismissed from their Hypothesis, being no Ways necessary in order to the Support of the principal Articles in that Scheme; but on the contrary, render it the more difficult to be received and defended. And what I to this End advance, I humbly submit to the Censure of the *Learned* and *Judicious.*

What is principally insisted on in this Essay, is, *That the Offer of Salvation made to Sinners in the Gospel, does comprise in it an Offer, or conditional Promise, of the Grace given in Regeneration.* I believe there is as really a conditional Offer of this made to sinful Men, in the Gospel of the Son of GOD, as there is of Pardon of Sin, Justification, etc. In this I think I differ from most that are in the *calvinian Scheme:* And I confess I was for many Years otherwise minded; but while I endeavoured to defend what I then believed, the Objections that offered themselves to my Mind against what I had admitted as true, prevailed on me first to doubt of it, and by Degrees to receive the Doctrine I now endeavour to defend: And if I make good what I assert I think I do not therein diminish, but exalt GOD's Grace.

I for several Years endeavoured in a more private Way to get Satisfaction in these Points, wherein I was fallen into a Way of thinking somewhat different from many others, before I entertained any Tho'ts of publishing my Sentiments. I frequently discoursed with and sometimes wrote to learned Divines, concerning the Matters here discoursed of; and had, I think, no Matter of Conviction that I was under any Mistakes; much less, that I had advanced any dangerous Errors. And I cannot deny but that some pious and learned Divines have spoken somewhat favoura-bly of my Hypothesis; and have expressed their Willingness that I should, by the Press, *shew my Opinion.*

I have in this Essay, endeavoured not to provoke or offend any Person whatsoever; and now profess, that I greatly respect and honour those, whose Sentiments differ from some of mine, discovered in this Discourse: And I have therefore chosen rather to argue on the Things considered, than meddle with the Persons from whose Opinions I dissent.

And after all that I have said for the Support of my own Hypothesis, (in the Explanation of which I have endeavoured to be very *free* and *open*) I think I am fully resolved seriously to weigh every Thing that shall be offered for my Conviction, according to the best of my Skill and Judgment; and I hope if I am in an Error, my Fault is not unpardonable.

I also hope, that if I am wrong in any of my Sentiments, I have taken such Care to secure the fundamental Articles in the Doctrine of *Grace,* that Men's Souls will not be endangered by any Thing advanced in this Attempt to set some Things in a clearer Light than they seem to me to be set in, in such Books as I have had Opportunity to read; but it may be thro' my own ignorance understand not.

I have not in this Essay had any Design against the Doctrine of *Original Sin.* GOD's *eternal Decrees* and *Providence,* the Difference betwixt *common* and *special Grace,* and the *Sovereignty of* GOD in the Affair of Man's Salvation. For according to my Hypothesis, as well as that I oppose, that is a great Truth maintained by the Apostle, Rom. ix. *It is not of him that willeth, nor of him that runneth, but of GOD that sheweth Mercy.* These Things I not only allow, but occasionally endeavour to defend; tho' this not being my principal Design, I have not much enlarged on them: But my main Design is that above expressed.

. . . .

The Grace of Regeneration cannot, on my Principles, be given according to Works; because, on my Hypothesis, no Man can perform any good Works, properly and strictly so called, 'till after he is regenerate or born again. That Grace may be given according to Works, two Things seem necessarily required, viz. (1) That the Works are really good and holy, with Regard to which the Grace intended is supposed to be given: For it is not likely that God should give his Grace as a Reward for Works not truly good and holy. (2) That the Works intended be done before the Grace is bestowed, which is supposed to be given as a Reward of them: For the Thing for which a Reward is given must needs be prior to that which is given as a Reward of it. But I, as well as those with whom I dispute, am fully of Opinion, that no Man can perform any good Action, (meaning by good what is in a proper and strict Sense so,) 'till after he is *born of the Spirit, or created anew unto good Works,* as in *Col.* 3. 10. with which compare *Ezek.* 36. 26, 27. and *Luke* 6. 43, 44, 45. How then should the Grace of Regeneration be given, on my Principles, according to Men's good Works or Merits?

If we duly consider what, according to my Principles, is really required of Sinners, in order to their obtaining the Grace of Regeneration, it will plainly appear, that Grace is not given to them according to Works. The Condition on which, according to my Opinion, Grace is offered to them, does neither consist in the perfect Obedience which the Covenant of Works required, not yet in such Holiness as the Gospel requireth of regenerate Saints: If it required the last of these no Person could even be regenerated or born again.

But what the Gospel requires of un-

regenerate Sinners, to the mentioned End, comprises in it such Things as these, viz. (1) That they acknowledge their Sinfulness, both by Nature and Practice, and that they deserve eternal Damnation. (2) That they acknowledge ·the Guilt of their many and mighty Sins, and that without the Pardon of them they never can be saved. (3) That they are sensible of the Corruption of their Natures, and their Need of regenerating Grace. (4) That they believe the good Tidings of that Salvation by Jesus Christ, which is revealed in the Gospel, and do not despair of God's Mercy. (5) That they seek earnestly to God for the Pardon of their Sins, and the regenerating Influences of his Spirit, seriously waiting on him in the the Use of those Means which he has directed to, in order to their obtaining these Mercies. (6) That they carefully avoid all those sinful Courses which tend to provoke him to deny his Holy Spirit, or with-hold the same from them. (7) That they persevere in the Way of their Duty, that has now been expressed. (8) That they confess, that in all this they are unprofitable Servants, and instead of doing more than their Duty, they fall infinitely short of it, and so are not worth of the least of God's Mercies, much less of Pardon of Sin, and the saving Graces of God's Spirit here, and eternal Glory hereafter. (9) That they earnestly plead with God the Promises of his Mercy, made to such as seek him for it; such as we have in *Matth.* 7. 7,—11. *Prov.* 1, 22, 23, *Luke* 11. 9,—13. *Prov.* 2. 1,—5. *Hos.* 6. 3.

If in this Way Sinners seek and obtain the saving Graces of God's holy Spirit, they will find no Occasion of boasting that they obtained them by Works of Righteousness which they have done, or by the Desert of their own good Works, and so have merited eternal Life at the Hand of God. There is not the least Appearance of any such

Thing in the Method proposed, of Sinners seeking Mercy of the Lord; they having Nothing to recommend them to him, or to plead with him, but their own Poverty and Misery, and the Riches of this Grace and Mercy, and most gracious Covenant: All which is nothing like trusting in, and pleading, their own Righteousness. Our supposing that to our obtaining the Grace of God, our begging God's Mercy, pleading the Merits of his Son, and his Truth and Faithfulness to his Covenant, is not, I think, to hold, that Grace is given according to Works, but well consisteth with that Eph. 2. 9. and Rom. 3. 27. *Where is Boasting then? It is excluded. By what Law? Of Works? Nay: But by the Law of Faith.*

. . . .

Now the great Question here is, Whether when Sinners are under such a Work of God's Spirit, with the external Means afforded to such as enjoy the Gospel, and yet do not come to Christ for Life; whether, I say, these remain, being under such Advantages, without any Power to believe to the saving of their Souls?

Now if this be affirmed by any, I confess I cannot agree with them in their Sentiments.

But for preventing Mistakes in this important Article, I shall here distinguish of Impotency, which is two-fold; and each of these Kinds does suppose there may be a Power opposite to it. The Kinds of Impotency I here Intend are by some, if I mistake not, called *natural* and *moral.* I shall speak of these two Kinds of Impotence according to the Notion I my self have of them.

And *first,* By what I call a natural Impotence, I intend such an Inability to do a Thing, as renders the Thing utterly impossible to be done by a Person without having a new Power or Powers given to him. Thus it is properly said of a blind Man, that he cannot see; and of a deaf Man, that he cannot hear: And thus I acknowledge that it may be truly said of a Person in a State of Nature; not being born of the Spirit, that he cannot perform any Actions that are truly spiritual or holy. This is as impossible as it is for a *Thorn-Bush* to bear *Figs,* or for a *Bramble-Bush* to bear *Grapes, Luke* 6. 44. Nothing less than changing the Nature of a Tree will render it capable of this. And thus he that is utterly destitute of saving Grace, cannot bring forth any Fruits of Holiness, till he is savingly renew'd and made a new Creature, *Eph.* 2. 10. No Arguments, Motives, or Persuasions can give Power to a Man in this Sense unable to do a Thing, to perform it.

But then, *secondly,* There is another Kind of Impotency, which arises only from Error in Men's Judgments, and Obstinacy in their Wills; and this does in some Sort disable Persons from doing some Things which otherwise they might do, were their Prejudices removed. However it may not be unfitly said of Persons under such Disadvantages, that they cannot for the present do this or that Thing, which they have an Aversion to, when yet such Persons want not a natural Power to perform what they are said to be unable to do. Thus when a Man is persuaded that his doing this or that which he is urged to do, will prove hurtful and injurious to him, it may be said, that at present he cannot do it, *i. e.* he cannot find in his Heart a Willingness to engage in doing that which he thinks will rather hurt him than do him good: Or if he thinks he might obtain some Benefit by doing the Thing, yet thinks the Advantages he might reap by it will not countervail the Difficulties he must undergo in that Self-denial which is requisite in order to it, he cannot bring himself to a Willingness to do it.

Persons are in Scripture in this Sense sometimes spoken of as unable to do this, that or the other Thing, which yet really they want not a natural Power to perform. Thus it is said of *Joseph*'s Brethren, and *they hated him so, that they could not speak peaceably of him,* (Gen. 37. 4.) Such Impotence as this is plainly spoken of by our Saviour, and the Nature of it unfolded in Luke 11. 5, 6, 7, 8. *He said unto them, Which of you shall have a Friend, and shall go unto him at Midnight, and shall say unto him, Friend, Lend me three Loaves; for a Friend of mine is come to me, and I have nothing to set before him: And he from within shall answer, and say, Trouble me not; the Door is now shut, and my Children are with me in Bed; I cannot rise to give thee. I say unto you, tho' he will not rise to give him because he is his Friend; yet because of his Importunity he will rise, and give him as many as he needth.* Note here, *I cannot rise to give thee,* in the latter End of Verse 7, is nothing more than, he *will not,* Verse 8. And this which he would not, he is by and by supposed to do. The same Kind of Impotency is pleaded in Excuse for not going to the great Gospel-Feast, Luke 14. 20. *I have married a Wife, and therefore I cannot come.* And our Saviour himself acknowledges this Sort of Impotency in some Men with Respect to their believing in him, John 5. 44. *How can ye believe which receive Honour one of another, and seek not the Honour that cometh from God only?* This Kind of Impotency is not an absolute and utter Inability to do the Thing which Men are sometimes said to be unable to do. This is often made evident by Persons actually doing what they have alledged themselves to have no Power for. Their *could not,* being indeed not more than this, that they *would not,* and not their being utterly unable to do the Thing intended. This is a Sort of *Cannot* which may be cured by good Instructions and Arguments which yet properly give no

new Power; and Men may help themselves against this Sort of Inability by reasoning themselves out of their Prejudices against the Things, which they and others may imagine they have no Power to do; so that they may see it was not Want of Power, but Want of a Will, that hindred them from doing as they should.

In the Sense now explained I acknowledge, that some cannot come to Christ for Life, and never will, except the Father draw them, as in *John* 6. 44. But then our Lord himself shews wherein this Inability consists. John 5. 40. *Ye will not come to me, that ye might have Life;* and Matth. 23. 37. *How often would I have gathered thy Children together, even as a Hen gathereth her Chickens under her Wings, and ye would not.* It would, in my Opinion, be very improper to charge Men's not coming to Christ merely on their wilful Rebellion, if a real Inability were the Cause of it.

If it be here said to be true of all that do not come to Christ for Life, that, in a strict and proper Sense, they have no Power so to do, I must crave Leave to dissent from this, 'till I can see otherwise than at present I can do.

And I shall only here insist a little more fully on one Argument against what I here oppose. I desire to know what Kindness it is to any Sinner, that he has an Offer of Salvation made to him in the Gospel, if he have no Power given to him to accept of that Offer. What Kindness is it to a Person that he has Tidings of a Saviour, and is promised that he shall be saved by him, on this Condition that he believeth on him, when, this notwithstanding, God never did nor ever will give him any Power to believe? Especially supposing that if he does not believe, he shall be punished with a much sorer Punishment than he should have been, if he had never had an Offer of eternal Life made to him; which will be the Case of such as enjoy the Gospel, and yet do not believe, *Matth.* 10. 15. I confess I think that God is much more merciful unto such as never have any Offer of Life, than he is to those who have an Offer on such Terms.

. . . .

On the Hypothesis pleaded for in this Discourse, I conceive some Grounds to hope for a better Accommodation of some of the Points in Controversy, betwixt those who are commonly called *Calvinists,* and such as are called *Arminians;* At least I hope that if my Hypothesis might be admitted, the Way would be thereby paved for the contending Parties to come to a better Understanding of some (at least one) of the most important Articles controverted betwixt them; and this without the least Damage to the Substance of that Hypothesis which *Calvinists* endeavour to support, against those who are for the *Arminian* Scheme, in which we think some of the Doctrines of Grace are not well asserted.

Many of those by whom several of the Arminian Doctrines seem to be something favoured, appear to me to be Persons of great Seriousness; and I cannot think that the Opposition which they sometimes make against some Things in the Scheme by Calvinists pleaded for, ariseth from an Enmity in their Hearts against the Grace of God; but rather, left while Men maintain the Sovereignty of God, in the Affair of Man's Salvation, in the Manner that many Calvinists do, they should thereby reflect some Dishonour on the Attributes of his Justice and Holiness, the doing of which they seem to dread. However, I believe it will be safest for us to be as charitable as may be, in our Opinion of such Persons; and that we take Care not to make the Difference more and greater than we need.

Now, suppose the Hypothesis which I have advanced and pleaded for, be a Truth, I hope our owning and allowing of it wou'd, as I have said, render several other Things contained in the Scheme maintained by the Orthodox, the more easy to be admitted by such as at present seem to be afraid to own and embrace them. And that I may make what I here say the more probable, I will give some Instances, in which I apprehend Things might prove as I hope and desire they may.

The *first* of these is the Case of *Original Sin. Calvinists* generally maintain, that the Guilt of *Adam*'s first and great Transgression, has fallen on all his Posterity; and that they are all thereby become naturally *Children of Wrath,* and *Heirs of Death.* They hold also, that on the Apostacy of our first Parents from God, they lost his Image, in which they were created; and their Natures were so depraved, that they were thereby rendered uncapable of performing any Actions truly gracious and holy, and as such acceptable to the Lord; and so were uncapable of Communion with him, and the Enjoyment of him, without the Pardon of Sin and renewing Grace. They also maintain that in this deplorable State all the Off-spring of the first *Adam* are involved.

And hereupon they further affirm, that before Men's Regeneration, they are utterly uncapable to accept the Terms, or perform the Conditions, required of Sinners in the Gospel, in Order to their Salvation; because they suppose the Gospel in this Case requireth something, the doing whereof supposeth Men first *born again,* and become *new* Creatures; which, they say, few ever attain to: Nor have Sinners any Offer of this Grace made to them. Now, if it be thus, thinks the Person inclining to *Arminianism;* (and who is there but by nature is not inclined to Error?) if this be the Doctrine of *original Sin,* and the Consequences following on it, I cannot, I will not receive it, 'till I can see such Evidences for it, as will compel me to yield my Assent thereunto. And now scarce any Evidence will convince such Persons that a Doctrine is true, that is so hard to be digested.

But now let such Dissenters from the *calvinian Doctrines* be told, that the Doctrine of *original Sin* is indeed a great Truth; and that the same may be defended, being duly stated and understood; but that it is true also, that God had a Design of glorifying his Grace and Mercy, in the Redemption of Mankind when fallen into a State of Sin; and that for this end, God sent his Son into the World so to die for all Men, that they might be saved on the Terms of a New Covenant, which Terms are not such as they are not able to comply with, by the Help of God's Grace afforded to them, nor such that they must be savingly converted or born again, before, and in order to, their Performance of them; but such as thro' God's Help, by his Word and Spirit, they may come up to in their present State; and so obtain Deliverance from Sin and Death, if it be not their own Fault in refusing the Mercies offered to them. If these Truths are owned and allowed, I think many People would not be so averse to the Doctrine of *original Sin* as they now seem to be: For thus the Gospel proposeth a Remedy against it, to every Person afflicted with the Sense of it, inasmuch as it tells every Sinner how he may come to have his Nature renewed, and the Image of God restored in him; and that the Condition unto this End required of him, is not such as a Person in a State of Nature cannot by God's Help perform.

Secondly, Another Point which I here intend is that of *Conversion* or *Regeneration:* In this I think *Calvinists* and *Arminians* differ greatly. Calvinists (at least many of them) hold, that true

saving *Conversion,* which they also call *Regeneration,* is a great Change wrought in the Soul of a Sinner by the Spirit of God, whereby he has a new Biass or Disposition given him. By this, according to them, the lost Image of God is restored to a Sinner: Of carnal he is hereby made spiritual, having *a new Heart given to him, and a new Spirit put within him,* as in *Ezek.* 36. 26. And this they think is an *instantaneous Change;* and that the Soul is *passive* in it, having no Hand in the working of it; but that it is wholly a Work of God by his Holy Spirit, creating Men anew in Christ Jesus unto good Works, as in *Eph.* 2. 10. *Psal.* 51. 10. *John* 3. 8. and Chap. I. 13. *Eph.* 2. 19, 20. and many other Places.

Add hereunto, that, according to Calvinists, Sinners can do no Actions that are spiritually good, or truly holy, 'till this Change be first wrought in them; and consequently, it is impossible, (as they think) that any Sinner should perform the Condition on which Salvation is offered to him, 'till he is first *converted* and *born of the Spirit,* as is above expressed. And they further think, (some of them at least) that God has no where offered or promised in his Work, on any Condition whatsoever, that he will work such a Change in any Sinner's Soul: And yet if any Sinner does not believe with such a Kind of Faith as can only be exercised by one already so converted, he shall be more severely punished, than if he had never had any Offer of Salvation made to him.

Now those who are inclined to *Arminianism* think this Doctrine is so harsh they cannot endure it: Nor does it seem to them any Way agreeable to the infinite Goodness and Mercy of God, made known and revealed in the Gospel. And then such seek to find some Flaws in the Doctrine mentioned; and what most readily offers it self to their Mind is, that those who thus hold are mistaken with Respect to the Nature of Conversion; and that Conversion or Regeneration is no such Thing, as they imagine it to be.

The Nature of Man (think they) is not so corrupted, as to need such a mighty Work of the Spirit of God, in order to the changing of it. The Ministry of the Word, they think, and those Motions and Convictions of God's Spirit, which he affords to Sinners under the Gospel, are sufficient to work all the Change in them that is necessary in order to their eternal Happiness: And what is talked of more than this, is a mere Fiction of some Men's Brains, and has no Foundation in the Word of God, on which it can be built.

But unto such as these I say, according to my Hypothesis, there is indeed a great Mistake relating to the Matter under Consideration; but it does not lye, as they imagine, in the Doctrine of *Regeneration* by *Calvinists* maintained. Sinners need by Conversion or Regeneration, such a Change as they hold necessary. The Depravation of their Natures by *original Sin*, renders such a Change indispensibly needful, as our Saviour himself teacheth, *John* 3. 3–8. and as is in many other Places of Scripture manifested.

But the *Mistake* lies in this, that it is not truly supposed and maintained, that the Condition required of Sinners in the Gospel, in order to their Salvation, is, that they believe and repent with a Kind of Faith and Repentance, of which no Sinner can be the Subject, who is not first *born of God, and so a new Creature;* and consequently in a State of Salvation, before ever he exerciseth such Faith and Repentance: When indeed, God's giving us that Grace whereof such Faith and Repentance is the Fruit and Exercise, is his saving us; not that whereby we are enabled and disposed to perform the Condition required of us. No: The Condition required of us, is, that we, *wretched* and *miserable,* and *poor,* and *blind,* and *naked* as we are, apply our selves to Jesus Christ, for *Gold tried in the Fire,* (true Grace) *that we may be rich;* for *white Raiment,* (his perfect Righteousness) *that we may be cloathed, and that the Shame of our Nakedness do not appear;* and for *Eye-Salve, to anoint our Eyes, that we may see.* We must not stay 'till we are renewed and sanctified by the Spirit of God, before we do this; but out of a Sense of our Misery, make Haste to Christ to do it for us: And awakened Sinners may, by the Help of that *Grace of God,* which they should not *receive in vain,* do thus. Tho' their Hearts are not yet changed by the Grace of Regeneration; yet they may go to him for that Grace. When God requires this of us, he requires not what is above our Power, and impossible for us, being furnished with that mentioned Grace of his, 2 *Cor.* 6. 1. Tho' we cannot regenerate our selves, yet it is not true, that we cannot apply our selves to Christ to work this great Change in us by his Spirit. And he invites and requires us thus to do; and has promised, that if we do, he will not *cast us out,* John. 6. 37.

Let this Doctrine be owned and preached among us, to awakened Sinners, tho' unsanctified, that we may thereby encourage them to lay hold on God's Mercy; and it is possible *Arminians* may then think, that they have far less to cavil against in our Doctrine of Regeneration, than they should have if this were denied. I am in Hopes, that if this Truth were duly acknowledged, such as are disposed to *Arminianism* among us, would be more inclined to receive our Doctrine, in such Articles of it as are indeed essential to it.

Thirdly, There is one Point more, which is very essential to the Scheme which I have endeavoured to explain and confirm; which being allowed, and clearly asserted among us, would have a great Tendency to gain over to us such as lean towards *Arminianism;* and make them more favourably inclined towards our Doctrine: And this is, That *God does not either by his Decree, or the Execution of it, lay a Necessity on any of his Creatures to sin against him.* This is one of the Things, about which the *Arminians* contend very earnestly with *Calvinists,* with Relation to our Doctrine: And tho' much of what they say on this Head, is, if I mistake not, very unjust; yet on the other Hand, I am of Opinion that some *Calvinists* have said Things with Respect to God's Degree, which have given too much Occasion of Offence to those who differ in Judgment from them. If it were granted on our Part, (1) That God does neither in his Decree, nor in the Execution of it, take away the Liberty of free Agents, such as Men and Angels are. (2) That when it is said, that God *wills* or *decrees* the Actions of Sinful Men, this must not be understood of an effective Decree, but permissive only: The

Nature of divine Permission being rightly understood. (3) That by the efficiency of God, whereby he executeth his Decree, he does not by any Action of his, lay his Creatures under a Necessity of doing Actions wherein they sin against him: The Concourse of the first Cause with the second, does not infer this. If these Things were well asserted and explained, it would, I think, tend much to quiet the Minds of such as are apt to be stumbled at the Doctrine of *Calvinists* about them.

What I have briefly said of such a Tendency, in this Essay, is not only designed as a Testimony to the Truth; but as what I hope, if allowed to be agreeable thereunto, might in some Measure serve to quiet the tumultuating Thoughts of those who have entertained such an Opinion of the Doctrine of God's Decree and Providence, as does not become the infinite Perfections of his Nature; and who are displeased at such as maintain the Truth in these Points.

34. The Selfless Love of God: Joseph Bellamy, *True Religion Delineated*, 1750

[Joseph Bellamy, *True Religion Delineated; Or, Experimental Religion, As Distinguished from Formality on the One Hand, and Enthusiasm on the Other, Set in a Scriptural and Rational Light, in Two Discourses,* in *The Works of Joseph Bellamy* . . . (Boston, 1853), I, 14–18, 50–52, 56–57, 97–100, 336–339, 341–343]

I am to show what is implied in love to God. And,

1. *A true knowledge of God* is implied; for this lays the foundation of love. A spiritual sight of God, and a sense of his glory and beauty, begets love. When he that commanded the light to shine out of darkness, shines in our hearts, and gives us the light of the knowledge of the glory of God; and when we, with open face, behold, as in

a glass, the glory of the Lord, then we are changed into the same image: the temper and frame of our hearts become like God's, to speak after the manner of men: we begin to feel towards God, in a measure, as he does towards himself; that is, to love him with all our hearts. (2 Cor. iii. 18; iv. 6.) For now we begin to perceive the grounds and reasons of that infinite esteem he has of himself, and infinite complacency in himself, and why he commands all the world to love and adore him. And the same grounds and reasons which move him thus to love himself, and command all the world to do so too, enkindle the divine flame in our hearts. When we see God, in a measure, such as he sees himself to be, and have a sense of his glory and beauty in being what he is, in a measure, as he himself has, then we begin to love him with the same kind of love, and from the same motives, as he himself does; only in an infinitely inferior degree. This sight and sense of God discovers the grounds of love to him. We see why he requires us to love him, and why we ought to love him—how right and fit it is; and so we cannot but love him.

This true knowledge of God supposes, that, in a measure, we see God to be just such a one as he is; and, in a measure, have a sense of his infinite glory and beauty in being such. For if our apprehensions of God are not right, it is not God we love, but only a false image of him framed in our own fancy. And if we have not a sense of his glory and beauty in being what he is, it is impossible we should truly love and esteem him for being such. To love God for being what he is, and yet not to have any sense of his glory and beauty in being such, implies a contradiction; for it supposes we have a sense of his glory and beauty when we have not; a sense of the beauty and amiableness of any object being always necessarily implied in love to it. Where no beauty or amiableness is seen, there can be no love. Love cannot be forced. Forced love is no love. If we are obliged to try to force ourselves to love any body, it is a sign they are very odious in our eyes, or at least that we see no beauty or amiableness in them, no form or comeliness, wherefore we should desire or delight in them. (Cant. viii. 7.) In all cases, so far as we see beauty, so far we love, and no further.

Most certainly that knowledge of God which is necessary to lay a foundation of genuine love to him, implies not only right apprehensions of what he is, but also a sense of his glory and beauty in being such; for such a knowledge of God as consists merely in speculation, let it rise ever so high, and be ever so clear, will never move us to love him. Mere speculation, where there is no sense of beauty, will no sooner fill the heart with love, than a looking-glass will be filled with love by the image of a beautiful countenance, which looks into it; and a mere speculative knowledge of God, will not, cannot, beget a sense of his beauty in being what he is, when there is naturally no disposition in our hearts to account him glorious in being such, but wholly to the contrary. "The carnal mind is enmity against God." When natures are in perfect contrariety, the one sinful, and the other holy, the more they are known to each other, the more is mutual hatred stirred up, and their entire aversion to each other becomes more sensible. The more they know of one another, the greater is their dislike, and the plainer do they feel it. Doubtless the fallen angels have a great degree of speculative knowledge; they have a very clear sight and great sense of what God is; but the more they know of God, the more they hate him; that is, their hatred and aversion is stirred up the more, and they feel it plainer. So, awakened sinners, when under deep and thorough conviction, have comparatively a very clear sight and great sense of God; but it only makes them see and feel their native enmity, which before lay hid. A sight and sense of what God is, makes them see and feel what his law is, and so what their duty is, and so what their sinfulness is, and so what their danger is; it makes the commandment come, and so sin revives, and they die. The clearer sight and the greater sense they have of what God is, the more plainly do they perceive that perfect contrariety between his nature and theirs: their aversion to God becomes discernible; they begin to see what enemies they are to him: and so the secret hypocrisy there has been in all their pretences of love, is discovered; and so their high conceit of their goodness, and all their hopes of finding favor in the sight of God upon the account of it, cease, die away, and come to nothing. "Sin revived and I died." The greater sight and sense they have of what God is, the plainer do they feel that they have no love to him, but the greatest aversion; for the more they know of God, the more their native enmity is stirred up. So, again, as soon as ever an unregenerate sinner enters into the world of spirits, where he has a much clearer sight and greater sense of what God is, immediately his native enmity works to perfection, and he blasphemes like a very devil; and that although perhaps he died full of seeming love and joy. As the Galatians, who once loved Paul, so as that they could even have plucked out their eyes and have given them to him, yet, when afterwards they came to know more clearly what kind of man he was, then they turned his enemies. And so, finally, all the wicked, at the day of judgment, when they shall see very clearly what God is, will thereby only have all the enmity of their hearts stirred to perfection. From all which it is exceedingly manifest, that the clearest speculative knowledge of God is so far from bringing an unholy heart to love God, that it will only stir up the more aversion; and therefore that knowledge of God which lays the foundation of love, must imply not only right apprehensions of what God is, but also a sense of his glory and beauty in being such.

Wicked men and devils may know what God is, but none but holy beings have any sense of his infinite glory and beauty in being such; which *sense* in Scripture language, is called *seeing* and *knowing*. "Whosoever sinneth, hath not seen him, neither known him." "He that doeth evil hath not seen God." "He that saith, I know him, and keepeth not his commandments, is a liar, and the truth is not in him." Because wicked men have no sense of his glory and beauty, therefore they are said not to know God; for all knowledge without this is vain; it is but the form of knowledge. It will never enkindle divine love. And, in Scripture, sinners are said to be blind, because, after all their light and knowledge, they have no sense of God's glory in being what he is, and so have no heart to love him. And hence also they are said to be dead. They know nothing of the ineffable glory of the divine nature, and the love of God is not in them. (John v. 42; viii. 19, 55.)

. . . .

1. This obligation which we are under to love God with all our hearts, resulting from the infinite excellency of the divine nature, is binding *antecedently to any consideration of advantage or disadvantage, of rewards or punishments, or even of the positive will and law of God himself.* To love God with all our hearts, naturally tends to make us happy, and the contrary, to make us miserable; and there are glorious rewards promised on the one hand, and dreadful punishments threatened on the other. And God, as Governor of the world, has, with all his authority, by his law, expressly required us to love him with all our hearts, and forbidden the contrary; and all these things are binding; but yet the infinite excellency of the divine nature lays us under bonds prior to any consideration of these things. So that if our interest did not at all lie at stake, and if there

had never been any express law in the case, yet it would be right, and our indispensable duty, to love God with all our hearts. His being infinitely lovely in himself, makes it our duty to love him; for he is in himself worthy of our highest esteem. He deserves it; it is in the nature of things his due; and that antecedent to any selfish consideration, or any express law in the case. To suppose the contrary, is to deny the infinite amiableness of the divine nature, and to take away the very foundation of the law itself, and the very reason of all rewards and punishments. For if our supreme love is not due to God, then he is not infinitely lovely; and if he does not deserve to be loved with all our hearts, why does he require it? And if, in the nature of things, it is not right and fit that we should love him, and the contrary unfit and wrong, what grounds are there for rewards or punishments? So that it is evident the infinite excellency of the divine nature binds us, and makes it our duty, antecedent to any consideration of advantage or disadvantage, rewards or punishments, or even of the positive will and law of God, to love God with all our hearts. And therefore our love must primarily take its rise from a sense of this infinite excellency of the divine nature, as has been before observed; and that seeming love, which arises merely from selfish considerations, from the fear of punishment or hope of reward, or because the law requires it, and so it is a duty and must be done, is not genuine, but is a selfish, a mercenary, and a forced thing. How evidently, therefore, do those discover their hypocrisy, who are wont to talk after the following manner: "If I am elected, I shall be saved, let me do what I will; and if I am not elected, I shall be damned, let me do what I can, and therefore it is no matter how I live." And again, after this sort: "If I knew certainly that God

had made no promises to the duties of the unregenerate, as some pretend, I would never do any more in religion." Surely they had as good say that they have no regard at all to the infinite excellency of the divine nature, but are entirely influenced by selfish and mercenary motives in all they do. They do not seem to understand that they are under infinite obligations to love God with all their hearts, and obey him in every thing, resulting from God's being what he is, and that antecedent to all selfish considerations. Such know not God. (1 John iii. 6.)

2. This obligation, resulting from the intrinsic excellency and amiableness of the divine nature, is *infinitely* binding, because this excellency and amiableness is in itself infinite. Our obligation arises from his desert, but he infinitely deserves our love, because he is infinitely lovely. When any person is lovely and honorable, reason teaches us that we ought to love and honor him, and that it is wrong to dislike and despise him. And the more lovely and honorable, the greater is our obligation to love and honor him, and the more aggravately vile is it to treat him with contempt. Since, therefore, God is a being of infinite dignity, greatness, glory, and excellency, hence we are under an infinite obligation to love him with all our hearts, and it is infinitely wrong not to do so. Since he is infinitely worthy to be honored and obeyed by us, therefore we are under an infinite obligation to honor and obey him; and that with all our heart, and soul, and mind, and strength.

. . . .

(2.) If we are under an infinite obligation to love God supremely, live to him ultimately, and take everlasting delight in him, because of his infinite glory and excellency, then the least disposition to disesteem him, to be indifferent about his interest and honor, or to disrelish communion with him; or the least disposition to love ourselves more than God, and be more concerned about our interest and honor than about his, and to be pleased and delighted in the things of the world more than in him, must, consequently, be infinitely sinful, as is self-evident.

When, therefore, the great Governor of the world threatens eternal damnation for the least sin, (Gal. iii. 10,) he does the thing that is perfectly right; for an infinite evil deserves an infinite punishment.

Hence, also, it is no wonder that the holiest saint on earth mourns so bitterly, and loathes and abhors himself so exceedingly for the remaining corruptions of his heart; for, if the least disposition to depart from God and disrelish communion with him, and to be careless about his honor and interest, is infinitely sinful, then the best men that ever lived have infinite reason always to lie as in the dust, and have their hearts broken. Although it be so with them, that all which the world calls good and great appears as dross to them; and it is nothing to them to part with friends and estate, honor and ease, and all, for Christ; and although they have actually suffered the loss of all things, and do count them but dung, not worth mourning about, or repining after; yet, notwithstanding all these attainments, attended with the fullest assurance of eternal glory in the world to come, they have infinite reason to do as they do, to dislike themselves, to hate themselves, and lie down in the dust all in tears, because still there is such a remaining disposition in their hearts to disesteem the Lord of glory; to neglect his interest, and depart from him; and because they are so far from being what they ought to be, notwithstanding the obligations lying upon them are infinite. O, this is infinitely vile and abominable, and they have reason indeed, therefore,

always to loathe and abhor themselves, and repent in dust and ashes; yea, they are infinitely to blame for not being more humble and penitent. A sight and sense of these things made Job lie down in the dust, and mourn so bitterly for his impatience under his past afflictions, though he had been the most patient man in the world. This made the Psalmist call himself a beast. And hence Paul called himself the chief of sinners, and cried out, "I am carnal, sold under sin; O, wretched man that I am!"—and hated to commend himself when the Corinthians drove him to it, and seemed to blush at every sentence, and in a sort, recalled his words—"I am not a whit behind the very chief of the apostles, yet I am nothing. I labored more abundantly than they all, yet not I." Such a sight of things kills a self-righteous spirit at root, in the most exalted saint; for he has nothing, all things considered, to make a righteousness of, but, in strict justice, merits eternal damnation every hour, and does nothing to make the least amends.

. . . .

Now, why does not God appear infinitely amiable in our eyes? Is it because he has not clearly revealed what he is, in his works and in his word? Surely no; for the revelation is plain enough. Is it because he is not infinitely amiable in being what he is? Surely no; for all heaven are ravished with his infinite beauty. What is it, then, that makes us blind to the infinite excellency of the divine nature? Why, it can be owing to nothing but a bad temper of mind in us, and to our not being of such a temper as we ought to be. For I appeal to the experience of all mankind, whether those persons and things which suit the temper of their hearts, do not naturally appear amiable in their eyes? And certainly, if God does not suit the temper of our hearts, it is not owing to any fault in him, but the fault must be wholly in ourselves. If the temper and disposition of God—that is, his moral perfections—be not agreeable to our temper and disposition, most certainly our temper and disposition are very wrong. "If God were your father, ye would love me; but ye are of your father the devil; therefore ye hate me;" that is, if you were of a temper like God, you would love me; but being of a contrary temper, hence you hate me. If you were of a right temper, I should appear amiable unto you; and it is wholly owing to your bad temper, that I appear otherwise. "If ye were Abraham's children, ye would do the works of Abraham."

Obj. But be it so, yet I cannot help being of such a temper as I am of: how, therefore am I wholly to blame?

Ans. You have as much power to help being of such a temper as the Scribes and Pharisees had; but Christ judged them to be wholly to blame, and altogether inexcusable. They could not like Christ or his doctrine: ye cannot hear my word, says Christ; but their *cannot,* their inability, was no excuse to them in Christ's account, because all their inability, he plainly saw, arose from their bad temper, and their want of a good disposition. And although they had no more power to help being of such a temper than you have, yet he judged them wholly to blame, and altogether inexcusable. (John viii. 33—47; xv. 22—25.) And now we know that his judgment is according to truth. But in order to help you to see into the reason of the thing, I desire you seriously and impartially to consider—

1. That sinners are free and voluntary in their bad temper. A wicked world have discovered a very strong disposition to hate God, even from the beginning. And the Jewish nation, God's own peculiar people, of whom, if of any, we might hope for better things, were so averse to God and his ways,

that they hated and murdered the messengers which he sent to reclaim them, and, at last, even murdered God's own Son. And now, whence was all this? Why, from the exceeding bad and wicked temper of their hearts. "They have hated me without a cause." But did any body force them to be of such a bad temper? Surely no; they were hearty in it. Were they of such a bad temper against their wills? Surely no; their wills, their hearts were in it. Yea, they loved their bad temper, and loved to gratify it, and hence were mightily pleased with their false prophets, because they always prophesied in their favor, and suited and gratified their disposition: and they hated whatsoever was disagreeable to their bad temper, and tended to cross it; and hence were they so enraged at the preaching and the persons of their prophets, of Christ and his apostles; so that they were manifestly voluntary and hearty in their bad temper. "We have loved strangers, and after them we *will* go." "But as for the word which thou hast spoken unto us in the name of the Lord, we *will not* hearken unto thee." "And the Lord God of their fathers sent to them by his messengers, rising up betimes, and sending; because he had compassion on his people, and on his dwelling-place; but they mocked the messengers of God, and despised his words, and misused his prophets." And so all wicked men are as voluntary in their bad temper as they were. The temper of the mind is nothing but the habitual inclination of the heart; but an involuntary inclination of the heart is a contradiction. And the stronger any inclination is, the more full and free the heart and soul is in the thing. Hence the bad temper, or the habitual bad inclination of the devil, is at the farthest distance from any compulsion; he is most perfectly free and hearty in it. And all sinful creatures being thus voluntary, free, and hearty in the bad temper of their minds—or, in other words, the bad temper of the mind being nothing but the habitual inclination of the heart—hence all must be to blame in a degree equal to the strength of their bad inclination. In a word, if we were continually forced to be of such a bad temper entirely against our wills, then we should not be to blame; for it would not be at all the temper of our hearts: but so long as our bad temper is nothing else but the habitual frame, disposition, and inclination of our own hearts, without any manner of compulsion, we are perfectly without excuse, and that whether we can help being of such a temper, or no.

. . . .

Obj. But I was brought into this state by Adam's fall.

Ans. Let it be by Adam's fall, or how it will, yet if you are an enemy to the infinitely glorious God, your Maker, and that voluntarily, you are infinitely to blame, and without excuse; for nothing can make it right for a creature to be a voluntary enemy to his glorious Creator, or possibly excuse such a crime. It is, in its own nature, infinitely wrong; there is nothing, therefore, to be said; you stand guilty before God. It is in vain to make this or any other pleas, so long as we are what we are, not by compulsion, but voluntarily. And it is in vain to pretend that we are not voluntary in our corruptions, when they are nothing else but the free, spontaneous inclinations of our own hearts. Since this is the case, every mouth will be stopped, and all the world become guilty before God, sooner or later.

Thus we see, that, as to a natural capacity, all mankind are capable of a perfect conformity to God's law, which requires us only to love God with all our hearts: and that all our inability arises merely from the bad temper of our hearts, and our want of a good disposition; and that, therefore, we are wholly to blame and altogether inexcusable. Our impotency, in one word, is not natural, but moral, and, therefore, instead of extenuating, does magnify and enhance our fault. The more unable to love God we are, the more are we to blame.

. . . .

Evangelical humiliation consists in a sense of our own sinfulness, vileness, odiousness, and ill desert, and in a disposition, thence resulting, to lie down in the dust full of self-loathing and self-abhorrence, abased before the Lord, really accounting ourselves infinitely too bad ever to venture to come into the divine presence in our own names, or to have a thought of mercy from God on the account of our own goodness. And it is this which makes us sensible of our need of a Mediator, and makes us desire to be found, not in ourselves, but in Christ; not having on our own righteousness, but his. No further, therefore, than these views and this temper prevail in us, shall we truly discern any need of Christ, or be heartily inclined to have any respect to him as a Mediator between God and us. There can, therefore, be no more of true faith in exercise, than there is of this true humility. When men, therefore, appear righteous in their own eyes, and look upon themselves as deserving well at the hands of God, on the account of their own goodness, they can feel no need of a Mediator, nor at heart have any respect to Christ under that character. (Luke v. 31.) This condemns the faith of the self-righteous formalist, who depends upon his being conscientious in his ways, and upon his sincerely endeavoring to do as well as he can, to recommend him to God. And this condemns, also, the faith of the proud enthusiast, who appears so good in his own eyes; so far from a legal spirit; so purely evangelical; so full of light and knowledge, humility and love, zeal and devotion, as that, from a sense of his own goodness, and how greatly beloved he is in the sight of God, he is encouraged and elevated, and feels greatly imboldened to come into the presence of God, and draw near, and come even to his seat, and use familiarity and boldness with God, as though he was almost an equal. Such are so far from any true sense of their need of Christ, as that they rather feel more fit to be mediators and intercessors in behalf of others, than to want one for themselves. And it is the way of such, from that great sense they have of their own goodness, to make bold with God, and to make bold with Christ, in their prayers, as if they felt themselves pretty nigh upon a level. Of all men in the world, I am ready to think that God looks upon these the worst, and hates them the most. (Luke xviii. 9–14. Isa. lxv. 5.) But did they know it, they would hate him as entirely as he does them. Hypocrites of all sorts fail in this point: they see no real need of Christ; they are not so bad but that, to their own sense and feeling, they might be pardoned and saved by the free mercy of God, without any mediator. Hence they do not understand the gospel; it is all foolishness to them. (1 Cor. ii. 14.)

6. [Faith] is a spiritual sense and firm belief of the truths of the gospel which encourages the heart to trust in Christ. (John vi. 45.) That the goodness of God is infinite and self-moving; that Christ, as Mediator, has secured the honor of God, the moral Governor of the world, and opened a way for the free and honorable exercise of his grace; that through Christ, God, the supreme Governor of the world, is actually ready to be reconciled, and invites all, the vilest not excepted, to return to him in this way—these truths, being spiritually understood and firmly believed, convince the heart of the safety of trusting in Christ, and encourage it

so to do. (Heb. x. 19. Matt. xxii. 4.)

7. Saving faith consists in that entire trust, reliance, or dependence on Jesus Christ, the great Mediator, his satisfaction and merits, mediation and intercession, which the humbled sinner has, whereby he is imboldened to return home to God in hopes of acceptance, and is encouraged to look to and trust in God through him for that complete salvation which is offered in the gospel. The opposite to justifying faith, is a self-righteous spirit and temper, whereby a man, from a conceit of, and reliance upon, his own goodness, is imboldened and encouraged to trust and hope in the mercy of God, (Heb. x. 19, 23. Luke xviii. 9, 14,) and accordingly, when such see how bad they really are, their faith fails; they naturally think that God cannot find in his heart to show mercy to such.

8. Faith imboldens the heart. In a legal humiliation, which is antecedent to spiritual light, the sinner is brought to a kind of despair. The things which used to imbolden him, do now entirely fail: he finds no good in himself; yea, he feels himself dead in sin; and upon this his heart dies within him. "I was alive without the law once; but when the commandment came, sin revived, and I died." And by spiritual light, in evangelical humiliation, his undone state, in and of himself, is made still more plain. But now faith imboldens the heart, begets new courage, lays the foundation for a new kind of hope—a hope springing entirely from a new foundation. "Having, therefore, brethren, boldness to enter into the holiest, by the blood of Jesus, let us draw near with a true heart, in full assurance of faith." By faith the heart is imboldened. 1. To return home to God, in hopes of acceptance. A spiritual sight and sense of the ineffable beauty of the divine nature begets a disposition to look upon it the fittest and happiest

thing in the world to love God with all the heart, and be entirely devoted to him forever; and enkindles an inclination to return, and everlastingly give up and consecrate ourselves unto him. "But may such a wretch as I be the Lord's? Will he accept me?" Now, the believer, understanding the way of acceptance by Christ, and seeing the safety of it, ventures his all upon this sure foundation, and hereby is imboldened to return. "He that cometh to God must believe that he is, and that he is a rewarder of them that diligently seek him;" that is, first, he must see what God is; behold him in his glory, or he cannot, in a genuine manner, desire to come to him. And secondly, he must see that he is ready to be reconciled unto and to save those who, from a genuine desire to be his, do heartily return to him through the Mediator he has appointed; or else he will not dare to come. But when both these are seen and believed, now the soul will return, and come and give up itself to God, to be the Lord's forever. 2. Faith in Christ imboldens the heart to look to and trust in the free grace of God through him, for all things that just such a poor creature wants; even for all things offered in the gospel to poor sinners. "Let us, therefore, come boldly to the throne of grace, that we may obtain mercy and find grace." Pardoning mercy and sanctifying grace are the two great benefits of the new covenant; and these are the two great things which an enlightened soul feels the want of, and for which he is imboldened to come to God by Jesus Christ. "I will be to them a God, and they shall be to me a people," saith the Lord in the new covenant. "And this is all my salvation, and all my desire," saith a believer.

. . . .

10. A heart to love God supremely, live to him ultimately, and delight in him superlatively; to love our neighbors as ourselves; to hate every false way; to be humble, meek, weaned from the world, heavenly-minded; to be thankful for mercies; patient under afflictions; to love enemies; to forgive injuries, and, in all things, to do as we would be done by—a heart for all this, I say, is always in exact proportion to the degree of true faith; for the same views of our own wretchedness; of God; of Christ; of the way of salvation by free grace through him; of the glory, reality, and importance of divine and eternal things, which lay the foundation for true faith, and always accompany the exercise of faith, do, at the same time, lay the foundation for this divine temper. And besides, this divine temper is what every true believer feels to be the fittest and happiest thing in the world, and, as such, longs for it, and goes to God to have it increased and strengthened; and, being unworthy to go in his own name, he goes in Christ's name; so that the obtaining more and more of this divine temper is one main end of his exercising faith in Christ. And whatsoever he asks the Father in Christ's name, he receives. God is readier to give his Holy Spirit to such a one, than parents are to give bread to their children, (John xvi. 23. Matt. vii. 11); and therefore every true believer does obtain the end of his faith; and not only has, but grows in this divine temper, and is governed by it, and brings forth fruit according to it; and thus shows his faith by his works, according to St. James's doctrine. (James ii.) And herein true faith stands distinguished from all counterfeits. Never had a hypocrite a spiritual sense of that ineffable beauty of the divine nature, which lies at the foundation of all the experiences of the true saint, and from whence all true holiness originally springs. The formalist may, from legal fears and mercenary hopes, be so strict and conscientious in his ways, as to

think himself a choice, good man; and the enthusiast, from a firm persuasion of the pardon of his sins, and the love of Christ, may be so full of joy and love, zeal and devotion, as to think himself a most eminent saint; but there is nothing of the nature of true holiness in either; for it is self, and nothing but self, that is the principal, centre, and end of all their religion. They do not believe in Christ, that through him they may return home to God, and be consecrated to him forever, and obtain grace to do all his will. They do not know God, or care for him, but are wholly taken up about their own interest. That Moravian maxim, "That salvation consists in the forgiveness of sins," exhibits the true picture of the heart of the best hypocrite in the world; while that in 2 Cor. iii. 18, is peculiar to the godly— "We all with open face beholding, as in a glass, the glory of the Lord, are changed into the same image, from glory to glory."

35. The Harmony of All Being: Jonathan Edwards, *The Nature of True Virtue, ca.* 1755

[Clarence H. Faust and Thomas H. Johnson, eds., *Jonathan Edwards: Representative Selections, with Introduction, Bibliography, and Notes*, rev. ed. (New York, 1962), 349–355]

Whatever controversies and variety of opinions there are about the nature of virtue, yet all (excepting some skeptics, who deny any real difference between virtue and vice) mean by it, something *beautiful,* or rather some kind of *beauty,* or excellency. It is not *all* beauty, that is called virtue; for instance, not the beauty of a building, of a flower, or of the rainbow: but some beauty belonging to Beings that have *perception* and *will.* It is not all beauty of *mankind,* that is called virtue; for instance, not the external beauty of the countenance, or shape, gracefulness of motion, or harmony of voice: but it is a beauty that has its original seat in the mind. But yet perhaps not *every* thing that may be called a beauty of mind, is properly called virtue. There is a beauty of understanding and speculation. There is something in the ideas and conceptions of great philosophers and statesmen, that may be called beautiful; which is a different thing from what is most commonly meant by virtue. But virtue is the beauty of those qualities and acts of the mind, that are of a *moral* nature, i.e., such as are attended with desert or worthiness of *praise,* or *blame.* Things of this sort, it is generally agreed, so far as I know, are not any thing belonging merely to speculation; but to the *disposition* and *will,* or (to use a general word, I suppose commonly well understood) the *heart.* Therefore I suppose, I shall not depart from the common opinion, when I say, that virtue is the beauty of the qualities and exercises of the heart, or those actions which proceed from them. So that when it is inquired, What is the nature of true *virtue?* This is the same as to inquire, what that is which renders any habit, disposition, or exercise of the heart truly *beautiful.* I use the phrase *true* virtue, and speak of things *truly* beautiful, because I suppose it will generally be allowed, that there is a distinction to be made between some things which are truly virtuous, and others which only seem to be virtuous, through a partial and imperfect view of things: that some actions and dispositions appear beautiful, if considered partially and superficially, or with regard to some things belonging to them, and in some of their circumstances and tendencies, which would appear otherwise in a more extensive and comprehensive view, wherein they are seen clearly in their whole nature and the extent of their connections in the universality of things. There is a general and a particular beauty. By a *particular* beauty, I mean that by which a thing appears beautiful when considered only with regard to its connection with, and tendency to some particular things within a limited, and, as it were, a private sphere. And a *general* beauty is that by which a thing appears beautiful when viewed most perfectly, comprehensively and universally, with regard to all its tendencies, and its connections with every thing it stands related to. The former may be without and against the latter. As, a few notes in a tune, taken only by themselves, and in their relation to one another, may be harmonious; which when considered with respect to all the notes in the tune, or the entire series of sounds they are connected with, may be very discordant and disagreeable. (Of which more afterwards.) *That only,* therefore, is what I mean by true virtue, which is *that,* belonging to the *heart* of an intelligent Being, that is beautiful by a *general* beauty, or beautiful in a comprehensive view as it is in itself, and as related to every thing that it stands in connection with. And therefore when we are inquiring concerning the nature of true virtue, viz., wherein this true and general beauty of the heart does most essentially consist—this is my answer to the inquiry:

True virtue most essentially consists in benevolence to Being in general. Or perhaps to speak more accurately, it is that consent, propensity and union of heart to Being in general, that is immediately exercised in a general good will.

The things which were before observed of the nature of true virtue, naturally lead us to such a notion of it. If it has its seat in the heart, and is the general goodness and beauty of the disposition and exercise of that, in the most comprehensive view, considered with regard to its universal tendency, and as related to every thing that it stands in connection with; what can it consist in, but a consent and good will to Being in general? Beauty does not consist in discord and dissent, but in consent and agreement. And if every intelligent Being is some way related to Being in general, and is a part of the universal system of existence; and so stands in connection with the whole; what can its general and true beauty be, but its union and consent with the great whole?

If any such thing can be supposed as a union of heart to some particular Being, or number of Beings, disposing it to benevolence to a private circle or system of Beings, which are but a small part of the whole; not implying a tendency to a union with the great system, and not at all inconsistent with enmity towards Being in general; this I suppose not to be of the nature of true virtue: although it may in some respects be good, and may appear beautiful in a confined and contracted view of things. But of this more afterwards.

It is abundantly plain by the holy Scriptures, and generally allowed, not only by Christian divines, but by the more considerable deists, but virtue most essentially consists in love. And I suppose, it is owned by the most considerable writers, to consist in general love of benevolence, or kind affection: though it seems to me, the meaning of some in this affair is not sufficiently explained, which perhaps occasions some error or confusion in discourses on this subject.

When I say, true virtue consists in love to Being in general, I shall not be likely to be understood, that no one act of the mind or exercise of love is of the nature of true virtue, but what has Being in general, or the great system of universal existence, for its direct and immediate object: so that no exercise of love or kind affection to any one particular Being, that is but a small part of this whole, has any thing of the nature of true virtue. But, that the nature of true virtue consists in a disposition to benevolence towards Being in general. Though, from such a disposition may arise exercises of love to particular Beings, as objects are presented and occasions arise. No wonder, that he who is of a generally benevolent disposition, should be more disposed than another to have his heart moved with benevolent affection to particular persons, whom he is acquainted and conversant with, and from whom arise the greatest and most frequent occasions for exciting his benevolent temper. But my meaning is, that no affections towards particular persons or Beings are of the nature of true virtue, but such as arise from a generally benevolent temper, or from that habit or frame of mind, wherein consists a disposition to love Being in general.

And perhaps it is needless for me to give notice to my readers, that when I speak of an intelligent Being's having a heart united and benevolently disposed to Being in general, I thereby mean *intelligent* Being in general. Not inanimate things, or Beings that have no perception or will, which are not properly capable objects of benevolence.

Love is commonly distinguished into love of benevolence and love of complacence. Love of *benevolence* is that affection or propensity of the heart to any Being, which causes it to incline to its well being, or disposes it to desire and take pleasure in its happiness. And

if I mistake not, it is agreeable to the common opinion, that beauty in the object is not always the ground of this propensity: but that there may be such a thing as benevolence, or a disposition to the welfare of those that are not considered as beautiful; unless mere existence be accounted a beauty. And benevolence or goodness in the Divine Being is generally supposed, not only to be prior to the beauty of many of its objects, but to their existence: so as to be the ground both of their existence and their beauty, rather than they the foundation of God's benevolence; as it supposed that it is God's goodness which moved him to give them both Being and beauty. So that if all virtue primarily consists in that affection of heart to Being, which is exercised in benevolence, or an inclination to its good, then God's virtue is so extended as to include a propensity, not only to Being actually existing, and actually beautiful, but to possible Being, so as to incline him to give Being, beauty and happiness. But not now to insist particularly on this. What I would have observed at present, is, that it must be allowed, benevolence doth not necessarily presuppose beauty in its object.

What is commonly called love of *complacence,* presupposes beauty. For it is no other than delight in beauty; or complacence in the person or Being beloved for his beauty.

If virtue be the beauty of an intelligent Being, and virtue consists in love, then it is a plain inconsistence, to suppose that virtue primarily consists in any love to its object *for its beauty;* either in a love of complacence, which is delight in a Being for his beauty, or in a love of benevolence, that has the beauty of its object for its foundation. For that would be to suppose, that the beauty of intelligent beings primarily consists in love to beauty; or, that their virtue first of all consists in their love to virtue. Which is an inconsistence, and going in a circle. Because it makes virtue, or beauty of mind, the foundation or first motive of that love wherein virtue originally consists, or wherein the very first virtue consists; or, it supposes the first virtue to be the consequence and effect of virtue. So that virtue is originally the foundation and exciting cause of the very beginning or first Being of virtue. Which makes the first virtue, both the ground, and the consequence, both cause and effect of itself. Doubtless virtue primarily consists in something else besides any effect or consequence of virtue. If virtue consists primarily in love to virtue, then virtue, the thing loved, is the love of virtue: so that virtue must consist in the love of the love of virtue. And if it be inquired, what that virtue is, which virtue consists in the love of the love of, it must be answered, it is the love of virtue. So that there must be the love of the love of the love of virtue, and so on *in infinitum*. For there is no end of going back in a circle. We never come to any beginning, or foundation. For it is without beginning and hangs on nothing.

Therefore if the essence of virtue or beauty of mind lies in love, or a disposition to love, it must primarily consist in something *different* both from complacence, which is a delight in beauty, and also from any benevolence that has the beauty of its object for its foundation. Because it is absurd, to say that virtue is primarily and first of all the consequence of itself. For this makes virtue primarily prior to itself.

Nor can virtue primarily consist in *gratitude;* or one Being's benevolence to another for his benevolence to him. Because this implies the same inconsistence. For it supposes a benevolence prior to gratitude, that is the cause of gratitude. Therefore the first benevolence, or that benevolence which has

none prior to it, cannot be gratitude.

Therefore there is room left for no other conclusion than that the primary object of virtuous love is Being, simply considered; or, that true virtue primarily consists, not in love to any particular Beings, because of their virtue or beauty, nor in gratitude, because they love us; but in a propensity and union of heart to Being simply considered; exciting absolute benevolence (if I may so call it) to Being in general. I say, true virtue *primarily* consists in this. For I am far from asserting that there is no true virtue in any other love than this absolute benevolence. But I would express what appears to me to be the truth on this subject, in the following particulars.

The *first* object of a virtuous benevolence is *Being,* simply considered: and if Being, *simply* considered, be its object, then Being *in general* is its object; and the thing it has an ultimate propensity to, is the *highest good* of Being in general. And it will seek the good of every *individual* Being unless it be conceived as not consistent with the highest good of Being in general. In which case the good of a particular Being, or some Beings, may be given up for the sake of the highest good of Being in general. And particularly if there be any Being that is looked upon as statedly and irreclaimably opposite and an enemy to Being in general, then consent and adherence to Being in general will induce the truly virtuous heart to forsake that Being, and to oppose it.

And further, if Being, simply considered, be the first object of a truly virtuous benevolence, then that Being who has *most* of Being, or has the greatest share of existence, other things being equal, so far as such a Being is exhibited to our faculties or set in our view, will have the *greatest* share of the propensity and benevolent affection of the heart. I say, *other things being* *equal,* especially because there is a *secondary* object of virtuous benevolence, that I shall take notice of presently. Which is one thing that must be considered as the ground or motive to a purely virtuous benevolence. Pure benevolence in its first exercise is nothing else but Being's uniting consent, or propensity to Being; appearing true and pure by its extending to Being in general, and inclining to the general highest good, and to each Being, whose welfare is consistent with the highest general good, in proportion to the degree of *existence** understood, other things being equal.

The *second* object of a virtuous pro-

* I say, in proportion to the degree of *existence,* because one Being may have more *existence* than another, as he may be *greater* than another. That which is *great,* has more existence, and is further from nothing, than that which is *little.* One Being may have every thing positive belonging to it, or every thing which goes to its positive existence in opposition to defect) in a higher degree than another; or a greater capacity and power, greater understanding, every faculty and every positive quality in a higher degree. An *archangel* must be supposed to have more existence, and to be every way further removed from *nonenity,* than a *worm,* or a *flea.* [Edwards's note.]

pensity of heart is *benevolent* Being. A secondary ground of pure benevolence is virtuous benevolence itself in its object. When any one under the influence of general benevolence, sees another Being possessed of the like general benevolence, this attaches his heart to him, and draws forth greater love to him, than merely his having existence: because so far as the Being beloved has love to Being in general, so far his own Being is, as it were, enlarged, extends to, and in some sort comprehends, Being in general: and therefore he that is governed by love to Being in general must of necessity have complacence in him, and the greater degree of benevolence to him, as it were out of gratitude to him for his love to general existence, that his own heart is extended and united to, and so looks on its interest as its own. It is because his heart is thus united to Being in general, that he looks on a benevolent propensity to Being in general, wherever he sees it, as the beauty of the Being in whom it is; an excellency, that renders him worthy of esteem, complacence, and the greater good will.

Tolerance

36. Against New Light Censoriousness: John Caldwell, *The Nature, Folly, and Evil of rash and uncharitable Judging,* 1742

[John Caldwell, *The Nature, Folly, and Evil of rash and uncharitable Judging. A Sermon Preached at the French Meeting-House in Boston, New England, July the 11th. 1742* (Boston, 1742), 12–17, 31–32]

To judge that a Man or Number of Men (who profess to *believe in GOD, and in CHRIST as the Messias, Son of GOD and only Mediator between GOD and Man, the Brightness of Divine Glory, and express Image of his Person,* and all his Doctrines the very Truth) will be damned, or are in a damnable State, by any other Way than the Wickedness and unrepented Immorality of their Lives, is judging without any Warrant or Authority. I shall here take it for granted that the Scriptures are to be our Rule in this as well as in other Cases of a religious Nature: And is it not self-evident, that Immorality unrepented of and persisted in, is always declar'd to be the Cause of Men's Condemnation (who believe as above) by our Saviour and his Apostles. The workers of Iniquity we know will be excluded from GOD's Favour, tho' they pretend to be his Children, and boast of their spiritual Attainments; *the Wicked will be turned into Hell, and all the Nations that forget GOD; the Wicked shall go away unto everlasting Misery.* GOD will call Men to an Account for their Actions, and reward or punish according to their Deeds, let them be good or evil. *Indignation and Wrath will be the Lot of the contentious, of such as obey not the Truth, but obey Unrighteousness; Tribulation and Anguish the Portion of every Soul of Man that doth evil; if we forgive not, we shall not be forgiven; if we judge we shall be judged.* And we may justly say, that such as continue to do evil shall not escape the Wrath of GOD. But are we not wise above what is written, when we declare a Man in a damnable State, whom we cannot charge as above, because he differs from us in such Points as we esteem sacred, or cannot express himself about such Things in the very Words we do? 'Tis, I think, clearly taught in Scripture, that GOD is a Spirit, Omnipresent, Omniscient, Omnipotent, Eternal, infinitely holy, just, merciful, good, etc. but 'tis no where said in the Scriptures, that if we differ in expressing our selves about these Perfections, that one Side has a Right to judge and condemn the rest: In like Manner, if *Calvinists* would suppose the distinguishing tenents of *Arminius* true, or *Arminians* the distinguishing Doctrines of *Calvin,* yet may not both ask where their peculiar Tenets are called damnable, or where 'tis said that

he who does, or does not believe as *Calvin* or *Arminus,* shall for that reason be saved or damned? How many then are wise above what is written! Suppose also Conversion was a sudden unintelligible Thing, produced by means of Terrors and Judgments (GOD's strange Work) the Evidence of which is talking well of our selves, arrogantly and evil of our Neighbours, yet may not any Person justly demand our Warrant to condemn such as cannot see with our Eyes? And is it not evident we have none but Pride, Evil-nature or Ignorance.

.   .   .   .

But perhaps some Persons may imagine I am mistaken in this, for tho' Men in general have not Qualifications to judge others, not Authority to do so, yet are there some who have, *Papists* say the *Pope,* or *General Councils,* or both in Conjunction are infallible, and therefore may judge others; their Judgments will also be decisive, because to him or them the Keys of the Kingdom of Heaven were committed, and he or they have Power to forgive or retain Sins, and open or shut Heaven as they please. Could this be proved, it would no doubt confute all the Arguments I have used or can use; but as the Foundation is weak, the Superstructure must fall; it being evident that the Gift of the Keys was to a particular Man, without any Relation to any real or supposed Successor, and that it had only a Reference to the first promulgating Christianity after our Saviour's Ascention, a common Sense of the Phrase, *the Kingdom of Heaven,* and in which Sense 'tis only true that *Peter* did open the Kingdom of Heaven.

BUT besides the Papists, there are who upon a different Foundation pretend to the same Power, because they are (they say) Converts, and have GOD's Spirit, they may judge all others, but none have a Right to judge them or their Experiences or Doctrines, Because *Paul* tells us, 1 *Cor.* 2. 15. *He that is spiritual, judgeth all things, yet he himself is judged by no Man.* And again, that only the Prophets have a Right to judge of the Prophets. This is taught from Pulpit and Press, and made a mighty Noise with by many who know neither what they say, nor whereof they do affirm.

AND truly it must be owned to be a cunning Device, to prevent their Errors from being confuted; for if none but such as believe or pretend to believe their Doctrines can judge of them, we need never expect to hear any absurdity discovered in them, tho' they believe ever so many. No, they will not give Things by their proper Names, which are done by themselves or Party; Ignorance will be called, *being under a Cloud,* a warm Imagination, *Impressions of the Divine Spirit,* boasting of their Righteousness, *telling their Experiences,* evil Nature, *Zeal,* etc.

BUT as cunning a Scheme as this is, are we to suppose that a Man who can think at all, will be perswaded to lay aside his Reason and Judgment, because others are bold and assuming? For suppose we should allow that converted Men have a Right to say and do, to save and damn whom and as they please, yet before we allow particular Men this Power, we should have clear Evidence that they are such Persons. In Cases of much less Moment we would not be content with Men's Words, and why should we in this? Is it because they are Men of Veracity? But if we will believe some Men because they are Men of Veracity in other Cases, why not all Men of Veracity? What will we say to a *Papist* or *Mahometan,* who will both confidently tell us their Way is the only one to GOD's Favour, that we must be damned if we come not into them, and that they feel the Spirit upon their Minds agreeing with their Principles,

and have seen the one the *Virgin Mary,* and the other *Mahomet,* in Visions and Dreams, ready to save them? Will we believe them because they confidently say so? Certainly if we had much Wisdom in Men or Things, we would demand Evidence of a superiour kind.

. . . .

LET us be careful of such Teachers as are leading us blindfold to their Opinions, nor will ever allow us to see until our Understanding are equally of the same Magnitude with theirs, or until we lay aside our Reason; and also of such who are for confining us to the hearing or reading only their Side of the Question in Controversies; telling us the opposite is damnable Doctrine, or terrible Heresy, and its Teachers and Authors Hereticks, who should not be heard nor read. This is intended to bypass our judgments, to prepossess us in Favour of their Doctrines, and a tacit Acknowledgment of their Fear lest the contrary Opinion would appear probable and better supported than theirs, if Men give them a fair hearing. And 'tis laying us under a kind of Necessity to judge without Evidence. For suppose the Doctrines such would have us believe true; yet how can we know that they are so, if we have not placed them in a just Point of View? And how can we place disputable Points in a View fit to be rationally judged of, if we have not placed the Arguments upon both Sides in a just Light before this Power? And how can we do this, if one Side only be known to us, and it be sinful to look into and examine the other or others? Besides, if such as oppose us are so absurd, why may we not see the Absurdity with our own Understandings, to prevent our being blind Zealots? How Deceiver like does it look, to say this Doctrine is true and founded upon Scripture, the opposite is most false, and without any Foundation in GOD's Word? But as you tender your

Souls Happiness you must not look into this false Doctrine, lest you should take that to be in the Bible which is not there. This is *Popery* with a Witness; and tho' such may believe Truth, 'tis plain they do not know for what Reason. Nay, it may be Error, and looks like its poor Shifts; 'tis what Truth needs not, its native Charms being sufficient to bear down Error when ever they are placed in a proper Light before an unprejudiced Mind.

No, my Brethren, be not thus captivated; examine and try, believe not a Doctrine true or false, because I or any other Man or Number of Men say so. Search the Scriptures, they are in your native Language, as to the main faithfully translated, the Enemies themselves being Witness; and where Men of Learn-

ing differ about the meaning of a Passage in the Original, let your own Judgments try which of them agrees best with the Design and Reasoning of the Author in the Place; read in all Controversies both Sides, compare both with the Word of GOD, and assent to what is best founded upon the same, or you are Believers you know not for what, and judge without Evidence: Understand with your own Understandings; see Evidence before ye believe or judge, (and say not, I am perswaded because I am perswaded.) This is your unalianable Right as Men and Christians, and bounden Duty; give not therefore up the one, nor neglect the other at the Desire of a few conceited, impudent, enthusiastick Men, or where you will end no humane Wisdom can discover.

37. A Separate Petition: Solomon Paine *et al.,* 1748

[Connecticut Archives, Ecclesiastical Affairs, X, 29abcd, Connecticut State Library, Hartford, Conn.]

To the Honourable general Assembly of his Majestys Colony of Conecticut in New England to be holden at Hartford in the said Colony, on the Second thursday of May A.D. 1748 The Memorial of Solomon Paine of Canterbury in the County of Windham and Mathew Smith of Stoningtown in the County of New London and Colony aforesaid and others Inhabitants of said Colony and most of them freemen of this Corporation, and all Leige Subjects to His Royal Majesty King George the Second Whome God preserve. All whose names are hereunto Subscribed, Humbly Sheweth, that Whereas the Living and true God in his holy word hath Commanded all Men to fear God and Honour the King, and that their fear towards God aught to be taught by his unerring word and not by the precepts of men, and hath given to Evry Man an

unalianable Right, in matters of the worship of God, to Judge for himself as his Conciance receives the Rule from God, who alone hath Right to Chalenge this Sovraignty over and propriety in them; and He hath shewed the Zeal he hath for his own Worship both by threatning and inflicting heavy Judgements upon those, who dare to usurp this authority over the Conciances of others, and teach for doctrine the Commandments of men; and also upon those Whose fear towards God is taught by the precepts of men: and also in his promising to and in Conferring great favours upon such as have appeared uprightly to stand for the Glory of God in Liberty of Conciance in all ages, and perticularly upon our fore Fathers, who Left their pleasent Native Country for an howling Wilderness full of Savage Men and Beasts that they might have

Liberty of Conciance, and they found the mercyfull and faithfull God was not a wilderness to them but drove out the Savages, planted Churches, and Colonys, he gave them favour in the sight of their Kings and Queens so that their Majestys have graciously granted to, and indulged their Subjects in this Colony, with a Charter in which among other great favours, this of Liberty is not abridged; and their Majestys King William and Queen Mary, tollerated Liberty of Conciance to all without any allowance to any Company or Body of Dissenters from the Church of England, to oblige or force any of a differant opinion from them to pay to the building of their meeting houses or the maintana[nce] of their Ministers; and forbid or dissalow of any of Whatsoever profession, to impose their opinion upon or to disturb or hinder others in their Worship, by fines, imprisonments etc. in Case they give Satisfaction (when Called thereto) that they do not hold treasonable Meetings, by taking the oaths etc. as in said act, which is still upheld by our gracious Sovraign King George; so that when his Majestys Subjects in this Colony, who were Conciance bound to worship in the way Called the Church of England and that of the Quakers, and also the anabaptists, were obliged by Some Laws Called Eclesiastical, of this Colony to Suffer the Loss of goods or imprisonment, and they made their aplication to the Honourable Assembly they had the force of said Eclesiastical Laws abated so far as respected their professions. Yet all this notwithstanding for as much as said Eclesiastical Laws are still understood, by those who have the Executive Civel power to stand in full force against all who do not worship with some one of them Churches or with the Major part of the people in the society where they Live: and whereas your Honours Memorialists and many more of their neigh-bours, who worship with them in the fear of God Cannot without doing violence to their own Conciances, profess to be of any one of the abovesaid Churches or of their way of worship and so neglect to worship God according to their own Conciances, as they understand the word of God by His Holy Spirit, but since the grace of God hath appeared to them Teaching them to deny all Ungodliness etc. they are determined (by Divine assistance) to obey God and worship Him in spirit and truth altho' that way is Called independent or Separate: and to Honour the King as Supreme and Governors as Sent by him, in yealding obediance to them in all civel Matters. And yet they are all Exposed either to Make shipwrack of a good Conciance, or to suffer by fines or imprisonment, as many of them have allredy Suffered for preaching the Gospel and other acts of Divine Service in obediance to the Commands, and by the power of Gods Holy Spirit, and great Quantitys of their temporal goods with which they Should Serve God and Honour the King, are taken from them to suport that worship which they Cannot in Conciance uphold; and they knowing that the doing of such violence, indangers Souls and also Commonwealths, and is threatened in the word of God with publick Calamitys or Eternal punishments; he shall have Judgement without Mercy who hath shewed no mercy, and mercy Rejoyceth against Judgement for they shall be Judged by the Law of Liberty: and seeing the Judgments of Allmighty God are a Coming upon this Land: and the abovesaid imposission and oppression still Caryed on: Whereupon your Honours Memorialists pray that your Honours may be the happy instruments of unbinding these burdens, and Enact Universal Liberty by Repealing all those Eclesiastical Laws that are or may be Executed to the Debarring of any in this Colony of the Liberty granted by God, and tolerated by our King, or forbid the Execution of said Laws, and they as in Duty bound shall Ever pray.

Dated in Canterbury May the 2nd A.D. 1748

the Number of Subscribers 330

38. Dissent in Virginia: Samuel Davies, Letter to the Bishop of London, 1752

[William Henry Foote, *Sketches of Virginia Historical and Biographical* (Philadelphia, 1850), 189–195]

I find I have been represented to your lordship as an uninvited intruder into these parts: for your lordship in your letter to Dr. Doddridge writes thus, 'If the Act of Toleration was desired for no other view but to ease the consciences of those that could not conform; if it was granted with no other view, how must Mr. Davies's conduct be justified? who under the colour of a toleration to his own conscience, is labouring to disturb the consciences of others. He came three hundred miles from home, not to serve people who had scruples, but to a country—where there were not above four or five dissenters within an hundred miles, not above six years ago.'

To justify me from this charge, my lord, it might be sufficient to observe, that the meeting-houses here were legally licensed before I preached in them, and that the licenses were petitioned for by the people, as the last license for three of them expressly certifies, as your lordship may see: which is a sufficient evidence that I did not intrude into any of these places to gain proselytes where there were no dissenters before.

But to give your lordship a just view of this matter, I shall present you with a brief narrative of the rise and increase of the dissenters in and about this county, and an account of the circumstances of my settling among them. And though I know, my lord, there may be

some temptations to look upon all I say as a plausible artifice to vindicate myself or my party: yet I am not without hopes that one of your lordship's impartiality, who has found it possible by happy experience to be candid and disinterested even when self is concerned, will believe it possible for another also to be impartial for once in the relation of plain, public facts, obvious to all, though they concern him and his party; especially when he is willing to venture the reputation of his veracity on the undeniable truth of his relation, and can bring the attestations of multitudes to confirm it.

About the year 1743, upon the petition of the Presbyterians in the frontier counties of this colony, the Rev. Mr. Robinson, who now rests from his labours, and is happily advanced beyond the injudicious applauses and censures of mortals, was sent by order of Presbytery to officiate for some time among them. A little before this about four or five persons, heads of families, in Hanover, had dissented from the established church, not from any scruples about her ceremonial peculiarities, the usual cause of non-conformity, much less about her excellent Articles of Faith, but from a dislike of the doctrines generally delivered from the pulpit, as not savouring of experimental piety, nor suitably intermingled with the glorious peculiarities of the religion of Jesus. It does not concern me at present, my lord, to inquire or determine whether they had sufficient reason for their dislike. They concluded them sufficient; and they had a legal as well as natural right to follow their own judgment. These families were wont to meet in a private house on Sundays to hear some good books read, particularly Luther's; whose writings I can assure your lordship were the principal cause of their leaving the Church; which I hope is a presumption in their favour. After some time sundry others came to their society, and upon hearing these books, grew indifferent about going to church, and chose rather to frequent these societies for reading. At length the number became too great for a private house to contain them, and they agreed to build a meeting-house, which they accordingly did.

Thus far, my lord, they had proceeded before they had heard a dissenting minister at all. (Here again I appeal to all that know any thing of the matter to attest this account.) They had not the least thought at this time of assuming the denomination of Presbyterians, as they were wholly ignorant of that Church: but when they were called upon by the court to assign the reasons of their absenting themselves from church, and asked what denomination they professed themselves of, they declared themselves Lutherans, not in the usual sense of that denomination in Europe, but merely to intimate that they were of Luther's sentiments, particularly in the article of Justification.

Hence, my lord, it appears that neither I nor my brethren were the first instruments of their separation from the Church of England: and so far we are vindicated from the charge of 'setting up itinerant preachers, to gather congregations where there was none before.' So far I am vindicated from the charge of 'coming three hundred miles from home to disturb the consciences of others—not to serve a people who had

scruples, but to a country—where there were not above four or five dissenters at the time of my coming here.

Hence also, my lord, results an inquiry, which I humbly submit to your lordship, whether the laws of England enjoin an immutability in sentiments on the members of the established church? And whether, if those that were formerly conformists, follow their own judgments, and dissent, they are cut off from the privileges granted by law to those that are dissenters by birth and education? If not, had not these people a legal right to separate from the established church, and to invite any legally qualified minister they thought fit to preach among them? And this leads me back to my narrative again.

While Mr. Robinson was preaching in the frontier counties, about an hundred miles from Hanover, the people here having received some information of his character and doctrines, sent him an invitation by one or two of their number to come and preach among them; which he complied with and preached four days successively to a mixed multitude; many being prompted to attend from curiosity. The acquaintance I had with him, and the universal testimony of multitudes that heard him, assure me, that he insisted entirely on the great catholic doctrines of the gospel, (as might be presumed from his first text, Luke xiii. 3,) and did not give the least hint of his sentiments concerning the disputed peculiarities of the Church of England, or use any sordid disguised artifices to gain converts to a party. 'Tis true many after this joined with those that had formerly dissented; but their sole reason at first was, the prospect of being entertained with more profitable doctrines among the dissenters than they were wont to hear in the parish churches, and not because Mr. Robinson had poisoned them with bigoted prejudices against the established church. And permit me, my lord, to declare, with the utmost religious solemnity, that I have been (as I hope your lordship will be in the regions of immortal bliss and perfect uniformity in religion) the joyful witness of the happy effect of these four sermons. Sundry thoughtless impenitents, and sundry abandoned profligates have ever since given good evidence of a thorough conversion, not from party to party, but from sin to holiness, by an universal devotedness to God, and the conscientious practice of all the social and personal virtues. And when I see this the glorious concomicant or consequent of their separation, I hope your lordship will indulge me to rejoice in such proselytes, as I am sure our divine Master and all his celestial ministers do; though without this, they are but wretched captures, rather to be lamented over, than boasted of. When Mr. Robinson left them, which he did after four days, they continued to meet together on Sundays to pray and hear a sermon out of some valuable book read by one of their number; as they had no prospect of obtaining a minister immediately of the same character and principles with Mr. Robinson. They were now increased to a tolerable congregation, and made unwearied application to the Presbytery of New Castle in Pennsylvania for a minister to be sent among them, at least to pay them a transient visit, and preach a few sermons, and baptize their children, till they should have opportunity to have one settled among them. The Presbytery complied with their petitions, as far as the small number of its members, and the circumstances of their own congregations, and of the vacancies under their Presbyterial care, would permit; and sent ministers among them at four different times in about four years, who stayed with them two or three Sabbaths at each time. They came at the re-

peated and most importunate petitions of the dissenters here, and did not obtrude their labours upon them uninvited. Sundry upon hearing them, who had not heard Mr. Robinson, joined with the dissenters; so that in the year 1747, when I was first ordered by the Presbytery to take a journey to Hanover, in compliance with the petition of the dissenters here, I found them sufficiently numerous to form one very large congregation, or two small ones; and they had built five meeting-houses, three in Hanover, one in Henrico, and one in Louisa county; which were few enough considering their distance. Upon my preaching among them, they used the most irresistible importunities with me to settle among them as their minister, and presented a call to me before the Presbytery, signed by about an hundred and fifty heads of families; which in April, 1748, I accepted, and was settled among them the May following. And though it would have been my choice to confine myself wholly to one meeting-house, especially as I was then in a very languishing state of health; yet considering that hardly the one half of the people could possibly convene at one place, and that they had no other minister of their own denomination within less than two hundred miles, I was prevailed upon to take the pastoral care of them all, and to divide my labours at the sundry meeting-houses.

And now, my lord, I may leave yourself to judge, whether the imformations were just, upon which your lordship has represented me as not 'coming to serve a people that had scruples, but as disturbing the consciences of others, under the colour of a toleration to my own, and intruding into a country where there were not above four or five dissenters, etc.' Your lordship must see if this account be true, (and thousands can attest it) that I had not the least instrumentality in the first gathering of a dissenting Church in these parts. Indeed I was then but a lad, and closely engaged in study. And I solemnly assure your lordship, that it was not the sacred thirst of filthy lucre, nor the prospect of any other personal advantage, that induced me to settle here: for sundry congregations in Pennsylvania, my native country, and in the other northern colonies, most earnestly importuned me to settle among them, where I should have had at least an equal temporal maintenance, incomparably more ease, leisure, and peace, and the happiness of the frequent society of my brethren; never made a great noise or bustle in the world, but concealed myself in the crowd of my superior brethren, and spent my life in some little services for God and his Church in some peaceful retired corner; which would have been most becoming so insignificant a creature, and most agreeable to my recluse natural temper: but all these strong inducements were preponderated by a sense of the more urgent necessity of the dissenters here; as they lay two or three hundred miles distant from the nearest ministers of their own denomination, and laboured under peculiar embarrassments for want of a settled minister; which I will not mention, lest I should seem to fling injurious reflections on a government whose clemency I have reason to acknowledge with the most loyal gratitude.

It is true, my lord, there have been some additions made to the dissenters here since my settlement, and some of them by occasion of my preaching. They had but five meeting-houses then, in three different counties, and now they have seven in five counties, and stand in need of one or two more. But here I must again submit it to your lordship, whether the laws of England forbid men to change their opinions, and act according to them when changed? And whether the Act of Toleration was intended to tolerate such only as were dissenters by birth and education? Whether professed dissenters are prohibited to have meeting-houses licensed convenient to them, where there are conformists adjacent, whose curiosity may at first prompt them to hear, and whose judgments may afterwards direct them to join with the dissenters? Or whether, to avoid the danger of gaining proselytes, the dissenters, in such circumstances, must be wholly deprived of the ministration of the gospel?

For my farther vindication, my lord, I beg leave to declare, and I defy the world to confute me, that in all the sermons I have preached in Virginia, I have not wasted one minute in exclaiming or reasoning against the peculiarities of the established church; nor so much as assigned the reasons of my own non-conformity. I have not exhausted my zeal in railing against the established clergy, in exposing their imperfections, some of which lie naked to my view, or in depreciating their characters. No, my lord, I have matters of infinitely greater importance to exert my zeal and spend my time and strength upon—To preach repentance towards God, and faith towards our Lord Jesus Christ—To alarm secure impenitents; to reform the profligate; to undeceive the hypocrite; to raise up the hands that hang down, and to strengthen the feeble knees—These are the doctrines I preach, these are the ends I pursue; and these my artifices to gain proselytes: and if ever I divert from these to ceremonial trifles, let my tongue cleave to the roof of my mouth. Now, my lord, if people adhere to me on such accounts as these, I cannot discourage them without wickedly betraying the interests of religion, and renouncing my character as a minister of the gospel. If the members of the Church of England come from distant places to the meeting-houses licensed for the use of professed dissenters, and upon hearing, join with them, and declare themselves Presbyterians, and place themselves under my ministerial care, I dare say your lordship will not censure me for admitting them. And if these new proselytes live at such a distance that they cannot meet statedly at the places already licensed, have they not a legal right to have houses licensed convenient to them, since they are as properly professed dissenters, in favour of whom the Act of Toleration was enacted, as those that have been educated in non-conformity? There is no method, my lord, to prevent the increase of our number in this manner, but either the prohibiting of all conformists to attend occasionally on my ministry; which neither the laws of God nor of the land will warrant: or the Episcopal ministers preaching the same doctrines which I do; as I humbly conceive they oblige themselves by subscribing their own articles; and had this been done, I am verily persuaded there would not have been one dissenter in these parts: or my absolutely refusing to receive those into the community of the dissenters, against whom it may be objected that they once belonged to the Church of England; which your lordship sees is unreasonable. 'Tis the conversion and salvation of men I aim to promote; and genuine Christianity, under whatever various forms it appears, never fails to charm my heart. The design of the gospel is to bring perishing sinners to heaven, and if they are but brought thither, its ministers have but little cause of anxiety and contention about the denomination they sustain in their way.

The Good Society

39. A Town Repents: Jonathan Edwards, The Northampton Covenant, 1742

[Jonathan Edwards, *The Works of Jonathan Edwards . . . ,* 2 vols. (London, 1834), I, ci–cii]

In the month of March, I led the people into a solemn public renewal of their covenant with God. To that end, having made a draft of a covenant, I first proposed it to some of the principal men in the church; then to the people, in their several religious associations in various parts of the town; then to the whole congregation in public; and then I deposited a copy of it in the hands of each of the four deacons, that all who desired it might resort to them, and have opportunity to view and consider it. Then the people in general, that were above fourteen years of age, first subscribed the covenant with their hands; and then, on a day of fasting and prayer, all together presented themselves before the Lord in his house, and stood up, and solemnly manifested their consent to it, as their vow to God. The covenant was as follows:

COPY OF A COVENANT,

Entered into and subscribed, by the people of God at Northampton, and owned before God in his house as their vow to the Lord, and made a solemn act of public worship, by the congregation in general that were above fourteen years of age, on a day of fasting and prayer for the continuance and increase of the gracious presence of God in that place.

March 16th, 1742. Acknowledging God's great goodness to us, a sinful, unworthy people, in the blessed manifestations and fruits of his gracious presence in this town, both formerly and lately, and particularly in the very late spiritual revival; and adoring the glorious majesty, power, and grace of God, manifested in the present wonderful outpouring of his Spirit, in many parts of this land, in this place; and lamenting our past backslidings and ungrateful departings from God, and humbly begging of God that he would not mark our iniquities, but, for Christ's sake, come over the mountains of our sins, and visit us with his salvation, and continue the tokens of his presence with us, and yet more gloriously pour out his blessed Spirit upon us, and make us all partakers of the divine blessings he is, at this day, bestowing here, and in many parts of this land; we do this day present ourselves before the Lord, to renounce our evil ways, we put away our abominations from before God's eyes, and with one accord, to renew our engagements to seek and serve God: and particularly do now solemnly promise and vow to the Lord as follows:

In all our conversation, concerns, and dealings with our neighbour, we will have a strict regard to rules of honesty, justice, and uprightness, that we don't overreach or defraud our neighbour in any matter, and either wilfully, or through want of care, injure him in any of his honest possessions or rights; and in all our communication will have a tender respect, not only to our own interest, but also to the interest of our neighbour; and will carefully endeavour, in every thing, to do to others as we should expect, or think reasonable, that they should do to us, if we were in their case, and they in ours.

And particularly we will endeavour to render every one his due, and will take heed to ourselves, that we don't injure our neighbour, and give him just cause of offence, by wilfully or negligently forbearing to pay our honest debts.

And wherein any of us, upon strict examination of our past behaviour, may be conscious to ourselves, that we have by any means wronged any of our neighbours in their outward estate, we will not rest, till we have made that restitution, or given that satisfaction, which the rules of moral equity require; or if we are, on a strict and impartial search, conscious to ourselves, that we have in any other respect considerably injured our neighbour, we will truly endeavour to do that, which we in our consciences suppose christian rules require, in order to a reparation of the injury, and removing the offence given thereby.

And furthermore we promise, that we will not allow ourselves in backbiting; and that we will take great heed to ourselves to avoid all violations of those christian rules, Tit. iii. 2. 'Speak evil of no man;' Jam. iv. 11. 'Speak not evil one of another, brethren;' and 2 Cor. xii. 20. 'Let there be no strifes, backbitings, whisperings;' and that we will not only not slander our neighbour, but also will not feed a spirit of bitterness, ill will, or secret grudge against our neighbour, insist on his real faults needlessly, and when not called to it, or from such a spirit, speak of his failings and blemishes with ridicule, or an air of contempt.

And we promise, that we will be very careful to avoid doing any thing to our neighbour from a spirit of revenge. And that we will take great care that we do not, for private interest or our own honour, or to maintain ourselves against those of a contrary party, or to get our wills, or to promote any design in opposition to others, do those things which we, on the most impartial consideration are capable of, can think in our consciences will tend to wound religion, and the interests of Christ's kingdom.

And particularly, that so far as any of us, by Divine Providence, have any special influence upon others, to lead them in the management of public affairs, we will not make our own worldly gain, or honour, or interest in the affections of others, or getting the better of any of a contrary party, that are in any respect our competitors, or the bringing or keeping them down, our governing aim, to the prejudice of the interest of religion, and the honour of Christ.

And in the management of any public affair, wherever there is a difference of opinions, concerning any outward possessions, privileges, rights, or properties, we will not willingly violate justice for private interest: and with the greatest strictness and watchfulness, will avoid all unchristian bitterness, vehemence, and heat of spirit; yea, though we should think ourselves injured by a contrary party; and in the time of the management of such affairs, will especially watch over ourselves, our spirits, and our tongues, to avoid all unchristian inveighings, reproachings, bitter reflectings, judging and ridiculing others, either in public meetings or in private conversation, either to men's faces, or behind their backs; but will greatly endeavour, so far as we are concerned, that all should be managed with christian humility, gentleness, quietness, and love.

And furthermore we promise, that we will not tolerate the exercise of enmity and ill will, or revenge in our hearts, against any of our neighbours; and we will often be strictly searching and examining our own hearts with respect to that matter.

And if any of us find that we have an old secret grudge against any of our neighbours, we will not gratify it, but cross it, and endeavour to our utmost to root it out, crying to God for his help; and that we will make it our true and faithful endeavour, in our places, that a party spirit may not be kept up amongst us, but that it may utterly cease; that for the future, we may all be one, united in undisturbed peace and unfeigned love.

And those of us that are in youth, do promise, never to allow ourselves in any diversions or pastimes, in meetings, or companies of young people, that we, in our consciences, upon sober consideration, judge not well to consist with, or would sinfully tend to hinder, the devoutest and most engaged spirit in religion, or indispose the mind for that devout and profitable attendance on the duties of the closet, which is most agreeable to God's will, or that we, in our most impartial judgment, can think tends to rob God of that honour which he expects, by our orderly serious attendance on family worship.

And furthermore we promise, that we will strictly avoid all freedoms and familiarities in company, so tending either to stir up or gratify a lust of lasciviousness, that we cannot in our consciences think will be approved by the infinitely pure and holy eye of God, or that we can think, on serious and impartial consideration, we should be afraid to practise, if we expected in a few hours to appear before that holy God, to give an account of ourselves to him, as fearing they would be condemned by him as unlawful and impure.

We also promise, with great watchfulness, to perform relative duties, required by christian rules, in the families we belong to, as we stand related respectively, towards parents and children, husbands and wives, brothers and sisters, masters or mistresses, and servants.

And we now appear before God, depending on Divine grace and assistance, solemnly to devote our whole lives, to be laboriously spent in the business of religion; ever making it our greatest business, without backsliding from such a way of living, not hearkening to the solicitations of our sloth, and other corrupt inclinations, or the temptations of the world, that tend to draw us off from it; and particularly, that we will not abuse a hope or opinion that any of us may have, of our being interested in Christ, to indulge ourselves in sloth, or the more easily to yield to the solicitations of any sinful inclinations; but will run with perseverance the race that is set before us, and work out our own salvation with fear and trembling.

And because we are sensible that the keeping these solemn vows may hereafter, in many cases, be very contrary to our corrupt inclinations and carnal interests, we do now therefore appear before God to make a surrender of all to him, and to make a sacrifice of every carnal inclination and interest, to the great business of religion and the interest of our souls.

And being sensible of our weakness, and the deceitfulness of our own hearts, and our proneness to forget our most solemn vows, and lose our resolutions, we promise to be often strictly examining ourselves by these promises, especially before the sacrament of the Lord's supper; and beg of God that he would, for Christ's sake, keep us from wickedly dissembling in these our solemn vows; and that he who searches our hearts, and ponders the path of our feet, would, from time to time, help us in trying ourselves by this covenant, and help us to keep covenant with him, and not leave us to our own foolish, wicked, and treacherous hearts.

40. The Millennial Day: Aaron Burr, *The Watchman's Answer*, 1757

[Aaron Burr, *The Watchman's Answer to the Question, What of the Night, etc. A Sermon Preached before the Synod of New-York, Convened at Newark, in New-Jersey, September 30, 1756*, 2d ed. (New York, 1757), 32–37]

The triumphing of the Enemies of Christ, will be short. When they think themselves most secure, and that there are none to oppose their Designs, *sudden Destruction shall come upon them, as on a Woman in Travail, and they shall not escape.* When the *Whore* of *Babylon,* or *mystical Rome,* shall say, *I sit as a Queen, am no Widow,* and *shall see no Sorrow;* then her Doom draws nigh; *her Plagues shall come in one Day; Death, Mourning & Famine; and she shall be utterly burnt with Fire.* Happy shall they then be, *who have come out from her, and are not Partakers of her Sin, that they may not receive of her Plagues.* The Destruction of *Antichrist,* will not be at once; yet on the *Resurrection* and *Exaltation* of the Witnesses, he shall receive a *deadly Wound,* of which he shall never be healed, but consume away by the *Breath of Christ's Mouth, and Brightness of his Coming.* Such sudden and awful Judgments will then be brought upon *him,* as shall affrighten the *Rest* of the World, and cause them to *give Glory to God.* This, with the passing away of the *second Woe,* in the Overthrow of the *Turkish Empire,* will open a Door for that *glorious Spread* of the Gospel promised in the *latter Days.* The *third Woe* under the sounding of the seventh Angel, which cometh quickly, will issue in the final and complete *Destruction* of *Antichrist* and

Confusion of all the implacable Enemies of the Church. Then shall be heard great Voices in Heaven, and the *joyful Sound* will spread far and wide on the Earth, saying, *The Kingdoms of this World are become the Kingdoms of our Lord and his Christ, and he shall reign for ever and ever.* Then, *My Brethren,* tho' we may be entering on the *darkest,* and most *gloomy* Part of the *Night,* which has continued so long, we may lift up our Heads with Joy, our Salvation draws near. The *Night is far spent, and the Day is at Hand.* The *Morning* cometh, and will usher in a glorious *Day,* when the *Sun of Righteousness shall arise,* and dispel the dark Clouds which now hang over his Church, become a *Light to the Gentiles,* and *a Glory to God's People Israel;* when *the Light of the Moon shall be as the Light of the Sun, and the Light of the Sun sevenfold as the Light of seven Days.* This Day of the Churches Prosperity, is to continue for a *Thousand Years;* some suppose, prophetically taken, 360,000 Years, that Christ may have a longer *Reign,* and greater *Number* of Subjects, than the *Prince* of Darkness has had; but this may be accomplished in the Space of 1000 Years, (literally taken) of such *Peace* and *Prosperity* as the Church will then enjoy, when the *Increase* of Mankind will be so much greater, and their *Destruction* so much less than at other Times. Some suppose Christ will reign personally here on Earth, during these 1000 Years, and that his *bodily Presence* will be the *Glory* of his Church; that the *Saints,* or, at least, the *Martyrs,* will be raised from the *Dead,* and *reign* with him. But such perplexing Questions and Difficulties, are started on this Head, as I have never yet seen answered; and since it is represented as a greater Blessing to the Church, to have Christ *interceding* in Heaven, and the Presence of *his Spirit* on Earth; I see no

Reason, either to desire or expect it. 'Tis expedient (says Christ) *That I go away; for, unless I go, the Comforter will not come unto you.* Without pronouncing any Thing decisively, about the *exact Circumstances* of these *glorious Times,* and the *Manner* in which they will be brought on, I will only say, That it seems evident, by the prophetic Description given of *those Times,* that their Glory will consist in the universal Promotion of *true Christianity* and *real Religion,* in the Gospel's having its *genuine Effect* on the Hearts and Lives of Men; such as were before *hateful,* and *hating one another,* will then have Hearts glowing with Love to God, and one another; such as were before the Plagues and Pests of Society, will then become its Ornament, Delight and Defence; such as were before fierce and savage, malicious and revengeful, barbarous and cruel, will then become kind and gentle, courteous and forgiving, meek and humble. The *Lyon* will be turned into the *Lamb;* and *there shall be Nothing to offend in God's holy Mount.* When supreme Love to God, and undissembled Affection to one another, reign, it will produce universal Harmony and Peace. Wars and Contentions, angry Jars and Disputes, will cease; *the Lamb shall lie down with the Wolf, and the Nations of the Earth will learn War no more.* Such a *glorious Change,* in such a corrupt apostate World, can be brought about by Nothing short of a *plentiful, outpouring* of the Spirit of all Grace, who has immediate Access to the *Hearts* of the Children of Men, by his enlightning, purifying, and all-conquering Influences. That the Change will begin *here;* that without *this,* all Means must prove ineffectual; and that *this* is sufficient to effect it, might be easily proved. Such *abundant Effusion* of the divine Spirit, will open an *effectual Door* for the Gospel, to have *free Course* and *be glorified,* which no Man shall be able to shut. A preached Gospel will be attended with such *Life* and *Power,* as will subdue and soften the *hardest Heart;* it will shine with such *Light* and *Glory,* as that the Remainder of *Pagan, Popish* and *Mahometan* Darkness, will flee before it, as the Shadows of the Night before the *rising Sun.* The Inhabitants of the Earth shall be filled with the *spiritual Knowledge* of God and Christ, *as the Waters cover the Sea;* Conversions will be greatly multiplied; Sinners will flock to Christ, as *Clouds,* and *as Doves to their Windows;* it will seem as if *Nations were born in a Day:* Then will God remember Mercy for his ancient People, the *Jews.* They shall be brought in with *the Fullness of the Gentile World, which will be Life from the Dead.* This is expressly promised, *The Children of* Israel *shall abide many Days without a King, and a Prince, without a Sacrifice, Image, Ephod, etc. Afterwards shall they return, and seek the Lord their God, and David, their King.* Then may it be said to the Church, *Arise; shine forth; for thy Light is come, and the Glory of the Lord risen is upon thee; his Glory shall be seen upon thee, and the Gentiles shall come to thy Light, and Kings to the Brightness of thy Rising.*

PRINCES and *Potentates,* will, I imagine, partake of this plentiful Effusion of divine Grace, whereby *Kings* shall be made *nursing Fathers,* and *Queens nursing Mothers* to the *Church,* disposed to cast their *Crowns* at the Feet of *Jesus,* and employ all their superior Advantages for the Honour of his Name, and Advancement of his Cause; and with what striking Beauty and Force will *Religion* then shine, when recommended by such distinguished Examples!

MINISTERS *of the Gospel,* will doubtless have a *double Portion* of the *Spirit,* when it is so remarkably poured forth.

They will then be like the *Angel* spoken of in *Revelations,* who *flew through Heaven, having the everlasting Gospel.* They will fly on the Wings of *Zeal* and *Love,* to publish the Wonders of *divine Grace* to a lost and ruined World. And their Meekness, Humility and Wisdom, will be equal to their Zeal. How different in that Day, will be the *Preaching, Conversation* and *Examples* of Ministers, from what we now behold? And what *glorious Effects* may be expected from the Gospel, when it is published by those whose Hearts are full of a Sense of its *Excellency, Truth* and *Importance;* and when this *shines* forth in their Lives. Alas! how little do we know of this in the present Day? what a mournful withdrawment of the divine Spirit! our Words freeze between our Lips; the divine Art of reaching the *Heart,* and alluring Souls to Christ is departed from us. Long experienced Unsuccessfulness damps our Spirits; we speak as those that expect to *labour in vain,* and *spend our Strength for Nought.*

CHRISTIANS, in general, will be favoured with unusual Communications of divine Grace, and *shine as Lights in the World.* There will be something convincing and alluring in their *Example:* That mean, low, sordid *Temper,* that contentious, jangling, quarrelsome Spirit, which now appears in most *Professors,* obscures the Beauty of our *holy Religion* in the Eyes of Strangers, and is one of the greatest *Obstacles* to the Spread of the *Gospel.* But when *true Religion* comes to be properly exemplified in the Lives of *Christians,* there will appear such a Charm, and *Excellency* in it, as will strike and allure the *Beholders,* and have a peculiar Tendency to propagate it throughout the *World.*

FAMILIES will then, 'tis probable, be as remarkable for being *Nurseries of Piety,* as they now are for being Scenes of *Disorder, Corruption,* and *Vice;* when *Children* will indeed be *trained up for God,* and come on the Stange of Action with Hearts animated with Love to *him,* and to all *Mankind,* and glowing Desires of being distinguished Blessings in their Day.

PUBLICK SCHOOLS, and *Seminaries of Learning,* will probably become Seats remarkable for *Virtue,* and *true Religion;* where it shall shine with divine *Lustre,* and diffuse its benign *Influence* far and wide: From those *Fountains* thus purified, will issue *Streams* that shall make *glad the City of our God.* I hint at these Things, as probable *Means* whereby the glorious Designs of God's Grace will be carried on, in the *latter Day,* that with our fervent *Prayer,* we may unite our earnest Endeavours for their Accomplishment.

WHAT a *glorious Change* will soon be produced, when God shall visit these dark Abodes, with such plentiful Effusions of his Spirit! What a new Face of Things must then appear in the *moral World. Behold I create a new Heaven, and a new Earth; be ye glad, and rejoice, for ever, in what I create, for I create Jerusalem a Rejoicing, and her People a Joy.*

SUGGESTED READINGS

COLLECTIONS OF DOCUMENTS

* Alan Heimert and Perry Miller, eds., *The Great Awakening: Documents Illustrating the Crisis and Its Consequences* (Indianapolis and New York, 1967).

William G. McLoughlin, ed., *Isaac Backus on Church, State, and Calvinism: Pamphlets, 1754–1789* (Cambridge, Mass., 1968).

* Clarence H. Faust and Thomas H. Johnson, eds., *Jonathan Edwards: Representative Selections* . . . (New York, 1935; rev. ed., 1962).

SECONDARY WORKS

Frank Hugh Foster, *A Genetic History of the New England Theology* (Chicago, 1907; reprint, 1963).

* Edwin Scott Gaustad, *The Great Awakening in New England* (New York, 1957; reprint, 1968).

Wesley M. Gewehr, *The Great Awakening in Virginia, 1740–1790* (Durham, N.C., 1930; reprint, 1965).

C. C. Goen, *Revivalism and Separatism in New England, 1740–1800: Strict Congregationalists and Separate Baptists in the Great Awakening* (New Haven and London, 1962).

Joseph Haroutunian, *Piety Versus Moralism: The Passing of the New England Theology* (New York, 1932; reprint, 1964).

Alan Heimert, *Religion and the American Mind, from the Great Awakening to the Revolution* (Cambridge, Mass., 1966).

Charles Hartshorn Maxson, *The Great Awakening in the Middle Colonies* (Chicago, 1920).

Sidney E. Mead, *The Lively Experiment: The Shaping of Christianity in America* (New York, 1963).

* Perry Miller, *Errand into the Wilderness* (Cambridge, Mass., 1956; reprint, 1963).

* Perry Miller, *Jonathan Edwards* (New York, 1949; reprint, 1963).

* H. Richard Niebuhr, *The Kingdom of God in America* (New York, 1937; reprint, 1959).

Leonard J. Trinterud, *The Forming of an American Tradition: A Reexamination of Colonial Presbyterianism* (Philadelphia, 1949).

*Williston Walker, *The Creeds and Platforms of Congregationalism* (New York, 1893; reprint, 1960) .

*Conrad Wright, *The Beginnings of Unitarianism in America* (Boston, 1955; reprint, 1966) .

* Books in paperback.

Richard L. Bushman

Born in Salt Lake City, Utah, Richard L. Bushman was educated at Harvard University. His books include *From Puritan to Yankee: Character and the Social Order in Connecticut, 1690–1765*. Mr. Bushman is Professor of History at Boston University.

Most twentieth-century Americans fail to appreciate the power of Christian conversion that characterized the eighteenth-century revivals, especially the Great Awakening of the 1740s. The common disdain in this secular age for impassioned religious emotion and language is merely symptomatic of the shift in values that has shunted revivals to the sidelines.

The very magnitude of the previous revivals is one indication of their importance. Between 1740 and 1745 literally thousands were converted. From New England to the southern colonies, people of all ages and all ranks of society underwent the New Birth. Virtually every New England congregation was touched. It is safe to say that most of the colonists in the 1740s, if not converted themselves, knew someone who was, or at least heard revival preaching.

The Awakening was a critical event in the intellectual and ecclesiastical life of the colonies. The colonists' view of the world placed much importance on conversion. Particularly, Calvinist theology viewed the bestowal of divine grace as the most crucial occurrence in human life. Besides assuring admission to God's presence in the hereafter, divine grace prepared a person for a fullness of life on earth. In the 1740s the colonists, in overwhelm-

(continued on back flap)

JACKET DESIGN: CHARLES E. SKAGGS